NIGERIAN HARVEST

A Reformed witness to Jesus Christ in Nigeria,
West Africa, in the twentieth century, including a detailed
history of the missionary ministry
of the Christian Reformed Church
in the Benue Province from 1940 to 1970

by Edgar H. Smith

BAKER BOOK HOUSE
Grand Rapids, Michigan

ISBN: 0-8010-7964-0

Library of Congress Catalog Card Number: 72-90326

Copyright © 1972
by The Christian Reformed Board of Foreign Missions
Printed in the United States of America
by Dickinson Brothers, Inc.

NIGERIAN HARVEST

Preface

I am pleased to pen a few opening words for *Nigerian Harvest*. That for two reasons. The story of God's great work in Nigeria should be told, and the writer of this story played such a vital role in its unfolding. For some two score years Nigeria missions have been in the hearts and prayers of God's people. This is because faithful missionaries serving in that land kept telling of what God was doing for the building of His church. And in this volume the story is told of much of the preaching and teaching and counseling and planning and building—with as much of the praying and agonizing and believing and singing. It is rich with the drama of God at work through His faithful servants.

Missionaries on the field as well as the leadership at home felt that Rev. Edgar H. Smith should be asked to write this book. His vital identification in heart and life with the entire effort to build Christ's church in Nigeria, and his personal involvement with almost every aspect of the work from its very inception made him the logical choice.

We are thankful for his service. It was done as a ministry to Christ, and with the author we pray that God may use this book to make known what has been accomplished through the ministry of Christ's Word in Nigeria.

Henry J. Evenhouse

Executive Secretary
Board of Foreign Missions
Christian Reformed Church

Contents

Foreword

The Board of Foreign Missions of the Christian Reformed Church completed thirty years of work in Nigeria, West Africa, at the end of 1969. That year it gave me a special assignment asking me to record the history of this activity and in the following pages I have attempted to do so. I served as a missionary for Nigeria for forty years and this creates a problem of my personal involvement in this history. However, I have made strenuous efforts to be objective and to resist the dangers inherent in such a situation, striving to record facts and not feelings.

One reason why the CRC became interested in Nigeria was that some of its members were missionaries there from 1920 to 1940. These were Johanna Veenstra, Mr. and Mrs. John Bierenga, Nelle Breen, Bertha Zagers, Jennie Stielstra and Tena Huizenga. Because of this involvement, unofficial though it was where the CRC was concerned, it was good to include something of that history, for it is very doubtful whether the CRC would be in Nigeria today but for the influence these early missionaries brought to bear upon their church in North America.

A further step back is necessary if we are to fully glorify God and extol His grace. At the opening of the twentieth century gross spiritual darkness held sway over all the land with which this history has to do. There was not a tiny gleam of gospel light anywhere. So if we begin where God began we can watch "the darkness turn to dawning and the dawning to noonday bright." The CRC's portion, which is somewhere between dawning and midday, will be more understandable if we begin with the darkness where God began. Moreover the two Nigerian churches involved in this record will enjoy greater satisfaction in reading this book if the whole history of God's work through Christ and His servants is given. Where the Benue Province of Nigeria is concerned, how true it is that in this century "the people who walked in darkness have seen a great light; those who dwelt in a land of deep darkness, on them has light shined" (Isa. 9:2).

To make this book possible I have had access to the minutes and monthly and annual reports of the Sudan United Mission (American Branch). I have also found a wealth of material in the acts of the Synods of the CRC and the minutes of its Board of Foreign Missions. This material has been augmented by the minutes of the CRC Nigerian mission. (I did not have access to personal CRC missionary correspondence, with the exception of my own file.)

Information was also gleaned from magazines such as *The Banner, The Missionary Monthly,* and *The Lightbearer.* Relatives and friends of Johanna Veenstra were gracious in allowing me to use the material quoted in this book. For all of this help I am most grateful.

I have also gathered information from the minutes of the EKAS Benue Church, the Rev. J. Lowry Maxwell's *Fifty Years of Grace,* and Johanna Veenstra's *Pioneering for Christ in the Sudan.* For this and all similar material I express my warmest thanks to those concerned.

I appreciate the help of so many who have encouraged me and made this work possible. My thanks to many colleagues who responded to my plea for information. My thanks also to the CRC Board of Foreign Missions for asking me to do this work and to its subcommittee for considering the manuscript when it was completed. Above all I thank my wife, Nelle, who has borne with me these many months and aided me continually with timely criticism and by doing masses of typing. We two have prayed much over this record of God's doings in one part of Nigeria. The views expressed and personal conclusions are solely mine and I accept responsibility for them. If I have erred it has not been done consciously.

I hope that this record will be a skeleton of basic and verifiable fact, a foundation on which others will be able to design comely images of various aspects of God's marvelous grace at work in the lives of men.

Edgar H. Smith

Holland, Michigan, USA.
May 1971

1

In the Beginning

God's Time for Nigeria

In the summer of 1939 the Synod of the Christian Reformed Church in North America told its Board of Foreign Missions to "take the necessary steps towards taking over this field [Lupwe-Takum] from the Sudan United Mission." In the months that followed final arrangements were made and on January 1, 1940 the CRC became responsible for the Christian mission work going on in the Lupwe-Takum district of the Benue Province of Nigeria. Officially this was the beginning of the Christian Reformed denomination's work in the continent of Africa.

However, "In the beginning, God—" is a Biblical quotation which should be remembered. The Trinity of the Godhead had plans made in eternity that the twentieth century was to be God's time for the redemption of Northern Nigeria. We cannot trace this plan from "before the world was," but we can follow it from the beginning of this century. In doing so we shall see that God uses all kinds of men, conditions, and organizations to effect His purpose. We shall also be able to place the Christian Reformed Church's contribution in a right perspective as related to the whole.

At the turn of the century little was known of the interior of Africa, of the vast three thousand-mile sub-Saharan stretch of territory then known as *The Sudan*. Men and nations, however, had slowly probed into the interior. One result of this was the wild scramble of European nations to carve up much of this huge con-

11

tinent between themselves, and to assert the right to rule the people whose home it was. Traders, explorers, political administrators, and, fortunately, Christ's messengers were among the first to go there.

Before Sir Frederick Lugard planted the British flag in Northern Nigeria, Rowland Bingham, founder of the Sudan Interior Mission, and his colleagues had made two attempts to penetrate into the north. As early as 1894 two of them had laid down their lives for Christ's sake. By 1904, a third party of the Sudan Interior Mission (SIM), men of the Sudan United Mission (SUM), and others of the Church of England (Church Missionary Society) were serving as Christian missionaries in different parts of the interior.

Dr. and Mrs. H. K. W. Kumm

Dr. H. K. W. Kumm was the leader of the SUM party of 1904. He was directed by the British high commissioner to settle in the town of Wase. This was some seventy miles north of Ibi, which is on the Benue River, and at the foot of the great volcanic rock which rises a thousand feet above the surrounding plain. Dr. Kumm was well suited for the task of pioneering a new mission field. In 1898 he said, "While still in England a voice often seemed to speak to me of the people of the desert, and the desire took possession of my heart to go and preach the Gospel to them. Now at last I have had the privilege of looking upon those dear people, and upon a portion of the vast desert of the Sahara, which is for me the promised land." [1] God created this longing for the desert within him and from his exploration of a part of it, Kumm realized two things. First, the hold that Islam had on the people living south of the Sahara Desert and, second, how the followers of the Prophet were winning the animistic peoples of the Sudan to the Muslim faith. It was this conviction that spurred him on to great activity so that these people might be won for Jesus Christ before Islam took them over. His vision was to set up a barrier of mission stations across the continent to counteract the penetration of Islam from the north.

What could this man and his wife, Lucy Guinness, do? Here were a brave, soul-winning German and a gentle, dedicated, English girl who left her well-to-do home to be a factory worker in order that she might learn by experience how the poor live and suffer. God drew this couple together in Egypt. There, in the presence of God and of two Sudanese students, they joined hands above those of their two black friends and made their marriage vows. They were united by Christ to win the Sudan for Him. This was a mustard seed from which a very great tree was to grow. Lowry Maxwell wrote, "Only eternity will reveal what great issues hung upon the meeting and union of these two, the linking up of his force and her fire, his drive and her depth of devotion, his vision and her passion."[2]

While Karl Kumm toured the British Isles looking for missionary recruits his wife, Lucy, and her zealous father, Dr. Grattan Guinness, tried to persuade the British Council of Free Churches to accept responsibility for the work projected in the Sudan. Although each church in the council felt unable to tackle a new field, nevertheless all expressed active sympathy for the proposal. This was expressed by many of them placing a representative on a committee, which committee formed the Sudan United Mission on June 15, 1904. This was unity in action and in it the Free Churches were joined by the Church of England. The churches concerned were not accepting responsibility as denominations but were by their sympathetic attitude telling their members that they favored this attempt to evangelize the Sudan. An interdenominational mission was born. The procedure set a pattern which was to be used in other nations.

Karl Kumm inspired many to devote their lives to Christ for His service in the Sudan. In 1909 he crossed the African continent from the Niger to the Nile. As far as European companionship was concerned he was alone. This daring journey provided him with firsthand information on the territory to be occupied. After it he not only sought further missionary recruits from the British Isles, but went to the United States and persuaded Americans to join in the mission. Interested Christians formed a committee, collected gifts, and sent out workers. In time South Africa, Denmark, Australia and New Zealand, Norway, Canada, France, and Switzerland became involved. Each country formed a national committee which was part of the SUM but at the same time was autonomous and responsible for its own workers and finance. Not only did the formation of the SUM in Britain help people of different denominations work together for the furtherance of the gospel while remaining true to their own creeds, it caused this to happen in the United States and many other lands as well. Moreover it drew together in a common task in the Sudan, Christian missionaries of various nations as well as of various denominations. It was in the best sense a "United Mission," nationally and interdenominationally.

The Involvement of America

When traders from Europe were no longer involved in the slave traffic they developed the export of farm and other produce. Since there were no roads they followed navigable rivers, setting up trading posts in riverside towns. The new colonial administrators sought out the principal cities and seats of major tribal influence and established their offices, law courts, and police or army quarters in them. The missionary's business was with the souls of men. Because men were to be found everywhere the missionaries went everywhere—not to enslave but, by the grace of God, to set free. Naturally the people, who were continually subject to raids by their tribal enemies, were not ready to fraternize with any strangers. This was especially true in the case of missionaries who neither ruled them nor sought gain from them. It was hard for them to believe that anyone was there to help them without reward of any kind. They felt there must be a hidden motive behind this disinterested service. They had never known love in the Christian sense.

In 1904 the SUM party settled at Wase by the direction of the British high commissioner. Between bouts of malaria fever it took the two men, John Burt and Lowry Maxwell, a long time to build a home and to learn a little of the Hausa language. But one or the other would take time to explore and in 1905 Burt traveled as far south as the town of Wukari. Late that same year Maxwell accompanied him on a second visit. These were the first attempts to preach the gospel in what was to become the CRC Nigerian mission field. By 1906, the Aku Uka, divine head of the Jukun people, encouraged Burt and Maxwell to come and live in the town of Wukari. The two missionaries paid local men to build for them "a little rectangular hut composed of two rooms, each twelve feet square, with a lean-to verandah in front."[3] This unpretentious and undecorated abode, with grass roof and beaten earth floor, was, with the presence of its owners, evidence that a seed of the tree of life had been planted in that place. It was occupied intermittently by missionaries for the next fifty years and was only removed in 1965 to make way for a magnificent church which now occupies the site.

As early as 1905 Karl Kumm had stirred up interest in America for the Sudan. One result of this was that the Rev. C. W. Guinter gave himself in total dedication to work for Christ in the Sudan. He was of the Evangelical Brethren Church and for his first seventeen years served under the SUM American committee. He with J. S. Derr and Walter Hoover arrived at Wukari in 1906. Guinter is still remembered in the area as a gentle man of love and kindness in action. It was in the year 1906 that the United States began its active part for Christ in the Benue field. The workers served under an interdenominational committee in the United States. This committee formed the American Branch of the Sudan United Mission. It was responsible for finding and sending workers to the field and for providing them with the money necessary to carry on the work.

Mr. Habu, evangelist, and Mr. Nyaliba became Christians during the 1910s at Donga. Mr. Habu led Istifanus Audu to faith in Christ.

Wase Rock is the heart of a volcano and rises one thousand feet above the surrounding plain. At its foot the Sudan United Mission began its work in Nigeria in 1904.

There was a common objective, namely, the evangelization of the entire Sudan from the Niger River to the Nile. Workers from Europe, America, or South Africa who served under the SUM banner in Nigeria had to work together harmoniously. The plan was for a defined area to be the concern of workers from one branch of the mission. This principle could not be strictly adhered to. For over thirty years American workers were often in short supply, for in those days poor health continually sapped the strength of those who were available. As a result the British Branch of the mission frequently loaned workers to serve in the American sector. From time to time this alone prevented a complete cessation of the work. This willingness to share workers has continued between the branches of the SUM and by it the meaning of the word *united* is clearly demonstrated in practice.

Mission Property

From the beginning of British rule it was recognized that the land in Nigeria belongs to the people. Generally it belongs to the people indigenous to a locality. Moreover, it does not belong to individual householders but to the community as a whole. In more recent years this was clearly illustrated when the Birom churches persuaded local Christian farmers to give to the Tekas Fellowship the land on which the Theological College of Northern Nigeria is built. The farmers were agreeable as separate individuals to do this without remuneration but the government would not permit them to do so. Payment was insisted upon and was made possible by a generous donation of $2800 from an anonymous Nigerian donor. This did not buy the land, however; it only reimbursed the farmers who were deprived of the use of arable soil. The land itself was leased to the Tekas Fellowship. Because the Fellowship is wholly Nigerian a term of ninety-nine years was permitted with the understanding, common to all leased property, that it may be taken away. Foreign companies such as a mission are only allowed to lease land for shorter periods of time up to, say, twenty-eight years. This restriction and a close control on the acreage which can be leased has had a distinct bearing on the history of Nigeria. Whereas in other African territories Europeans purchased and possessed huge estates of the better land and pushed the indigenous residents into small and poor reservations, in Nigeria this never happened. In 1960, when Nigeria declared its independence, there was no conflict with dissatisfied foreigners since the land belonged to its own people.

In order to lease a parcel of land for a mission station a formal certificate of occupation was issued by the government to an incorporated body. The SUM sought and obtained incorporation in Britain in 1907, at which time sixteen directors were elected and a constitution and by-laws were adopted. From that time until the present, land leased by any branch of the SUM in Nigeria has been legally obtained through that incorporation. Various missionaries in Nigeria in behalf of one or another sector of the mission have been granted power of attorney. In the CRC this is held by its secretary on the field. The government only recognizes one SUM even though it is made up of different branches. There has never been any dispute between branch and branch as to ownership of land or buildings.

Problems have arisen with the government itself. The CRC inherited free of charge from the British a very fine house at Donga. Due to official delays, not mission carelessness, the lease expired and the mission buildings became government property and were scheduled to be auctioned off—and the auction was planned for a Sunday afternoon. However, God supplies all needs. Legal advice which could not be obtained for weeks was desperately needed when a friend suggested sending a telegram pleading with the governor of Nigeria for clemency. His Excellency responded favorably to the appeal and gave his permission for the CRC to buy back its own property for $200. He allowed one week to remove the building. The only male missionary, assisted by willing workers, dismantled the building, all of which, apart from the bricks and concrete, had come from England thirty years earlier. Considering the fact that it rained seven inches in one night that week, this was a memorable feat. The metal roofing, girders, doors, and windows supplied the needs of the first home at Baissa and an office in Lupwe. The sale of some of the material enabled the mission to pay the $200 to the government for the property.

Another property problem was of a different nature and occurred at Katsina Ala in Tivland. At the public high school there the Dutch Reformed Church Mission (DRCM) built a chapel for the use of the teachers and students. Many years later the school was visited by the lieutenant governor of the North. He saw the chapel, said that Christian services were not to be held there, and ordered it to be closed. It was closed, but the chairman of the mission knew something of the law and pointed out to the proper authorities that the chapel had been consecrated at a religious service. He added that land so consecrated under British law was outside the jurisdiction of the government. The lieutenant governor had no alternative but to agree and withdraw his order. The chapel was reopened. When it fell into disrepair another was built to replace it. Recently the CRC has replaced this also with a better and more commodious building. The site for this was granted by the Muslim principal of the school. For over forty years the mission has served Christ in the school without hindrance, a service which has proved most rewarding. At present the Rev. Shimrumun Yakobu, who graduated from Calvin Seminary in 1969, is chaplain at the school.

The Constitution of the SUM

The constitution of the SUM was written in 1907, only three years after the formation of the mission and before there were any Nigerian converts to Christ. It reveals the wisdom of God and the faith and vision of the founders of the mission. It states that its object is ". . . to carry the Gospel to those regions in the Sudan that are at the time unoccupied by other Protestant missions, and by evangelizing the pagan tribes to counteract the Moslem advance. The Mission desires to take its part in the formation of an African Union Church."[4] This is a vital statement and has governed the mission's thinking throughout the years.

The idea of evangelizing people to counteract the Muslim advance has a negative ring to it. During the earlier decades the missionaries were very few and could serve only limited numbers of non-Muslim people. In general the Muslims were neglected; moreover the Christian converts for the most part had vivid memories of slave raiding perpetrated by Muslims and so were not inclined to love them. For a long time the term "counteracting the Moslem advance" promoted an attitude of antagonism. However, for the past ten years a positive and more pleasing tone has been introduced into the churches and most, though not all, are adopting a different attitude. This is one of realizing that the Muslim also is a sinner in need of salvation and that the gospel of Jesus Christ is as powerful for him as for any other person. This confidence does much for the Christian witness himself and for his Muslim neighbor.

Another important aspect of the aim of the mission which has always been kept in view refers to "the formation of an African Union Church." Seeking the implementation of this expectation had a pronounced effect on the growth of Christ's church in Nigeria. It will be referred to again but is noted here as being a basic intention of the mission when there were yet no African Christians in Northern Nigeria.

Because of this intention and because missionary personnel working with the SUM were drawn from diverse church denominations a statement of doctrine was found to be necessary. The one chosen was that of the Evangelical Alliance which had been written in the middle of the nineteenth century. At no point is it at variance with the teachings of the CRC and in 1939 the CRC Synod approved of it. The articles of the statement are evangelical in nature. All the bodies cooperating in the SUM whether denominational or interdenominational accept it and conduct their work in accordance with it. So from a doctrinal point of view all involved in the SUM are able to work harmoniously together while at the same time each is able to follow his own denominational trend. As Christian Nigerians were added to the church the effect of a basic harmony with the addition of varying denominational emphases was evident and suited the different branches of the work.

Stations Established at Donga and Ibi

Our first roots as an American branch of the SUM were planted at Wukari. Before the advent of motor roads it was difficult to reach. The towns of Ibi and Donga are on navigable rivers so mission stations were opened at both places, and during the rainy season it is possible for steamboats to reach them. This made it possible for heavy prefabricated materials for the buildings to be imported from Europe. Homes made from metal and concrete could resist fire and termites. They did, however, soak up so much heat from the sun that at certain seasons life was almost unbearable for those who lived in them. One home was equipped with steel doors but the missionary sold them and they were made into farm implements.

Ibi, which was an important port of call during the days of river traffic to Adamawa and the Cameroons, was headquarters of the SUM until 1934 when they were transferred to Gindiri. It served Langtang station to the north, Wukari, Donga, Sai, and Takum to the south. It also served all the mission stations on the upper reaches of the Benue River and from it Lokoja and Burutu, a port for ocean steamers, could be reached by canoe or barge.

Notes

1. J. Lowry Maxwell, *Half a Century of Grace,* London, 1954, p. 22.
2. Ibid., p. 23.
3. Ibid., p. 60.
4. SUM Constitution, p. 2.

A young Tiv woman carries a pot and calabashes. Note the "tear-drop" tribal face marks.

2

The People of the Benue and Tiv Areas

Coastal, Middle, and Northern Belts of Nigeria

We have written about the missionaries who first penetrated into
Western Sudan and worked with the SUM. Their purpose was to
spread the gospel of Jesus Christ among the non-Muslim people living
south of the Sahara Desert. Of these people there were several tribes
located in the Wukari and Tiv divisions of the Benue Province. It is
with these and the Muslim groups that are scattered among them that
this history has to do.

Nigeria has been divided in many ways. For our purpose I suggest
three broad divisions. Most of the coast of Nigeria faces south and
for some 150 miles in depth it forms the coastal belt comprising
about one sixth of the country's land surface. In 1970 this area
accounted for six of its twelve states. It was in the eastern half of this
belt that the civil war raged during the 1960s. A prominent feature
of the coastal belt is the almost impenetrable swamps and thick
forests. Here may be found valuable oil and coconut palms, and
rubber and cocoa plantations. Here also, inland and off the coast, are
the new and very productive oil wells. The annual rainfall is heavy
and at one or two points near to Mount Cameroon is as high as three
hundred inches.

Next from east to west stretches the middle belt. Its center line is
roughly the Benue River. Here the rainfall diminishes and ranges
between forty and seventy inches, all of which falls between March
and October. The terrain here is more open and may be classed as

savannah or bush country. The word *bush* sometimes refers to the trees which are stunted and twisted by the annual burning of the grass. This is a popular term and is part of Nigeria's English language. The bush is good farming country. Although farming methods are primitive and backbreaking, the land produces abundant root and grain crops even though fertilizers are used only minimally.

North of the middle belt and also reaching right across the country is the wide northern belt. The rainfall diminishes considerably so that the land is semidesert in its more northerly parts. There the farming season is very short but crops of grain are good, and cotton and peanuts not only satisfy Nigeria's needs but are valuable exports.

The Slave Traffic

In earlier centuries the coastal people had contact with the rest of the world. In the nineteenth century, when the export of slaves died down, concurrently with more peaceful trading pursuits missionaries from Britain and the United States settled along the coast and at towns not far inland. They brought with them the benefits of education and medicine. Thus the Yoruba, Ibo, and other tribes living near the coast obtained an advantage over those who lived inland, for fifty years elapsed before even a small beginning was made in the interior.

To help understand the middle belt reference must be made to the traffic in slaves. The current race problem in North America arises from the hundreds of thousands of West African people who were exported to America in the eighteenth and nineteenth centuries. Plantation owners bought these people from the shippers. The English and Dutch were prominent among these; they risked the serious health hazards of African seaports in order to fill their ships with suffering mankind. They themselves did not capture the people but bartered for them with beads, trinkets, and cheap gin. It was the powerful coastal Africans, whose followers went to the interior as far as the middle belt, who captured men, women, and children. By way of illustration, over a hundred years ago a German linguist in Sierra Leone chose a hundred key words and interviewed slaves to obtain the equivalent words in their mother tongues. In the 1950s another linguist took these same words from a Benue hill tribe and found them to be so similar as to leave no doubt that at least one of the people who had been interviewed in Sierra Leone a century before had been of the same people.

The coastal trade in slaves ceased long ago. Within the country of Nigeria this was not so; it continued there into the present century. In this also the middle belt suffered; some towns of the Benue

Province had to pay an annual tax of slaves to the emir of Sokoto. Some of these were used within Nigeria, while others were forced to stagger across the desert to North Africa or across the continent to Arabia. As it is true that Europeans and Americans were wrong in this slave trade activity, it is equally true that Africans were wrong in the part they played in enslaving their fellow men.

The slave trade is mentioned because of its far-reaching effect on the inhabitants of the middle belt. In the past they were open to attack by residents from coastal and northern belts and sometimes by tribesmen of their own area. This affected their way of life. Many small tribes sought safety by living in isolation on the sides and tops of hills which were difficult of access. In the Benue area I recall climbing one of these hills to the village of Furum. The path was steep, narrow, and dangerous. After hours of sweating upwards in the tropical heat the path petered out. At that point we approached the protective device the villagers had contrived. There a tree trunk, and beyond it another, were suspended by ropes from above. Each man, facing the sheer rock wall, had to step first onto one tree trunk and then the other one, slowly edging his way across to the other side. A false step would precipitate a fall of a thousand feet to death below. Every night and at times of danger the drawbridge was removed.

Farmland and water were almost nonexistent on such rocky eminences. When a people for the whole of their lifetime lived under such conditions of privation and fear the effect upon their culture can be imagined. When water had to be carried up such steep slopes it would be used for drinking and cooking. Since very little water could be spared for washing or doing the laundry such people might not be as clean as others. Farming could be done only in the valleys so that time and energy were lost and the harvest was limited. So much hard work with meager rations and a diet low in proteins had a marked effect on the physique of the people. The hill was a fortress and none strayed very far from it. Spears, knives, and bows and arrows were the equipment of every man and boy; there was continual fear of the enemy. Under these conditions social intercourse with other tribes was very limited in pre-British times. Consequently there were many marriages between near relatives in small tribes with its consequent problems. Many of the people in the Wukari Division lived under these conditions when the missionaries first arrived among them.

The Tiv Tribe

It is believed that the Tiv people entered Nigeria from the Cameroon hills to the east. Before the twentieth century they lived in the plains on gently rolling country south of the Benue River and on both sides of the Katsina Ala River, which is a tributary of the Benue. In 1910 a rough estimate of their numbers was two hundred thousand. Little was known about them and in their territory there were only one or two very small riverside tribes and trading settlements favored by Hausa transients at Katsina Ala, Gburuku, and Abinsi. At that time the provincial capital of Makurdi did not exist, nor did Gboko. At the time the Benue River was a main thoroughfare, and overnight camping on the sandbanks was common. Travelers preferred the north bank, for then the river formed an effective barrier between themselves and the hostile Tiv tribesmen.

The Tiv lived in open bushland and for the most part they had no hills to turn to for safety. They never lived in towns or villages and preferred homesteads of one, two, or three families. They still do so. This is a tribal characteristic and differentiates them from the rest of the tribes around them. Because of it the gospel witness and building up the church of Christ has had to follow a different course among them. It may be supposed that because they lived in such small groups they were easy to attack and defeat, but it is not improbable that this led to their safety. In case of attack the African drum telegraph immediately went into operation, homes would be emptied, and the Tiv would go into hiding or lie in ambush and make life dangerous for the invaders.

Because of their separated mode of life the Tiv had no paramount chief, and clan heads had little authority. In order to carry on government by indirect, native rule the British developed the clan concept and ultimately a paramount chief, Tor Tiv, was installed. In 1930 Gboko was an uninhabited place on the watershed between the Cross and Katsina Ala rivers. It was chosen to be the center of Tivland and was slowly developed into the government administrative center of Tiv Division. It is now a thriving and fast-growing city and the Tor Tiv has his home and headquarters there.

The Tiv are a virile, fertile people and under the peaceful control of Britain their aggressive nature took them far afield beyond their own borders into the north and northeast. They have settled far to the east beyond the Donga and Taraba rivers and many of them are now living north of the Benue River, some as far as sixty and eighty miles from that river.

The Jukun and Chamba Tribes

The Jukun people are to be found scattered through the wide plains to the east of the Tiv. It is said that they originated in Egypt.

Although this is difficult to substantiate, they do carry out certain customs native to Egypt. For example, upon attaining a certain age the men are allowed to wear a double queue of plaited hair at the back of their heads, and these men never wear anything above the navel when in the presence of their divine king. In the seventeenth century they were a powerful nation, a conglomerate of animistic peoples who were able to threaten the city of Kano on one occasion. During the eighteenth century Jukun power began to wane and in the nineteenth century it was necessary for the tribe to move from Kororofa to Wukari. This enabled them to be near the valuable salt mines of Akwana and Awe which they controlled. They, like all other tribes, were forced to submit to the British when they came in 1900. Wukari became the divisional headquarters but in 1931 the extent of its jurisdiction was greatly reduced when a new divisional headquarters for the Tiv was started at Gboko eighty miles to the west. The remainder of the Wukari Division was divided into three districts and a small piece of trust territory held under a mandate of the League of Nations. In time the three districts became coequal parts of a federation and the League of Nations territory became part of the Adamawa Province. In this way the Jukun empire was greatly reduced.

The well-developed animistic religion of the Jukun has had a very firm hold upon the people. As a result they are well disciplined and display respect for authority and age. When in the 1920s they permitted the British to place the deposed emir of Sokoto and his retinue at Wukari it emphasized the influence of the Muslim religion among their people. They also permitted the Christian mission to function freely in the area and, although the response was very light for forty years, ultimately Christ has found a place in Jukun hearts also. The triumphant history of the Jukun of long ago leaves a proud imprint in the lives of the remnant which lives today.

The Chamba tribe is indigenous far to the east of the Wukari Division and is not within our area of mission activity. However, in the latter part of the nineteenth century a warlike segment of this tribe invaded the land, entering through the Cameroon foothills at Gashimbilla. It set up small towns there and at Galumje, Chenchenji, Donga, and Suntai. The people along their line of march were overcome. One physical evidence of this is the moldering town walls which may be found hidden in the tropical growth in places like Lupwe and Kwambai. These walls were built by order of the Chamba people. A number of towns still have Chamba chiefs but for the most part their people living in the Wukari Division no longer speak their mother tongue; instead they use Jukun.

Muslims in the Area

The Hausa people number several millions in Nigeria and with the Fulani are heavily concentrated in the emirates of the far north. Many of them are able traders and travel far to carry on their business. They settle in towns and a company of them will be found in any sizable community. This is true in the Wukari and Tiv divisions, and in towns like Ibi and Chinkai they form the major element in the mixed population. As the Tiv did not live in towns this did not affect them except that in these later years Tiv and Hausa intermingle in such places as Makurdi and Gboko. Nearly all Hausas are Muslims. Although they are not active missionaries of their faith, wherever they go they do proclaim it. Five times a day they offer prayers and will do this in whatever place they happen to be. Their Koranic catechism classes are held openly along the roadside and every Friday they congregate together in the early afternoon for public worship, regardless of the difference in sects. These manifestations of their faith with their annual fast and feasts proclaim their faith and bear an influence in the community. The Islamic faith in Nigeria has been adulterated by the animistic and superstitious cultures practiced by those surrounding it and makes it different in some ways from that found in other parts of the world.

To sum up, in the Wukari, Tiv, and United Hills divisions of the Benue Province there are many tribes. The Tiv tribe is very large and is migrating well beyond its original borders. The Kuteb, Ndoro, Tigum, Ichen, and other smaller tribes are found in the hilly country near to the Republic of Cameroon. There are one or two riverside groups and the Jukun and Chamba are scattered in the eastern plains. In earlier days all of these were animistic in their religious beliefs. Groups of Hausa people are found in the towns and are of the Islamic faith. With the exception of the Tiv people a great many of the men of the other tribes speak the *lingua franca,* the Hausa language. Many of them also speak one form or other of Jukun as a second language. In 1910 these all were on the threshold of a new and different life. At that time all were poor, food was not plentiful, and clothing was not available to the average home owner. Fear reigned and cruelty was common. There were no schools or hospitals, consequently ignorance and disease were very common. It was to this situation that a few missionaries addressed themselves. Those who would reach the Tiv people had to learn their language for they knew no other. The other missionaries after some experimenting decided to first learn Hausa and to use it as a medium of communication. It was not ideal but with the limited personnel available it was the best approach when interpreters were used. The use of Jukun was not ignored and before 1920 missionaries had translated and had printed three versions of the Gospel of Mark, each aimed to suit a different locality.

The Rev. J. E. I. Sai was chairman of the Tiv Church for many years. His father established the village of Sai where the mission to the Tiv people first began.

3

South Africa and the Tiv at Sai

Dr. Kumm Visits South Africa

During 1907 Dr. Karl Kumm visited South Africa in search of more Christian workers and support for the Sudan. Enrico Casaleggio tells us that before his arrival a conference was held at Stellenbosch and at one of the meetings the Rev. C. T. Wood pointed to the Sudan on a map and said, " 'Here lies the greatest unevangelized territory in Africa.' Rev. J. G. Botha said these words hit him like an arrow." [1] To him they were the call of God so that when Dr. Kumm appeared on the scene, Botha took steps immediately to serve Christ in the Sudan. After his ordination he went to England for a short course of instruction in tropical diseases. Then in October 1908 he and V. H. Hosking left for Nigeria. Hosking was a Methodist and Botha was of the Dutch Reformed Church, the first Reformed witness in this field. The two men were the first missionaries of the South African Branch of the SUM. In 1909 other workers joined them; two of them were single women. This was a new and brave venture for women in so primitive a land and they were the forerunners of hundreds who have served Christ there.

Hosking and Botha began work at Dilli, two or three hundred miles to the east but it was in 1911 that C. W. Guinter of Wukari helped Botha look for a site for a mission station twenty-three miles south of Wukari. Government officials had indicated that it was permissible to witness in the villages east of the Wukari-Takum road and that the Tiv people living to the east could also be ministered to.

At the time the name *Tiv* was not known and another less courteous term from the Hausa language was used. The mission was allowed to build on the west side of the track but in 1911 owing to adverse reports about the warlike behavior of the Tiv no mission work was allowed for more than one hundred and fifty miles westward of that point. Still, it was a beginning.

The British government made the offer to the Americans in Wukari that they begin work in the Tiv tribe. Guinter wrote to Botha immediately telling him of the offer and saying, "our branch cannot hope to open work among the Tiv for some years." This information reached Botha and his colleagues at Dilli when they had already decided not to carry on there. They had considered Tangale but the same day that Guinter's letter arrived, word was received from the government that they would not allow work to be opened there. After a day of prayer and consideration of the offer to enter Tivland they decided to accept it. It took Botha thirteen days of horseback riding to reach Wukari. Even so he left immediately for the south with Guinter and they chose the site at Salatu or Sai. The step of faith had been taken promptly.[2]

At the time only the Tiv living east of the road could be reached, but soon afterwards, the remainder, then believed to be two hundred thousand in number, were allowed by the authorities to listen to the gospel. For a long time it was thought that the Tiv were too dangerous to allow the movement of strangers among them. Eventually, however, the government found that missionaries promoted peace since they were not out to exploit the people but wished instead to help them. The missionaries were glad to take the message of the love of God to the Tiv regardless of whatever danger they might encounter.

The South Africans settled in Salatu. Casaleggio points out that this was a mispronunciation of the Tiv expression *Saa i utu,* meaning "matters of the night."[3] *Sai* is the name of the place. It was a Tiv homestead and its respected father, Mr. Sai, allowed the missionaries to settle there. One of his sons, J. E. I. Sai, was among the first four men to be ordained into the Tiv Church. A knowledge of Hausa was of no use to Botha and his colleagues. The Tiv did not know it and they did not like the Hausa people; so the Tiv language had to be reduced to writing and a vocabulary and grammar had to be written in it. Casaleggio quotes Baikie who met the Tiv (Mitsji) in 1854 as saying, "The Mitsjis, as far as we can judge, are wilder and less intelligent than the other African tribes with whom we came in contact, [on the Niger and Benue rivers] except the Baibai-

Jukuns."[4] After the briefest of contacts explorers record snap judgments. This was one. A stocky, strong Tiv, whose facial markings had been enlarged by keloids might look wild if he didn't smile. But for him, or a Jukun, to be described as "less intelligent than the other African tribes" is grossly wrong. Both Tiv and Jukun are intelligent people and once granted the advantage of education are equal to any others.

The Dutch Separate from the SUM

From 1908 until the present there has always been a South African Branch of the SUM. It is interdenominational in character and is governed by a committee in South Africa. By 1915 there were four couples of the Dutch Reformed Church serving this branch. They were Rev. and Mrs. J. G. Botha, Rev. and Mrs. A. J. Brink, Rev. and Mrs. W. Malherbe, and Rev. and Mrs. J. Strydom. At that time their church requested permission to leave the SUM and to work independently of it. This appeal was granted and the separation took place on July 1, 1916, eight years after Botha and Hoskin came to Nigeria. Hoskin, A. S. Judd, and other members of the South African Branch as a branch of the SUM went to Keana, north and west of the Benue River and started a new field there. Later on the SUM regretted that this step of complete separation had been permitted and when other denominations wished to do the same thing it was arranged that they remain part of the mission. They had their own area of service, autonomy in personnel and finance, and ecclesiastical control of the work.

Denominational fields were not unknown in the mission work in Northern Nigeria. The Anglicans of the Church Missionary Society had been in Lokoja since 1865 and Zaria from 1905. The Mennonites and Church of the Brethren of North America began work in the early decades of this century. Within the SUM organization and before the separation of the DRCM there were Lutheran branches from Norway and Denmark. The formation of the DRCM Nigerian mission field was with goodwill and complete understanding on both sides. It did mean that for more than forty years the work among the Tiv developed tribally, linguistically, and ecclesiastically without reference to other churches and tribes within the SUM orbit. This conformed to the traditional nature of the Dutch Reformed Church of South Africa and the separatist attitude of the Tiv people. The DRCM did have contact with the Conference of Missions of Northern Nigeria and later, the Northern Missions Council. Soon after its formation the Tiv Church became a member of the Tekas Fellowship of Churches.

Notes

1. E. Casaleggio, *The Land Will Yield Its Fruit*, p. 8.
2. Ibid., p. 12.
3. Ibid., p. 13.
4. Ibid., p. 17.

4

Johanna Veenstra

The CRC Defers Involvement in Africa

It was in 1918 that advice was given to the Christian Reformed Synod to investigate Central Africa and China as possibilities for the expansion of mission work. One of the first grounds stated for this investigation was the conclusion that mission funds would go much further in conducting foreign missions in comparison with work in New Mexico. It said concerning work in Central Africa (and this is a free translation from the Dutch language), "Because in recent times various voices in our church have called for the opening of a mission field in Central Africa, very favorable reports from the mission field there have been received and indeed a member of our church has already been accepted for work there."[1] Dr. Lee Huizenga and Dr. J. C. De Korne made a report favorable to the initiation of mission work in Africa and this was submitted to the Synod of 1920. Synod's committee, however, advised, "That our church begin the work of missions in China and not in the Sudan." This advice was accepted.[2] The reasons against the choice of the Sudan are of interest, especially since the church did take up work in the western Sudan (Nigeria) twenty years later. Translated from page 92 of the Agenda for Synod which was written in the Dutch language, we read that:

> (a) Mission work in the heart of such a tremendously huge land with very poor highways brings with it all manner of practical difficulties. (b) The danger of political

33

complications. (c) Little or no opportunity for the education of the children of the missionaries. (d) The peoples of the Sudan belong to the types of mankind from which one cannot expect the most in the Kingdom of God. (e) The climate presents serious objections. (f) The close cooperation with churches of less pure confession which are associated with the Sudan United Mission fills us with fear for the maintenance and propagation of our Reformed principles.[2]

There is no purpose in evaluating these statements since later the CRC did enter the Nigerian field with enthusiasm and vigor, and in view of the fact that the Lord blessed the work to a measure far above the fondest expectations of the most ardent proponents for entering that field. Since the sentiment of the Synod was such in 1920, it was perhaps wise for it not to accede to the recommendation of Huizenga and De Korne to go to the Sudan. Besides, when it decided not to go to the Sudan it did decide to go to China. In doing so it stepped outside the North American continent and began its foreign mission work. Even though political issues eventually closed the door to China, by a thread it held on to a Christian witness in the Far East, and the work in Japan and other places is now eloquent testimony to the goodness of God to the CRC. Moreover God's design to use the CRC in Africa was there in 1918. That thread was sometimes one CRC member, sometimes three or four. After twenty years God's purpose for the CRC came to pass in the Sudan.

Miss Veenstra's Early Years

The First World War was harsh and although Karl Kumm had become a naturalized British citizen, yet because he was born a German, he was unacceptable in Britain. He found asylum in the United States and there his zeal for the Sudan continued unabated. His public appearances inspired many, among them, Johanna Veenstra. In the summer of 1915 at Lake Geneva in Wisconsin, Dr. Kumm gave a stirring address which greatly moved Miss Veenstra. She was called of God by this means and after spending three days in prayer "she yielded her will to the Lord to obey Him."[3] It was because of this young woman that the CRC eventually worked in Nigeria.

Miss Veenstra was the third of six children born to Mr. (later the Rev.) and Mrs. William Veenstra. Mr. Veenstra was a carpenter by trade. When he felt the call of God to the ministry he and his family left their home in New Jersey to go to Grand Rapids to study. In 1900 he was ordained in the Christian Reformed Church of Zutphen,

Michigan, but before he had served that church for a year, he died of typhoid fever. Johanna, born April 19, 1894, was almost eight years old when her father passed away. The family moved back to New Jersey where her mother opened a store. After her fourteenth birthday Johanna took a job in New York as a stenographer to help her family financially. There came a critical point of decision for her when she was fifteen years of age. She tells about her spiritual life in her book *Pioneering for Christ in the Sudan*. Of the conflict in her soul she said of herself, "But why all this struggle? The Holy Spirit made it clear to me. I wanted peace, but in my own way. I was very willing, more than willing, to give my *heart* to the Lord, but I shrank from giving my *all*. I wanted to be a child of the King, but I fought desperately against consecrating my *life* unto the service of that King! But who was I to withstand the power of the Almighty? He prevailed" (p. 32).

It was at the Park Avenue Baptist Church of Paterson, New Jersey, which she sometimes attended, that she surrendered to her Lord one Sunday evening. "She walked to the front of the auditorium, knelt down, and definitely gave her heart to the Savior."[4] This was her first public confession. A few months later she did so again, together with forty-four others, when she became a communicant member of her own Christian Reformed Church. For Johanna it was not only asking Jesus Christ to be her Savior but also making a total and complete commitment of her whole life to Him. Many Christians never reach this point and most of those who do, do so some time after their conversion. But Johanna's struggle had been concerned with total surrender and when she did so she did so altogether so that henceforth Jesus Christ would be her Lord indeed. To her this was a very real experience.

She had received her grade school education in a Christian school. After a course at a business college she served for a time at the Star of Hope Mission. Then she took a three-year course at the Union Missionary Training Institute in Brooklyn. While in training she responded to God's call given her during Dr. Kumm's visit in Wisconsin and was accepted for service in Nigeria by the American Branch of the SUM. However, the Mission's rule was that she must be twenty-five years of age before going to Nigeria, so she filled in the time by serving the Eastern Avenue CRC in Grand Rapids as a mission worker half-days and studied Reformed doctrine for the other half. Later she took a seven-month course in midwifery and practical medicine at Bellevue Maternity Hospital and worked at the Paterson Hebrew Mission for a few months. So she had business ability, a good knowledge of the Scriptures and doctrine, some ideas on how to meet medical and maternity emergencies, and a lot of practical mission experience with Jews and Gentiles.

Her Life in Nigeria

Not only by her church membership but by her never wavering loyalty Miss Veenstra linked the CRC with Nigeria for thirteen years. She left New York on October 2, 1919, aboard the S. S. Mauretania. A page of a letter she wrote when she left America after her first furlough is reproduced here. The underlining is by the author. The reader will see the large place her Lord had in her heart and how joy and prayer are emphasized. She says that her life motto was, "Be strong and of good courage; be not afraid, neither be thou dismayed: for the Lord thy God is with thee whithersoever thou goest."[5] During student days she wrote, "Seek to do hard things and beware of easy tasks," and in physical trials and spiritual challenges she carried this out. The title of her book, *Pioneering for Christ in the Sudan*, is a fair and good one. It takes a full quota of courage to travel "alone" on an African river for two weeks, resting at night on the sandbanks and listening to the call of a wild animal or the splash of a crocodile nearby. Fortunately she almost always had missionary companions. Together they endured the hardships as pioneers are supposed to do.

She made light of physical trials. In 1925 she wrote, "We are now in the thick of the rainy season, pools everywhere. Just now there is a lovely shower. It is so cozy under a grass roof—by a kerosene lamp—heaps of insects flying about for company—crickets singing and frogs croaking—dear Africa. And for a touch of home we will have the 'Hallelujah Chorus' or so on the victrola."[6] When she was thirty-five years of age she could write to some friends and say, "I only returned a few days ago, and got a proper drenching on my way home. I pushed the wheel [bicycle] 23 miles, and over a steep mountain pass in the heavy rain, so I was pretty tired. But am all over it now, and happily busy as ever, rejoicing more and more as the days go by."[7] Although a devoted and serious person, she could see the humorous side of life and once wrote, "I am told the photo makes me look fatter than I really am. I don't mind that, you know. Africans favor fat women, and so I am more in their favor by having added weight, and so I just think it is lovely to be of good size." When one can call a grassroofed shack a "cozy home," and when insects, crickets, and frogs have ceased to be a burden, and when climbing a steep mountain pass makes one rejoice more and more, then one really has arrived.

36

The day has been a glorious one in nature, and a large crowd came to N.Y. to see me off. My mother was there & I choked the tears but would not permit them to fall. And there was every reason to rejoice. The Lord has been so good. His grace so abounding, and I was heavily laden with all His tokens of loving care. My relatives and friends showered me with gifts of money and useful things, and _I lack nothing_.

Thank you for the beautiful card with the precious message. It was in my room together with a few others from such. And in the last few days I had so many letters and callers that my heart was overwhelmed and I could only utter "O Lord how good Thou art." I sat quietly alone on the upper deck this evening in the beautiful twilight - reflecting on His love, and only praying - Lord - may I love Thee more! May I be more faithful unto Thee and Thy service.

Mr. Stam was also with the group. We sang and prayed on the boat, and then they sang after they got off - "Take the name of Jesus with you" and "anywhere with Jesus I can safely go." Dr. Kumm and Mrs. K. were also in the group. It was not a sad parting, and surely there must have been much prayer - for the Lord wonderfully sustained and restrained. I wanted it to be a time of rejoicing as there is so much to call for the high note of praise and it seems more

---

A page from a letter written by Johanna Veenstra shortly after she sailed for Nigeria after her first furlough. (Underlining by the author.)

Critics speak harshly about missionaries employing domestic help. This is hardly fair if, for instance, all water must be carried a quarter of a mile and then boiled and filtered; or if the cooking must be done over an open fire of wet wood; or the laundry be done in cold water in a galvanized tub in the backyard. A full day's work for others had to be done and the bush missionary was on call at all hours of the day and night. If third class help could be employed to help with the simpler chores it was a sensible thing to do and not beyond the limited means of the missionary. Miss Veenstra supervised the erection of new buildings and the repair of old ones. She attended the sick and was called out at all hours and under adverse conditions to help expectant mothers. She taught the Scriptures, preached on Sundays and weekdays, made reports, kept the accounts, traveled continually, and stirred up interest in America by writing letters and magazine articles in order to encourage hoped-for support. In February 1930 she wrote, "There is constant blessing in the work. It has grown to that point where the supervision of it just about takes all my time and nerve energy." She had at that time just finished a trek with Mrs. D. Forbes which had lasted twenty-four days. This companion, who was older and heavier than Johanna, had valiantly climbed the mountains also, being propelled upwards by three men, one on each side and one behind.

There were sorrows to endure and share. She tells of George Botha and his wife and two-year-old daughter, who was seriously ill. "Near midnight I was called to help and later on through the mud and water, I went down to the beach over half a mile away, to the [river] steamer where the parents and sick child were. I saw the little one was very ill. . . . At dawn we walked to the mission station. At nine o'clock that same morning the little one died in my arms. The father said, 'Safe in the arms of Jesus, my darling.' The mother prayed for grace. I tenderly washed this little corpse, dressed it for burial and sat in the hut until the little box coffin was made." In such ways she shared the sorrows of others.

I have visited this little grave and near it is a larger one. For a time two members of the CRC, Mr. and Mrs. John Bierenga, were colleagues of Miss Veenstra. Mrs. Bierenga laid down her life for Christ in Nigeria five years before Miss Veenstra did, and was buried at Ibi. She died of malaria fever before she had spent a year in the country. While in her last illness she was carried, in a hunter's net, on the shoulders of African porters for eighty miles in order to get help. But at the end of that rugged journey she died and was buried near Botha's daughter. This was a terrible blow to Mr. Bierenga. He continued at Lupwe without a colleague for another year but illness forced him to return to America. He and his wife were two of those who strengthened the tie between Nigeria and the CRC.

After her arrival in Nigeria early in 1920 Miss Veenstra spent a year as a probationer at Donga. She then worked at Lupwe under the Rev. C. Whitman throughout 1921. For several years before that missionaries had visited Takum and the villages on the mountains around it. In the Donga logbook we read, "From April 6 to May 3 [1917] Mr. Whitman was on an investigating and evangelistic tour among these hill people. Some sixty services were held where more than 2600 persons heard the gospel. Lissam is recommended as a suitable place for an outstation." Already in 1916 the interest in the gospel was so great that a young Nigerian Christian of Donga, Timon Mama, had been persuaded to settle in Takum as a witness for Jesus Christ. He was followed by Irmiya and Filibbus Ashu, who were of Wukari town. These were resident missionaries in Takum District before there was a mission station there. It is important to note this use of newly born-again men and women right from the beginning of the Nigerian work. A basic principle of missions in Northern Nigeria has always been that every believer must be a vocal witness to his or her Savior. Truly, missionaries went about "preaching" and doing good and this was fruitful in a limited way. In addition each Christian, even before he became a church member, was telling his friends the good news of Jesus Christ. Some of these ardent converts left their homes at the suggestion of overworked missionaries and went to other towns to be resident witnesses for Christ. They also went about preaching and gathered fruit of converted souls. These were the first home missionaries of the yet unfounded Nigerian church. The harvest increased in volume as the number of Nigerian witnesses increased. It proved to be a blessing that foreign missionaries were kept in short supply because it encouraged the use of local men and women.

First Buildings at Lupwe

Towards the end of 1919 when Irmiya and Filibbus Ashu were resident in the area, the first missionary was posted to Lupwe. He was William M. Bristow who had recently left the British armed forces after serving during the First World War. He arrived at the end of the wet season when the grass was at its highest and he had to struggle with the untamed bush in order to build a home. The stone and clay for the foundations, walls, and floors; the poles, grass, and fibers for the roof all had to be won from the surrounding countryside. Wood from packing cases met the need of doors and window

The first church at Kwambai was built about 1930.

The first simple home at Lupwe was built in 1919 by W. M. Bristow.

The chapel at Lupwe was built in 1936 as a memorial to Johanna Veenstra. Funds came from special offerings taken in CRC Sunday schools each Palm Sunday.

shutters. Add to this large quantities of perspiration, and much frustration caused by a completely unskilled labor force speaking an unknown language and yet Lupwe obtained its first home of two circular rooms with a large veranda, all under one roof. This was another mustard seed from which a great tree was to grow. Some years before there had been a town at Lupwe, but its inhabitants moved away to become part of the town of Takum. A visitor who cares to force a way through the heavy undergrowth will be able to find the wall of the old town and walk around it. At one corner he will find a spring of fresh water, the beginning of the Bika stream which was invaluable to the mission for a great many years.

As early as 1915 a training center had been established at Wukari in order to train seekers after Christ to know the Bible and become leaders. Our present efforts at Lupwe, Wukari, Baissa, Harga, and Serti were inspired by the original school at Wukari. It was hoped that village chiefs would send suitable lads to Lupwe to be trained. For this reason the site was chosen four miles from Takum town to lessen the temptations of an urban area. It had a good water supply, plenty of farmland, and plenty of people in nearby villages to be evangelized. For the missionaries who came from temperate zones the location was trying because the circle of high hills on every side cut off cooling breezes and made the location hot and humid. After fifty years it makes up fourteen acres of well-kept grounds, with many tropical fruit and shade trees, several homes, two or three offices and a large school complex with a chapel at its center. The training program at Lupwe has seen a number of changes, but it still is the station's main function. At present it is a training center preparing men for theological studies. A large medical ministry was also carried on from this station until 1967.

Mr. Bristow finished his buildings early in 1920 but it was not until February 1921 that the Rev. C. L. Whitman of Canada and Miss Veenstra went there from Donga. Mr. Whitman was in charge and added to the buildings at Lupwe while Miss Veenstra did simple medical work. Both were active in trekking to other villages, many of them on the tops of hills. The records show that at different times they carried the gospel to the people on Kunabe mountain, a place which was to resist the message of Christ for forty years. It is now blossoming out for Jesus Christ.

In addition to the evangelists already mentioned three other Nigerian workers appeared about this time. In the Lupwe station report for October 1920 we read, "At Takum a man named Audu, who during the war was a headman of porters in East Africa, made public confession of Christ."[8] He was baptized and became a full church

41

member on April 6, 1922, after attending catechism classes for eighteen months. He was destined to become the Rev. Istifanus Audu, the first ordained minister of the Ekas Benue Church. At the time of his conversion he had been practicing the Muslim faith, but he had been brought up in a Jukun animist home. Then there was Habu of Ibi who was an evangelist and led Audu to faith in Jesus Christ. Afterwards he became a government worker in charge of the town medical clinic and served as a church elder at Ibi until his death more than forty years later. The third man was Jonathan Wamada, who was baptized the same day as Audu and Pa'ana, who was known as the daughter of prayer. Pa'ana and these men were chosen vessels of God and, with Filibbus Ashu, remained in the faith until God called them to higher service. Only Audu is still with us, serving the Takum Church.

Orphans Saved to Serve

When the British took control in Nigeria, the Hausa/Fulani practice of enslaving men and women, girls and boys of the Middle Belt died out slowly. For many years travelers, especially river travelers, were stopped by the police and their belongings and canoes were searched. Children were often found hidden under the matting on the floors of the canoes. These youngsters had been stolen from far-off places and knew nothing of the whereabouts of their homes. In time the authorities turned to the SUM for help in caring for these children and a home was established for them. Missionaries brought them up until they reached their midteens, by which time the boys were able to fend for themselves and the girls could be married. Many of them became Christians and the girls were sought out by new converts so that they might set up Christian homes. This was a wonderful provision made by God to meet the needs of the men when girls of their own tribes had not yet responded to the gospel.

Jonathan Wamada married one of these orphaned girls, Ra'utha (Ruth) and Filibbus married another, Astira (Esther). They were and are fine women of God. Astira had seven children, the last being born after Filibbus died. Contrary to local custom she refused to marry again and insisted on raising her children herself. They are now leading Christians in church, community, and government. Ra'utha had no children but they adopted eleven children and kept them until they became of age to marry. One of the sons, a teacher, was secretary of Ekas Benue Church for many years. So God turned the sorrow of early childhood days into long lives of blessing. This happened in very many cases. God used the mission to bring Christ to lost orphans and thereby strengthened the life of the Christian family and church.

Slow Growth of the Work

In 1923 Mr. Whitman, who in the meantime had married, had to retire to Canada due to ill health. At the same time the Guinters of Wukari left the area and started a new work much farther to the east. That year, upon her return to Lupwe from America, Miss Veenstra took charge, helped by colleagues loaned by Britain and Canada. It was in 1925 that other Americans, the Rev. and Mrs. W. Hood, joined her. Miss Veenstra handled her leadership role well, was firm in her decisions, and followed the pattern laid down by the SUM. Her justice was tempered with mercy. She continually cast herself upon God for wisdom and help. Any case of sinfulness in the little flock cost her much emotional distress and heartache, as did the discipline carried out in order to restore the erring one to Christ. Signs of progress, no matter how humble, caused her to rejoice in God. In his day Abraham of old had only one true son of faith but in time his descendants became a great multitude. Compared with the 1960s Miss Veenstra saw only a small and erratic advance in her days, but compared with the 1900s she witnessed a mighty blessing from the Lord.

Without reference to Takum and other towns and villages the first record for Lupwe station shows that an average of five persons per service listened to the gospel. Five years later it had risen to sixteen and averaged only twenty-three in 1930. The same was true of the medical ministry when in 1921 an average of only twenty patients per month were recorded and in 1930 this had risen to forty-four. Only very slowly was the confidence of the people built up in these pale and sickly looking strangers. For much of that time the number of missionaries averaged only two and they had much more to do than is indicated in "preaching" and healing. Each person healed helped to break down suspicion and distrust and was a step forward. The boarding school in which the Bible and other subjects were taught shows the same trend. It was begun in 1923 when it taught nine boys. By 1930 this number had risen to thirty, which included some girls and women. It succeeded in teaching some to read and write, and the value of possessing and being able to read the New Testament in the Hausa language was very great when 99.9 percent of the population at that time was illiterate. Persistence, patience, and great faith were needed by the workers.

However, most of their energy and a great deal of their time was

These two old people at Kwambai urged the people there to turn to the Christian way. With the exception of one or two families they all did so in 1930, rejecting their traditional religion.

This photo, taken about 1930, pictures some of the first Christians in the Takum and Lupwe area.

spent away from Lupwe—and the above statistics reveal nothing of this activity. To trek through the countryside demanded courage and physical strength. In November 1924 Miss Veenstra wrote, "After the Council meeting I pushed the pedals of our good friend, the bicycle, for eighty miles and came back to my own station. It was 'Home sweet home' and there was plenty of good hard work to be done." It would take her five days to cycle the eighty miles from Ibi to Lupwe and two days to recover from the trials of the journey. It was over rugged footpaths, patches of deep sand, twisted tree roots, and hidden stumps designed to send the unwary headfirst over the handle bars. It was in the tropics with high humidity which soaked one with perspiration. Where there was no ice or cold water six or even eight cups of tea would be needed to help one recover from dehydration. Bush journeys uphill and down, through streams and miles of lonely uninhabited country or heavy forests were the lot of most missionaries until the 1950s. These trips, though time-consuming and a drain on energy and health, were gladly made that people might hear that Jesus saves. Single women, married couples, bachelors—all will tell you that they were very worthwhile and rewarding.

This is true even though the fruit gathered for Christ was so meager in those early days. This was partly because the missionary aimed for perfection in the "convert" and was often disappointed by a lapse which did not measure up to the ideal. The ideal might be the observance of one day in seven as a day for worship and rest, and for one who had never known or practiced this custom it was easy not to keep it. The records show that many were disciplined for not observing the Sabbath. They also show that many seekers who were not yet baptized were erased from the register for drinking strong drink, committing adultery, or gambling and the like. When the number of believers were few to start with, the statistics take a dive downwards when one or two were set aside for lapses in moral conduct. There is criticism of what was done in earlier days, but what was done was done in faith and good conscience in an attempt to lay the foundations for a pure church. To have had no discipline would have produced a church built upon sand which would have disappeared in time of adversity. In 1924 the reports show that seven Africans partook of the Lord's Supper at Lupwe; by 1932 the number had risen to twenty-one, a gain of fourteen in eight years. This was slow indeed, but more understandable when we read that two adults were baptized who had been "faithful enquirers for at least six years" and so learn that it was not easy to become a communicant member. Thirty years later the pendulum had swung to the other extreme and crowds were baptized after only six weeks instead of six years of instruction.

In the efforts to create a holy church it is interesting to note the emphasis placed on conferences for the deepening of spiritual life. These recurred frequently. In October 1927 Miss Veenstra reported: "During this month we have held special services for two and a half days for our Christians. These meetings were for prayer and heart searching. As a result there has been a great confession of sin and failure. No less than twelve Christians arose to confess sin, and others are still desiring to do so. Among the sins confessed are: coldness of heart, lack of zeal to witness for Christ, adultery, stealing, lying to God, lying to man, beer drinking and palm-wine drinking, evil communication, fighting. On the part of some, especially the baptized Christians, it was a great struggle, and while at first we thought there would be no break, suddenly the Holy Spirit gave liberty and there was a great humbling followed by many confessions. We are asking God to cleanse us altogether and to empower us by the Holy Spirit—that Christ Jesus may reign in our lives and through our witness come to rule in the hearts of the people all about us."[9] Records of such meetings are frequent. In 1932 Miss Veenstra wrote: "At Kwambai we also had special days for heart searching and prayer. Over thirty of the Christians arose to confess some sin of which God convicted them. These meetings were full of spiritual power."[10] Public, spontaneous confession of sin and manifestation of the outpouring of the Holy Spirit were common, and from time to time have recurred up to the present. In North America we are often suspicious of public manifestations of repentance or other public manifestations of the work of the Holy Spirit. However, God does work that way, as can be vouched for in our ministry in Nigeria. Perhaps in North America we are missing something special from God.

Self-Support

By unanimous consent the five branches of the SUM working in Nigeria adopted a far-reaching principle of procedure. It accepted the ideal of indigeneity as proposed by Roland Allen. Although it was very difficult to implement, it was wise that this step was taken. In the beginning it meant that the SUM tradition of paying Nigerian Christians to witness and teach had to be stopped. This change was resented by those who had benefited and for over thirty years the writer was to hear complaints about this action taken by the mission. The plan was that the believers indigenous to a locality should govern, support, and propagate the Christian faith themselves. The free use of Nigerians as witnesses, even long before they were church members, has been mentioned. After 1923 it was up to the Nigerian converts to pay their own workers and to build their own churches, pastors' homes, schools, and other facilities. This required a lot of persuasion. A difficulty which has always contributed to misunderstanding is that from the Nigerian point of view the missionary appears to be so rich whereas the peasant farmer has so little by comparison.

To promote the new scheme of self-support Miss Veenstra introduced the system of giving something every week in envelopes. The promise in those early days was for the husband or the wife to give one or two pennies weekly which at that time could be compared with a casual laborer's wage of eighteen pence per week. But this low giving was augmented by tithing farm produce. Since everybody farmed this was a big help, especially when many gave a full tithe of their harvest. When a family harvesting a hundred bundles of grain gave ten of them to God, or ten families gave, say, a hundred bundles, then there would be sufficient to feed their evangelist's family for a year. Chickens, sheep, or goats would frequently be given and the money from the sale of them helped to swell the village church's treasury.

Churches and other necessary buildings of a simple nature were erected by the Christians donating material and free labor. The women worked as hard as the men and carried in rocks, earth, and water to make clay for the walls, and roofing poles and grass for thatching purposes. Earthen floors would be beaten by singing women and seats and pulpit furniture made from clay by the men. The missionary pitched in to help and was especially useful to ensure good bonding for the bricks and in assembling and erecting the main rafters for large roofs. These simple structures lasted for only a few years but during that time the group had grown stronger and was able to build a better building. Moreover the principle that the believers must build their own place of worship had been firmly established. If they wished the second or third building to have a concrete foundation or a metal roof they knew that they must collect money to buy the necessary materials. Loans are unheard of and a building progressed as the money came in so that some buildings took three or four years to build.

With some tears and frustration on the missionary's part, self-support came to stay. In May 1929 Miss Veenstra wrote to a friend, "During the past year quite a few workers have been removed from Missions here in Nigeria and one cannot but ask, 'If the Lord removes me, will the work be so that the Christians can carry it on?' I want to teach them to be wholly dependent upon the Lord, and take away every crutch that we missionaries give them to lean on. It is not fair to the work of God's Kingdom to train them to be so dependent upon us. More and more I see the need of a self-supporting, self-governing church here in Africa. And because this is not the way our CRC works in China or on the Indian field, probably the Lord saw best that they should not take this field. Mission work costs so little if the self-supporting policy is strictly adhered to. But it is the hardest way. And the missionary has to move to the background. We humans do not always like to choose the hardest and the most humbling path of duty."[11] Hard and humbling indeed!

The first full-time worker at Kwambai was sent there by the Takum congregation which promised to support him. The Kwambai people at the time were not believers and, unfortunately, the Takum Christians forgot their financial obligations. The worker, Danyelu Nasamo, frequently complained of hunger and after twelve months he died. It was said that he died of starvation and the missionaries were blamed for his death but it was an unfounded criticism. Sometimes the missionary was unwise. At the time of her death Miss Veenstra had made it known that all useless items of her property were to be burnt or buried. What is useless to one person is not so to another who is poorer, and the missionary was foolish to follow the advice. In his zeal he complied with the request and it was only years later that he discovered how badly some of the Christians rightly felt about his action. Through trial and error a way had to be discovered how to apply a good principle diplomatically.

Self-Government

Teaching the young church self-government was a slow process and demanded patience; but it was steadily pursued and has been very successful in common with the other aspects of indigeneity. The plan of our Lord Jesus was followed. Jesus chose His disciples and they went everywhere with Him, learning from Him, and learning by serving. Paul did the same with Timothy, Titus, and Luke. Whitman had Timon; Miss Veenstra had Filibbus, Kazo, and Danyelu; and the Smiths had Istifanus, Yohanatan, and Siman Audu. It was an excellent method and practical experience obtained by traveling and witnessing together was invaluable. Sometimes a governing principle would evolve from a happening in the small company of believers. A rumor of ill behavior needed the procedure laid down by Christ in Matthew 18. But language difficulties and cultural problems drove the missionary to confer with his Nigerian helpers. To delve into the subtleties of a way of life so different from that of the foreign missionary required the help of those who were used to it. When it came to divine direction concerning a problem, the missionary knew God's Word and could instruct the Christians from it. Together they would struggle with the matter and with much prayer reach a decision. As decisions were made they formed a background of tradition which eventually became an integral part of the church order for a church not yet formally organized.

These decisions were not the dictatorial action of a missionary. They were taken by Nigerian church leaders in consultation with missionaries. Any matter of more than minor importance was also referred to the leaders of other branches of the SUM for their consideration when a principle was involved. Some were so weighty as to encourage consulation with all the Protestant missions working in Northern Nigeria. The outcome of such consultations was not binding on any one mission or church, yet at the same time the course of action which found general approval became the practice throughout the region.

The Christians were new in the faith and, having turned to Christ from animism, had had no Christian influence in their homes. They naturally believed and followed whatever the particular missionaries taught them. Miss Veenstra was the leader for ten years in the Lupwe-Takum District and her views on doctrine and church practice often prevailed. In this way a Reformed tradition was planted there. For instance, when the question of small children and their relationship to the church had to be faced she called the believers together and explained the Reformed view on infant baptism and the concept of the covenant. She then arranged for a Baptist minister, the Rev. D. Forbes, to place before the same group his teaching on believer's baptism. The Christians considered these two views for a year and then, not long before Miss Veenstra's death, decided in favor of the covenant teaching. It is interesting to learn that Mr. Forbes baptized the first thirteen children in August 1933. In reference to this same subject, however, it is also true that the Ekas Benue Church did not then, and does not now, baptize a child until both parents are confessing members of the church. This is because of the Nigerian way of life and the extended family system. A child is almost wholly under the control and discipline of the mother during its early years and later it is at the disposal of its father who might be inclined to have the child reared in the home of a heathen relative or married to an unbeliever. The church ruled that one could be more certain of the fulfillment of parental obligations if both parents were in the faith and not one only. Here is an illustration of how Western custom must give way to African culture. Suffice it to say that self-government was a basic principle and was learned in the school of experience. Many decisions were born out of much travail and prayer.

Continued Interest of the CRC

It was a sorrow to Miss Veenstra that organizationally her ministry was not officially under the Christian Reformed Church. She had been firm of purpose in going to Nigeria in obedience to her Lord. This was not made easier when ministers sought to persuade her to leave Nigeria and go to China. In 1921 she wrote to a close friend, "I have been asked to change and go to China (not officially) but by one minister at home and by _____ from China. I expect when home more ministers will probe me on the matter. God only knows I want His will in the matter. I am often hungry for my own people and feel a great lack, but His grace is and will be sufficient if I am to continue here. I have fought hard this term for our high standards and discipline, and have been told, 'Keep on, you will yet win.' If God would use me here for His glory I am willing, though my flesh and nature cry for the fellowship of 'eigen bloed en soort [own blood and flesh].' But also I can enjoy the oneness of believers in Christ and have heart fellowship with them."[12]

During her missionary career Miss Veenstra spent four periods away from Africa; one of these was spent in England, the others in the United States. She was an able speaker and had access to many CRC churches. She attracted large audiences and was well liked by the women. In 1922 she was a valuable asset to the semiannual gatherings of the Women's Missionary Unions, which movement began in the twenties. It in turn did much to encourage her by prayer and gifts. Her gracious ways and public speaking did much to endear her to the CRC denomination.

In 1928 three classes of the CRC, those of Muskegon, Grand Rapids East, and California brought overtures to the Synod to consider favorably the taking up of the work in Nigeria. However, the Synod's committee of preadvice proposed that "Synod not go into this matter on ground of decisions taken re China and Indian fields."[13] This proposal was adopted. After this the Synod of 1930 had a communication from Miss Veenstra before it which was referred to the Board of Missions for investigation and report to the Synod of 1932.[14] But when the two years had elapsed, the Board proposed "to defer action on this matter to the Synod of 1934 because of the present economic situation, and of the need of further study of the subject by the Board."[15] By 1934 Johanna Veenstra had gone to her eternal reward. That year Synod accepted the Board's recommendation not to assume responsibility for the SUM field. The reason given was "the economic situation. This work would involve an expense of $10,000 annually."[16] At the time there were three single CRC women working in Nigeria. At the Synod of 1937 requests were presented by Classis Holland and the consistory of Second Fremont CRC regarding the Nigerian work and the Board was told "to investigate this field of labor [Sudan Mission], and to advise Synod at its next meeting whether or not our Church should adopt it as its own."[17]

Reference will be made to other decisions of the CRC later. These will show that from time to time various parts of the denomination were interested in the CRC becoming involved in Africa but this did not take place during Miss Veenstra's lifetime nor for several years afterwards. Ultimately her prayers and the prayers of many others were answered. She adhered to the Reformed faith, and at the same time she adopted practices which promoted the speediest possible spread of the gospel and the economic soundness of the Benue Church as it pertained in the Nigerian situation. She also enjoyed close fellowship with many other evangelical Christian missionaries.

Johanna Veenstra's death

For many years Miss Veenstra was a member of the Field Council of the SUM which met once a year. In 1933 after attending this council which met on the high plateau she sought the advice of Dr. P. W. Barnden. There was evidence of chronic appendicitis. Since the plateau climate was good and since there was a hospital nearby, whereas Lupwe was a long way from one, Johanna decided to have an operation before returning to the lowlands. Five days after the operation, at dawn on Palm Sunday, April 9, 1933, she died at Vom Hospital. An autopsy revealed that the appendectomy was successful but death was caused by an obstruction and heart failure. On March 18, three weeks before her death, she wrote to some friends and in speaking about Nelle Breen's early departure for Nigeria said, "I don't doubt . . . they [her dear ones] will ask, 'What may the future hold in store for each of us?' And how kind of our Father to veil that future. How little we long to know the distant scene lest it should be to us a revelation of fear and tears. And when the day comes for any experiences of sorrow or keen disappointment He supplies the grace

Johanna Veenstra first went to Nigeria in 1919 and served Christ there until her death in 1933.

The cross marks Miss Veenstra's grave. She was buried here in April 1933, the first missionary to be buried at Vom.

for the trial. So we look forward by faith, knowing that we are His, and that He will never leave us. We are very eager to see Nellie again, I especially so, and then we may be able to give some longer visits to our newest outcenters." Before this letter reached its destination her relatives, her colleagues—Nelle Breen, Bertha Zagers, and Jennie Stielstra—her children in Christ and the whole of the CRC were plunged into grief. So godly and dedicated a woman, not yet forty years of age, called home to be with God just when there was a breakthrough of blessing, now no longer to be enjoyed and tended by the one whom God had chosen to nurture its beginnings.

Two hymns were sung at her funeral. The first, "Jesus Triumphant," set the right note for a life lived fully for Christ. The other, a favorite of Johanna's, is a clear testimony to the aim and undeviating purpose of her life. It was F. Brook's hymn:

My goal is God Himself, not joy, nor peace,
 Nor even blessing, but Himself, my God;
'Tis His to lead me there—not mine, but His—
 At any cost, dear Lord, by any road.

So faith bounds forward to its goal in God,
 And love can trust her Lord to lead her there;
Upheld by Him, my soul is following hard
 Till God has full fulfilled my deepest prayer.

No matter if the way be sometimes dark,
 No matter though the cost be ofttimes great,
He knoweth how I best shall reach the mark,
 The way that leads to Him must needs be straight.

One thing I know, I cannot say Him nay;
 One thing I do, I press towards my Lord;
My God my glory here, from day to day,
 And in the glory there my great Reward.

Notes

1. CRC Acts of Synod, 1918, p. 86.
2. Ibid., 1920, pp. 49, 50.
3. Veenstra Memorial Booklet, 1933, p. 6.
4. Recker, Sunday School Notes, *The Beginnings of Christianity in Africa*, p. 2.
5. J. Veenstra, *Pioneering for Christ in the Sudan*, 1926, p. 68.
6. J. Veenstra, Private letters, June 10, 1925.

7. Ibid., August 9, 1929.

8. This was a person's declaration before the congregation to say that he was seeking Jesus Christ. Baptism and acceptance into church membership might take place at a later date.

9. Lupwe Station Report, October 1927.

10. Ibid., November 1932.

11. J. Veenstra, Private letters, May 1929.

12. Ibid., September 1921.

13. Acts of Synod, 1928 Article 52, IV, 2, i.

14. Ibid., 1930, p. 35, (2).

15. Ibid., 1932, Article 80, 3.

16. Ibid., 1934, Article 77, 2.

17. Ibid., 1937, Article 121, c.

18. J. Veenstra, Private letters, 1933.

5

The Work Continues

Available Personnel

The field of labor to be covered stretched from Wukari and Donga in the north through Takum and Lupwe to Katsimbilla, 100 miles to the south. There were small but fluctuating churches at Donga, Wukari, and Takum with a total of some thirty or forty communicant members. At Takum three men, Filibbus, Istifanus, and Umaru Matta had been installed as elders in the church for which office they had been trained by Miss Veenstra. Those at Donga and Wukari had been trained by other missionaries. Although the believers were few in number and many of them had not yet been baptized, nevertheless they were keen witnesses for Christ and many served as voluntary workers. The outreach of the elders, evangelists, and missionaries into the Kuteb hills had been greatly blessed in some places where it had become a mass movement towards Jesus Christ. This was to become a lavish harvest but it had been preceded by many hard years of steady, plodding gospel testimony.

Takum town had first been visited in 1907 and the earliest reference to the "Takum hills" relates to Mr. Whitman's activities there in February 1913.[1] It was early in 1916 that the first resident Christian witness settled in Takum; he was a Nigerian evangelist from Donga. The following year there was extensive trekking into the surrounding hills. This exploration with the gospel was carried on regularly for many years by one or two missionaries and Nigerians but with very meager results. In June 1926 the record shows that two villages were holding Sunday services with 7 people attending at Lissam and 14 at Kwambai. By 1930, four years later, the service at Lissam had been abandoned but the meeting at Kwambai had risen to an attendance of 120. After another six years we find that three other Kuteb villages had joined the Kwambai breakthrough and the four meetings showed a total of 335 persons attending Sunday worship. In marked contrast to the tribally mixed and transient city groups, the villages of Kwambai, Fikyu, Jenuwa, and Acha were farming communities and were all of a single tribe, the Kuteb. They had openly rejected their tribal religious practices and publicly burned their witchcraft emblems. They were of one culture and language.

At the time of Miss Veenstra's death there were three other women, members of the CRC, working with her. At Lupwe there were Bertha Zagers of Fremont, Michigan, a trained nurse, and Jennie Stielstra of Hardewyk, Michigan, a trained teacher. Both of these had been in Nigeria for nine months. Then there was Nelle Breen of Holland, Michigan, who was completing her rest period in America after serving as a teacher in Nigeria for two years. The SUM American committee decided to carry on the work left by Miss Veenstra and sent Miss Breen back to lead the little group of workers and believers. When passing through London she sought the advice of the general secretary of the SUM there and he urged her to retain the Wukari-Donga-Lupwe District as a distinctly American venture. She and her colleagues accepted this advice and the believers supported them in their decision.

It was not easy to implement the decision to carry on. The leader, a powerful personality, was gone. The three women were new, struggling to learn the Hausa language and trying to get used to each other. There were African Christian leaders who had been in the work for a long time and it took much time and patience to get used to each other and to accept one another for Christ's sake. In October 1934, just before Miss Zagers and Miss Stielstra left for their furlough in the United States, Miss Breen married Edgar Smith. He was a missionary of the British Branch of the SUM and had served at Ibi for a term in the headquarter's office there, and before going to England had transferred that office to Gindiri about 150 miles to the north. In the autumn of 1934 he returned to Nigeria and was loaned to the American Branch to work at Lupwe. After his marriage to Miss Breen he continued on secondment from Britain until the close of 1939. This move was considered to be wise by SUM authorities in order to keep personnel at Lupwe rather than deprive it of missionary staff when the work was proving to be very fruitful.

It was a joy to the young couple that Miss Veenstra had been

Johanna Veenstra (seated) and (left to right) Nelle Breen, Jennie Stielstra, and Bertha Zagers constituted the entire Lupwe staff in 1932. They were all members of the CRC but were serving the Sudan United Mission at that time.

In 1934 Ed (Edgar H.) Smith and Nelle Breen married and he was loaned for several years to the American SUM by the British to work at Lupwe.

aware of their proposed union. In September 1932 she had written to Smith, who was an English Baptist, "The thing that astounded me was that *I* felt so given to let you have your own way, that it never occurred to me to discourage Baturiya. . . . From the moment she told me about you I never felt a single vexation of spirit. I had and still have a calm confidence and assurance that God will have His way in the matter. What a help it is to feel 'He is leading.' But *how* I miss her. Especially since here in Donga. She was such a genuine sharer in the trials I had with all the palavers. Such a sympathizer and 'bearer of my burdens.' " Smith was not an ordained minister but he had had thirty months of rugged training at the Missionary (Pioneer) Training Colony in London and two terms at Livingstone College, studying the basics of tropical diseases and medicine, whereby the Nigerian government permitted him to help in the mission's medical ministry.

The Medical Ministry in the 1930s

Smith was able to assist in the medical work for many years, especially when visiting the villages, but the heavy burden of the department was borne by the nurses. Bertha Zagers served until 1936. In 1937 Tena Huizenga, of Chicago, took up the work and four years later she was joined by Anita Vissia of Grand Rapids, Michigan. Each of these women was totally dedicated and worked under difficult and very primitive conditions. There was no doctor to diagnose the cases which came for help nor to prescribe suitable medicines. The nurse had to do this and then treat the patient with the aid of Nigerian nurses' aides. When visiting in the villages this work had to be carried on under a shade tree, working from a wobbly card table, and sterilizing instruments by boiling them in a cooking pot placed on an open fire. Crowds gathered to watch the proceedings, the giving of injections being a very popular feature. There was no privacy while it was being done. It is fair to say that the work which these nurses and their African helpers accomplished under very adverse conditions was phenomenal.

The first full year under the control of a registered nurse, Bertha Zagers, was 1933, and the average number of new patients treated each month rose sharply to 110. Although Johanna Veenstra had done a little medical work, it fell to Miss Zagers to set a course for a fuller medical ministry. A new treatment clinic had been built at Lupwe and was a great help. Those patients who had to stay for a few days were given very simple rooms in which to live. Miss Zagers started the treatment of lepers, a ministry which continues until the present time. The medical treatment in the thirties was hydnocarpus oil given by injection. It had only limited success. Yaws, an unsightly disease afflicting especially children, did respond to treatment. This seemed miraculous to the relatives—seeing bodies covered with ulcers completely healed in three weeks time. This was not always so. A quack medicine man brought two of his children to Miss Zagers, but they died despite several days of careful nursing care. Some time later the father, Ndechifun, became the first Christian believer at Fikyu. When he was asked what turned him to Christ he said it was the love and sympathy which the nurse had shown to his children.

During Tena Huizenga's early years at Lupwe she had to contend with epidemics of smallpox and meningitis in addition to the full daily routine. Both diseases were very contagious and the death rate was high. Grass shelters had to be erected away from the mission station in the bush where the relatives could stay with their patients. The nurse and her aides did what they could to nurse them back to health. Sometimes because of fear the relatives would abandon their own kin, making burials a major problem. Even though they were simple and took place a few hours after death it was difficult to get graves dug, especially when the relatives had run away. The scare over smallpox helped the missionaries very much in their campaign to promote vaccination. Year after year all on the mission compound and those living in the villages around were encouraged to be vaccinated. Although frequent repetition of vaccination was unnecessary the missionaries gladly stood in line and were vaccinated every year in order to assure the fearful ones that it was all right. Muslims did not in those days respond to the invitation as it was rumored that bodies marked with this scar would be kept out of the Islamic hereafter.

The mission at Lupwe was able to make one large contribution to the better health of the Benue Province in the 1930s. Sleeping sickness, *trypanosamiasis Nigeriense*, was increasing rapidly as the population moved more freely through the countryside. At first government health authorities were not aware of this, but Ed Smith as he traveled about collected specimens of the tsetse fly in each place that he visited and sent them to the center for trypanosamiasis research hundreds of miles away. After three years had passed, this evidence was conclusive, and in July 1938 a large team of workers was sent by the government to Takum. This invasion by a hundred strangers scared the populace for some days but after a while they submitted to having their necks examined for enlarged glands. If a smear from these examined under the microscope revealed the germ the person was treated over a period of a few weeks. Without treatment death would ensue, often preceded by a most distressing period of madness. The inquiry, started at Takum, systematically proceeded throughout the district and ultimately throughout the whole Benue Province. At the end it was estimated that an average of 10 percent of the population was treated for the disease. At some points of the Takum District it reached 30 percent. Today the incidence of the disease is very low in that province and is almost unknown to the general public.

By 1936 Lupwe had two Nigerians who had been trained at Vom Hospital. One of them, Audu Siman of Galumje, had been a school-boy at Lupwe in the 1920s. He was not only a capable nurse but also a great spiritual influence in the district. On one occasion he was called to see his father, the chief of Galumje, who was seriously ill. The mission report for September 1937 records, "The witch doctors were at their wits' end. They had done their divining and performed their fetish rites, but the chief grew worse. As a last result they sent to another village for a 'specialist' witch doctor. Before he arrived Audu Siman came. He asked whether now that they had done their best would they let him prove his God. He administered the medicines he had taken with him, and gathered a few who are interested in Christianity for prayer. After a couple of days of improvement there was a relapse. The witch doctors wanted to try again, but Siman assured them that there would be improvement next day. There was much prayer offered here and there and God heard. Ten days after he left, Siman returned to us rejoicing in the Lord not only for the restoration of his father but for the glorious victory over the evil one." This dear brother's testimony was a lasting blessing. He was bedridden for many months, slowly dying of tuberculosis, but his love for Christ was so radiant that every visitor to his bedside, Christian, Muslim, or pagan left with a blessing from God. He was God's man to demonstrate the quality of the new Christianity.

Education of Illiterates

Through the first years of the Lupwe boarding school, village chiefs had been persuaded to allow likely boys to attend. When the Lord turned the Kuteb people to Himself the young and not-so-young adults clamored to be taught and some of them came to Lupwe to study for a period of six months each year. During the dry weather which was not good for farming the farmers could take time to attend school if relatives would lend a hand at home. Both Nelle Smith and Jennie Stielstra were trained teachers and had taught in Christian schools in Michigan. As Mrs. Smith continued a full-time teaching schedule after she was married, these two, with such assis-

Several of this class of schoolboys at Lupwe about 1930 became pillars in the church. Daniel Ndeyantso (front, fourth from left) is now chairman of EKAS Benue Church.

tance as they could get from Nigerians, slowly developed an educational system. The farmer students were mostly married men who had never known paper or pencils when they were children. It was no light task to teach an undisciplined mind to read or untrained fingers to write. But it was done because both teacher and pupil were determined that it should be done and Jesus Christ was a living and present incentive to make it possible.

School attendance show these figures for 1932 and 1940. Attendance at Takum went from 20 to 39, at Donga from 17 to 18, at Wukari it declined from 22 to 18, but at Lupwe it increased from 49 to 60 and in the Kuteb villages from 46 to 120. As late as 1940 these were very simple schools and their main purpose was to enable the illiterate to become literate, thereby helping the seeker after Christ to meet one of the requirements for baptism, viz. to be able to read the Bible. The Lupwe boarding school went further as it trained Christians to become leaders and farmer-evangelists in their own communities. The school building was at first a very simple structure, open to the winds with no doors or windows and no furniture at all except a blackboard, and a table and chair for the teacher. However, an indirect result of the death of Miss Veenstra was the taking of an offering in many CRC Sunday schools on Palm Sunday each year, the Sunday on which she died. A first use of this money was to erect the Johanna Veenstra Memorial Chapel and School at Lupwe. This was erected by Smith and Sulle Carpenter and comprised a chapel and four classrooms. The latter had doors and glass windows as well as furniture for all the students. It was destroyed by fire thirty years after it was built but the chapel was restored and continues in use until the present time.

In the decade of the 1930s the government slowly evolved its education policy for Northern Nigeria and the fruit of this became clearly defined a few years later. Both it and missions had the uphill task of inculcating a desire for education into the minds of the people. This took much time and patience. Where the town and village chiefs became interested they encouraged their people to seek education, and schools were opened. Where they were indifferent or opposed to the peasantry being educated there was no progress at all. After thirty years, into the 1960s, in the northern belt where opposition was common, educational ignorance enveloped 95 percent of the youth. On the other hand, in the middle belt where there had been encouragement, after thirty years of steady growth as many as 30 percent of school-age children were receiving a primary education.

When free of their boarding school duties at Lupwe the teachers spent much of their time living in other towns and villages. They set up simple literacy classes where there were none, and the Nigerian teachers in these and the longer-established centers were encouraged by visits of as long as a month's time. More important still the missionary nurses and teachers were primarily evangelists and served the spiritual needs of the community and church. They spent many weeks of each year away from home living with the people. Women as well as men conducted worship services, held instruction classes for the leaders, developed the catechism ministry, taught in the schools, treated the sick, and reached new places with the gospel story. It was a full though tiring life which gave immense satisfaction.

Transport and Trekking

Miss Veenstra had once tried to use a motorcycle but she fell and hurt herself. A friend helped her to finish her journey in his motorcycle and sidecar. On the journey they hit a hardheaded ant hill hidden in the grass and turned upside down. No one was hurt but this was enough of motorcycles for Miss Veenstra. In 1934 two American school teachers supplied the field with another machine. This provided transportation to keep the workers in touch with the world and with hospitals. It was a great advance over the bicycle and Shank's mare. The motorcycle with sidecar often took three adults, a baby and sixty pounds of luggage a distance of 350 miles on dirt roads to the fresh air and fresh food of Miango on the high plateau. Like its motorcar successors it took many patients to hospital. One was a woman who had been in labor for sixty hours, transported to hospital, propped up in the sidecar, one of the driver's arms being used as a head rest. But after twenty miles of travel she died. Very late at night her body, shrouded in a piece of canvas but still sitting up, had to be transported back to Lupwe. The corpse had to be returned to the relatives as evidence that she had really died and had not been spirited away by the missionaries. She was buried at dawn and then the "ambulance" driver had to preach at the nine o'clock service.

In the thirties two children were born to the Smith family, Alyce Jean and Paul Edgar. These proved to be a blessing to the community. A common belief was that white people were not born, but that they came grown up. The advent of the children dispelled this impression. First one and then the other "trekked" on the handlebars of their parents' bicycles. By living among them the people

A three-wheeled motor-
cycle was the first mecha-
nized transport at Lupwe.
It could carry three adults,
a child, and sixty pounds
of baggage. Many journeys
of three to four hundred
miles on dirt roads took
three days to complete.

Crossing a stream on a
bush bridge can be ex-
citing.

This dirt road near the
Baissa forest is typical of
those traversed by cycle
and car.

could feel them, count their toes, see them laugh and cry. Sometimes, if they could find a peek hole, they could see them nurse. When one woman saw this she flung her arms around Mrs. Smith and said, "Thank you, thank you for having this baby. You are just the same as we. Now your God can be our God too." In such simple ways barriers of doubt, distrust, and fear were removed and confidence was built up to lead to the acceptance of the gospel message. This was true whenever the missionary lived in the homes of the people. The very fact that he or she would stay overnight in a village had a marked effect for good relationships between the two races. In earlier days many places had suffered grievously at the hands of foreign traders and it took many years of visiting and of bringing medicines, sympathy, and love before real confidence was established.

These journeys were always made with Nigerian Christian companions. In addition there would often be a few porters as well who were usually Christians. In the evening or in the moonlight when a crowd had gathered there would be singing. In the Jukun or Kuteb languages this singing would be antiphonal, often taking the form of questions and answers. This was a most valuable way to teach the gospel as the tune and words would remain with the hearers months after the missionaries had passed that way.

In 1936 Ed Smith and Siman Atajeri of Donga made their maiden trek to Gindin Dutse, now known as Nyita. It was memorable because the small, white-haired chief was so captivated with the message of Christ that he insisted on it being repeated again and again. Like others untouched by civilization he was a perfect gentleman. Within a few months this man encouraged his people to turn to Jesus Christ. He was not to live long but it was long enough for him to die in the faith. When he was dying he left strict orders that he was to be buried as a Christian and not according to the customs of his forefathers. Fortunately two Lupwe Christians were near at the time to help the bewildered relatives know what to do and what not to do when a Christian died. His death was a turning point for Gindin Dutse and it is now a flourishing Christian community.

In January and February 1937 another forward step was taken when Istifanus and Smith with Musa Chiroma and Habila Adda trekked through Ndoro and Tigum territory and climbed the Mambila Plateau. They left Miss Stielstra and Mrs. Smith at home to do the work at the station and school and Audu Siman to care for the sick people. They were away for forty-five days on their 350-mile journey by foot. Every day the sick were helped and the gospel was preached. On this journey the first contact was made with the village

Several weeks of each year were spent by the missionaries visiting the villages. This type of one-room accommodation would be their home. Canvas cots and chairs for ease, bush lanterns for light, but no bathroom.

When unable to walk or cycle to the villages, Mrs. Smith and others sometimes used this one-wheeled push-about. It suited the narrow footpaths. Note the tall grass.

Even the babies went into the bush. Here William Recker rides comfortably in a basket.

of Baissa which led to the opening of a mission station there twelve years later.

Brief though the visits were they were valuable. By them firsthand information was obtained as to what needed to be done. Further knowledge was gained by subsequent journeys. The forest tribes got used to those from bush tribes. Many of them saw a white man for the first time and were distressed at his sickly color, which they didn't favor at all. But this man and his friends had a message, and as far as could be seen had no ulterior motive but to tell about a strange God who loved them. The value of a passing contact is illustrated by the account of two Christians who climbed into the hills south of Lupwe where they met " . . . a certain Umaru who had been a believer for seven years. He had heard Filibbus and Istifanus preach in another village seven years before. For all that time he had refused to take a second wife although she had been paid for. He also kept Sunday and had caused nineteen others to follow [Jesus] with him."[2]

The Church Grows

Whereas the women were mainly engaged in teaching and nursing, it was Smith's primary task to care for the spiritual work of the whole area. He preached regularly, often with the aid of a Christian interpreter who, sentence by sentence, translated the message from Hausa into Jukun. He rotated his ministry so as to serve as many regular preaching centers as possible. These included the long established places of Wukari, Donga, Lupwe, and Takum, and the newly emerging villages of Kwambai, Fikyu, Jenuwa, and Acha. These places not only met for worship every Sunday morning but there were also catechism classes, Sunday school for adults and children, and public prayer meetings on Wednesdays. Lupwe and the newer centers had early morning prayers every day. The sun was the clock. With the first streaks of dawn a bell (usually a strip of metal) was rung and at sunrise it was rung a second time when morning prayers were offered. This service included the singing of a hymn, reading from the Bible with an explanation of the passage followed by prayer, and was concluded with the Lord's Prayer said in unison.

Catechism classes were open to any who had shown the church leaders at a regular monthly meeting that they were ready for instruction. They were called inquirers and for many years had official recognition in the church. An inquirer was a long step ahead of a church attender. They were not yet baptized but they had declared their faith in Jesus Christ, consequently as has been said

The fifth church built at Takum. Three of its forerunners burned down and one was destroyed by a hurricane.

This, the second Fikyu church building, was abandoned in favor of a third. The ''jungle'' is reclaiming the site.

earlier, lapses in conduct necessitated disciplinary action. While exercising discipline to these or to church members it was discovered that there was a strong tendency for discipline to become legalistic and so lose some of its spiritual purpose. But standards had to be set. In Africa standards are naturally affected by African cultures. Matters pertaining to marriage and sex have always been the most prominent. In those days stealing was rare but lying was common. Lapsing into idolatrous and fetish practices was even more so. It continues to be difficult for missionaries with American or European cultures to understand African ideals in the building up of the church. Yet when African churches (denominations) have been organized it is essential that they be permitted to make their own decisions on matters of discipline.

After Miss Veenstra's death the church leaders were glad to have a male missionary join them and they worked well together. There were six of them in the Takum area and of these Yohanatan was full-time worker at Kwambai and Filibbus was in charge in Takum town. In September 1935 Filibbus died suddenly of a cerebral hemorrhage. His death was a shock to the church and mission. He had served Christ faithfully for seventeen years after graduating from Wukari Bible Training Institute and the loss of so outstanding a leader was a great blow to the Christian community.

Later on Istifanus Audu was recognized as leader of the Takum area but it was several years before he became a full-time worker. He earned his living as a tailor.

In those days it was not easy to be a Christian. For a long period Istifanus was subjected to much vile abuse, especially by the local political hierarchy and the Muslims. Formerly he had been a Muslim. Unwholesome songs and unclean remarks were publicly shouted along the streets at his and his family's expense. He was the Takum church leader and he was especially grieved when a frog, an evil creature in the eyes of the people, was inscribed with a curse on its yellow belly and laid at the door of his home. This sort of persecution turned none from the faith; instead, their faith was strengthened by it.

It was the same in the mountain village of Acha when the village elders were so severe on the new Christian converts; many were the beatings that they had to endure for Christ's sake. The most dangerous enemies of all were backslidden converts. When Nyita was turning to the Christian faith a chief, who had once been a church member, so arranged it that one of his wives was found in the leading Christian's room. He was wrongly accused of committing adultery and had to endure the red pepper ordeal, the suffering of which was intense. Through suffering, Christ builds His church and such happenings did not diminish but rather increased the number of believers.

Missionaries were not exempt from danger. One illustration must suffice. Two women missionaries were alone in a mountain village. Their quarters for the night was a doorless dwelling large enough to contain only two cots and a small table. The sun-baked walls were four inches thick and in this shell they had to spend a sleepless night. Many of the villagers were drunk and worked up to a pitch of mad hatred. The frenzied crowd danced and drummed and yelled and cursed their way around and around the tiny building until the dawn appeared. But "the peace of God which passeth all understanding shall keep your hearts and your minds through Christ Jesus." There is restraining grace to protect those who are on business for their King.

The oldest organized congregation in the Benue field is located at Donga on the river by that name. It was established on June 17, 1917, with twelve charter members, six men and six women. It has had a checkered history with much backsliding. In the thirties it dwindled to almost nothing. But the faith and persistence of Kwancha Dawuda, a carpenter by trade, maintained a witness there and eventually he was to see it become a very fine indigenous ministry in the Benue Church. The work at Wukari, where the SUM had been so active in the 1910s and early 1920s, also dropped very low in the 1930s. Here also Iliya Gani, a humble gentleman, held on for Christ through bitter persecution. The following decade Christ began to manifest Himself in saving souls. Imagine then the distress of the missionaries when at this point Iliya who had once been poisoned for Christ's sake and who had endured a thousand insults should later estrange himself by becoming a bigamist.

In the 1930 to 1940 decade the church in Takum town held its own, the churches at Donga and Wukari lost much ground, but the new ones in the Kuteb country grew in faith and gained greatly in numerical strength. In those ten years attendance at Sunday worship services in Takum grew from 70 to 145, at Donga it remained at 54, at Wukari it rose from 32 to 67, and at Lupwe with the eight Kuteb centers it went from 130 to 820.

During that time there were physical misfortunes which disheartened the believers and tended to retard growth until fresh courage and faith enabled them to overcome their losses. One incident will do to illustrate this. During the weekend of an annual Christian convention being held in Takum, a fierce wind blew tufts of burning grass from a bush fire on to the thatched roofs of homes at the south end of town. It was late at night and within an hour half of the town was destroyed by fire. Many homes belonging to Christians, the church, school buildings, and the mission house were all destroyed. At dawn all that was left were masses of smoldering ashes surrounded by clay walls newly baked by the fire. It was Sunday and the Lord's Supper was to follow the sermon. Soon the Christians had removed the hot ashes, the clay seats were dusted, and the pulpit furniture, which had been saved, was replaced. Then the service was held beneath the blue sky and the saints rejoiced in the Lord. Tomorrow was another day and slowly from the ashes of the past would arise evidences of hope for the future.

In 1936 the church made another important decision. From the point of view of affluence it may seem absurd in its insignificance but as a principle it has borne rich fruit. The station report records, "A long conference was held with Takum leaders. One thing was of great moment, a real advance was made. the leaders agreed to [set up] a general fund, separate from the usual church funds of each village. You will know that the funds of each congregation are used for the welfare of that congregation. It is now, at last, agreed that each place allocate one tenth of its income to a general fund. This fund will be used in helping nearby places and in sending the gospel into unresponsive areas."[3] Four months later we read, "It should also be noted that gifts were given to the British and Foreign Bible Society and that the collections for 1936 were much increased and nearly every place had a good balance in hand after helping others."[4] When set against a monthly offering at Takum of sixteen shillings, eleven pence, and eight tenths of a penny, say $3.40, a tithe of this would be one shilling, eight pence, and four tenths of a penny, or 34¢. For that month Donga gave a total of 65¢, a tithe of which was 6¢. The sum may appear ridiculous, but the principle was valuable, for the tiny church began to cultivate a concern for those who were outside their own constituency. There were annual harvest tithes for the use of the local village church and by 1940 the Kuteb villages were offering a thousand bundles of grain to God. Of this, one tenth, or a hundred bundles, was kept separate for the mission ministry of the church. This procedure continues until the present time and the evangelism account is the only one in the Benue Church which always has a good credit balance.

The remaining nine tenths of the offerings were used locally. They enabled the place where they were collected to pay a little to the Christian who came from elsewhere to be their leader. These workers were farmer-evangelists, just as the apostle Paul was a tent-making preacher. The money, especially in those days of world depression,

71

amounted to very little, but it was sufficient to buy salt and on rare occasions a length of cloth for the family wardrobe.

By 1940 there were fifteen Nigerians serving eleven hundred churchgoers in a dozen different places. At this time Smith was not ordained, but by a special provision of the British Branch of the SUM he was annually granted a license enabling him to administer the sacraments. In February 1936 he baptized the first eight men at Kwambai and of this he wrote, "It was a packed service and one which will ever be remembered for the amazing stillness which was over all for the whole length of the service. Representatives came from Fikyu, Jenuwa, and Acha. Istifanus supported me in the service and twelve [people] confessed faith."[5] The eight men who were baptized had been under instruction for four years and had been examined by the church elders at Takum. They were all married and were steady home owners, two of them being quite old. Three of them became full-time workers in the church and served for many years.

Notes

1. Donga Station Monthly Log Book.
2. Lupwe Station Report, February 1936.
3. Lupwe Station Report, August 1936.
4. Lupwe Station Report, December 1936.
5. See footnote 8, chapter 4.

6

Change of American Control

The American Interdenominational Committee

Apart from brief comments this history has not discussed the American committee which controlled the Lupwe-Takum field. There was an SUM committee in America comprised of individuals of various denominations who desired the spread of the gospel in the Sudan and this committee was the channel for obtaining personnel and funds for the work. In 1923 the Evangelical Brethren Church of North America, whose Rev. and Mrs. C. W. Guinter had served in Nigeria from earliest days, arranged with the SUM to divide the work in Nigeria. One part was to remain under the SUM committee, the other part would be taken over by a committee of the Evangelical Brethren Church[1] and would become a separate branch of the SUM. When this division took place the original committee which looked after the Lupwe missionaries arranged with the British Branch of the SUM to do so only on condition that in times of personnel and financial stress that branch would support the ministry in the now CRC area. For the seventeen years which followed Britain frequently helped out by loaning missionaries, paying their wages, and giving other financial aid. This will help to explain why later on Britain figured so largely in the transfer arrangements made with the CRC.

In those years the American committee sent out ten workers, including Miss Veenstra. Three of these were of other denominations and the others, a married couple and five women, were all members of the CRC. About 1934, two of our CRC ministers, the Rev. John

73

Beebe and the Rev. Jacob Hoogstra, were appointed members of the SUM American committee because of the increasing interest the CRC was showing in the Nigerian field. Two years later a Calvin seminary student was interested in becoming a missionary to the Sudan and inquiries were made as to the possibility of his being ordained to serve under the SUM. Because of the nature of the church order this could not be done and the matter was dropped.

Before leaving the SUM American committee, we note from its minutes that in January 1939 it agreed "to recommend to the British Branch the following: 'American Branch is of the opinion that the Lupwe field should be given to the C. R. Church in which said field this Church be autonomous ecclesiastically and doctrinally." In September of the same year, when it knew that the CRC desired to accept responsibility for the work, it decided "that the British Branch [S.U.M.] has the jurisdiction to negotiate the transaction."[2] This opened the way for the SUM of Britain to conclude the negotiations for transfer and the committee of the American Branch of the SUM terminated its organization on January 18, 1940.[3]

The Christian Reformed Church Takes Action

In the thirties the interest of the CRC in Nigeria steadily increased until in March 1937 the secretary of its Board of Missions, Dr. H. Beets, wrote to the SUM in London saying, "A voice has been heard to have our C. R. Church become responsible for a part of the Sudan United Mission field."[4] Later that same year the Synod entertained overtures from Classis Holland and the Hardewyk CRC urging it to inquire into the possibilities of becoming responsible for the work. As a result the Synod charged the Board of Missions to investigate this field of labor and to advise Synod whether to adopt it as its own.[5] In May of the following year a subcommittee said in its report to the executive committee of the Board, "according to its opinion, there are no insurmountable obstacles against taking over the field, and because of the considerable preponderance of arguments in favor of the work, humbly advises the Executive Committee and the Board to go on record as favoring the adoption of this field by the Church, and to advise Synod accordingly, provided, of course, that satisfactory arrangements can be made with the S.U.M."[6] A few weeks later the Synod requested the Board "to fully ascertain the conditions on which the Lupwe-Takum district of the S.U.M. field in Nigeria can be taken over by our Church and report to the next Synod."[7]

The Board did this and in its report it quoted a letter written by Gilbert Dawson, secretary of the SUM in Britain, adding its own explanation of the three points raised by him. From the Board's minutes we quote:

III. The response of the British Branch to the proposal of the American Branch is given in a letter from Mr. Gilbert Dawson, Secretary:

After careful consideration, my Committee have instructed me to say that they are prepared to hand over the care and control of the work in Lupwe district to the Christian Reformed Church on the same basis as that of the work carried on by the two bodies mentioned above, the Danish Branch (Lutheran) and the Evangelical Church of U.S.A.; that is, autonomy on the field and in control of the work, but association with the Sudan United Mission as part of the Mission, provided:

1. The Christian Reformed Church accepts the Doctrinal Basis of the Sudan United Mission and holds no doctrinal views which are not in accord with the principles of that Basis. A copy of the Doctrinal Basis is enclosed herewith.

2. The Church is willing to co-operate with the rest of the S.U.M. work in Nigeria, by appointing a representative on the Field Council, and by showing sympathy with the African Church aims of the Mission.

3. The Church is willing to continue the work along the Indigenous Church lines on which it has been conducted from the beginning, and which were so dear to the heart of Miss Veenstra.

IV. The Board herewith passes this information on to Synod, and further informs Synod:

1. That it sees no difficulty in the way of taking over this field as far as the doctrinal basis is concerned, because the S.U.M. has declared itself satisfied with our doctrinal standards. As soon as the decision of the British Branch, quoted above, was received our Secretary mailed to the London office of the S.U.M. a copy of our Doctrinal Standards, informing the brethren there that our Church carries on its work on the basis of our own Doctrinal Standards and asking them to peruse these carefully and to notify us at once if there is anything in them which would make them hesitate to have our Church work in the Sudan field. A cablegram from the Executive Secretary of the S.U.M. states, "Doctrinal Standards acceptable."

2. That it sees no difficulty in the way of taking over this field as far as ecclesiastical control is concerned. The S.U.M. offers us this field on the same basis as that of the work carried on by the Danish Branch of the Lutherans and by the Evangelical Church of the U.S.A. Synod has already learned from the report submitted in 1938 that these Churches enjoy autonomy in their mission work: "They (i.e. the S.U.M.) have no control over our work. We are directly responsible to our own church in America." The present attitude of the S.U.M. is thus more favorable than it was a year ago; at the time the previous report was submitted to Synod, the S.U.M. did not feel inclined to hand over the work to an independent body; now it is prepared to give us full control. Its proviso that we be willing to co-operate with the rest of the S.U.M. work in Nigeria cannot mean, in the light of other statements it has made, any curtailment whatever of our authority to conduct mission work along the Reformed lines which we consider essential. We now co-operate with other churches on our Indian and China fields, but in neither case has this ever meant a limitation of our authority.

Rev. John Beebe and Dr. J. T. Hoogstra, who are officers of the American Branch of the S.U.M., have submitted the following written statement:

"The second proposal is self evident. As the field council is administrative in character and advisory in emergencies, we think wisdom will dictate that, in the event we take over the field, our mission personnel be represented on this field council. Such questions as mission technique, relation of natives to chiefs, etc., are best dealt with on the field."

3. That it sees no difficulty in the S.U.M. proviso that we be willing to continue the work along the indigenous church lines on which it has been conducted from the beginning, subject only to the provision that everything be in accordance with the Word of God and Reformed principles.[8]

After considering this information the CRC Synod of 1939 authorized the Board to take the necessary steps toward taking over the Lupwe-Takum field from the SUM. It granted it permission to call new workers, stipulated that workers' salaries were to be according to British SUM schedules and that the budget was not to exceed $6,000 per annum. The reasons for taking the field were given in detail and may be summarized by saying that the field had a large

Dr. J. C. De Korne with Reta De Boer and Harry Boersma managed CRC mission affairs for many years after Dr. H. Beets resigned as secretary.

Dr. J. C. De Korne and Rev. H. J. Evenhouse display a young leopard. It had been killed that day (January 1947) by the men with the spears.

place in the hearts of CRC people who were already contributing a good amount of money toward its support. The field itself was acceptable because it was needy, it was fertile, and it was in a peace zone under British protection. It also pointed out that most of the workers were from CRC churches and the ecclesiastical and doctrinal control would be with the CRC. The price for carrying on the work was considered to be low.[9]

On July 7, 1939, the secretary of the Board, Dr. J. C. De Korne, wrote to the SUM in London and said, "I am happy to be able to inform you that our Synod authorized our Board to proceed to taking over the Sudan field, usually known as Lupwe-Takum field. All arrangements connected with the transfer of this field have been left to the Board and its Executive Committee and we hope to have further word from you on the matter soon. Questions such as the precise date for transfer and what to do about the present force on the field still remain to be considered with you."[10] Two months later De Korne wrote to the Smiths in Nigeria, "You have perhaps learned from other sources by this time of the action of the Christian Reformed Synod at its 1939 meeting. By unanimous vote it was decided to take over from the Sudan United Mission the Lupwe-Takum district in which several of our own people have been and are working. Since by your contacts with our people and by your addresses while on furlough you have had a part in establishing this connection, I want to congratulate you on the warm place that your field has already won in the hearts of our people. It certainly was providential that you were led to begin that work and that our people have become so enthusiastic about it."[11]

The British Branch secretary wrote to Dr. De Korne in September 1939 and urged the CRC to send a representative to Nigeria in order to get firsthand information on several points before the transfer was made. This was not done. As far as can be ascertained there was no formal transfer of the Nigerian work to the CRC. In America no references can be found regarding the work actually changing hands. If there were any in England, they were lost when the SUM office there was destroyed by enemy action during World War II. We only conclude that points raised in various letters written by the British SUM and the CRC were acceptable to and considered binding on both parties. The passage of time was to show that there were misunderstandings which might have been avoided had members of the London committee and of the CRC Board of Missions met in person and, after a full discussion, issued a joint statement of agreement.

Remaining a Part of the SUM

A major difference of interpretation was the relationship between the SUM and the CRC. This difference did not become apparent until 1947 when our secretary in Nigeria was invited to add to his duties those of field secretary for the five branches of the SUM active in Nigeria. He was nominated because the Lupwe-Takum field was one of the five branches of the SUM and had always had a seat on the Field Council of those branches. The CRC Board did not understand this relationship. The editor of *The Banner* commented on this matter in his editorial of September 8, 1938, where he quoted a letter written by the SUM British committee saying that the Lupwe-Takum field "should remain part of the work of the S.U.M. carried on along the same lines and on the same principles as the work of the mission generally." To make this plain the same letter continued by saying:

> My Committee had before them the fact that about twenty-five years ago the Dutch Reformed Church of South Africa had asked to be allowed to take over a portion of the work of the S.U.M., several members of that Church being then missionaries of the S.U.M. This request had been granted, what is known as the Munchi field being handed to the D.R. Church, but my Committee now felt that had this proposal been made some years later, they would have suggested to the D.R. Church that instead of taking over the field as an independent body they should rather work with the S.U.M. and as part of the S.U.M., in the same way as the Danish Branch of the Mission subsequently arranged to do, and as has been done in the case of the Evangelical Church of the U.S.A. My Committee do not feel that it is in the best interests of the work that it should be split up into various independent Missions but that the promotion of the African Church, which is their ideal, will best be obtained by conserving as far as possible the unity of the work which is leading to the formation of that Church. Although the S.U.M. appears to consist of various National Branches which are more or less independent, the Mission is one body in the sense that a similar Constitution has been accepted by each Branch and the doctrinal basis of the Mission is the same in every Branch.

The following week the editor continued his comment and said concerning the letter from London:

We cannot interpret his letter to mean anything else than that *his committee is definitely committed against handing over any part of the work to another body.* He writes that his committee does not want the work to be "split up into various independent missions." The reason is that this would not promote the ideal of the African church, since this can best be attained by conserving as far as possible the unity of the work. Again, Rev. Dawson writes that his committee "had no wish to hand over the work as to an independent body"; on the contrary they "desired that it should remain a part of the work of the S.U.M." The same expression is used a little farther on. The committee feels that, instead of giving part of its field to the South African D.R. Church, as an independent body, as was done about twenty-five years ago, it should have suggested that "they should rather work with the S.U.M."

What do these statements mean? That, though the S.U.M. is willing that our Church should provide all the workers and funds needed to carry on the work in the Lupwe district, the field, strictly speaking, will not be ours. It will still be "part of the work of the Sudan United Mission."[12]

The Banner editor's opinion was his own, but in the light of Mr. Dawson's statement, it does not seem unreasonable. Dawson spoke for his London committee and went out of his way to make it plain that the Lupwe-Takum field must remain part of the SUM. However, the Board's report to the Synod of 1939 on this point only said: "Its proviso that we be willing to cooperate with the rest of the S.U.M. work in Nigeria cannot mean, in the light of other statements it has made, any curtailment whatever of our authority to conduct mission work along the Reformed lines which we consider essential. We now cooperate with other churches on our Indian and China fields, but in neither case has this ever meant a limitation of our authority."[13] The last sentence was the Board's interpretation saying that the CRC in Nigeria would work in harmony with the SUM the same as it was doing with other missions in New Mexico and China. This interpretation was incorrect. Had it been made known to London or Nigeria a reconsideration of the matter of transfer would have been called for. The committee in Britain and the missionaries who were involved were agreeable that the administrative work in the United States be transferred from one committee to another. In Nigeria the work was to remain a part of the SUM. The difference in interpretation meant that for many years the Home Board of the CRC did not acknowledge that it was a part of the SUM, whereas in London and Nigeria it was known that it was. The message and methods of the 1930s continued unchanged in the 1940s. Where the missionaries were concerned the only change was that the official mailing address in America became Grand Rapids instead of Philadelphia.

Ecclesiastically and doctrinally no problem arose. The CRC agreed to the doctrinal basis of the SUM which was easy to do as that basis was at no point at variance with the teachings of the CRC. Although the CRC doctrines are set out in greater detail they do not differ from the evangelical position of the SUM. Since 1923 the field had been subject to Reformed teaching only. The final decision as to the Smiths becoming workers for the CRC was left until they came to the United States in 1941. At that time the special license to administer the sacraments which he had received from Britain was dropped. Smith had become a member of the CRC and the Calvin Seminary adviser to the Board of Foreign Missions advised that he be ordained if examination showed him to be acceptable. The Synod encouraged the Board in this line of action, Classis Holland examined the candidate, and he was ordained in October 1941 by Ninth Street Christian Reformed Church in accordance with a special provision of the church order. History shows that he served the CRC as a foreign missionary for thirty years.

An African Union Church

Another problem involved in the transfer of the Lupwe-Takum field was the establishment of an African Union Church. In 1939 the CRC had been assured that the field would be doctrinally and ecclesiastically autonomous. In its turn it had assured the SUM that it was in sympathy with the aim of creating one African church. These two assurances appear to be at variance with each other. The constitution of the SUM drawn up in 1907 says, "The Mission desires to take its part in the formation of an African Union Church." In 1944 the CRC Synod decided:

> The second problem deals with the matter of Church Union in Africa. It is a problem because it is evident that the Sudan United Mission, from whom we took over the Lupwe station, contemplates one union church throughout the entire area which it occupies and this desire of the S.U.M. was clearly made known to the Christian Reformed Church before it took over the Lupwe field. On the other hand, the Christian Reformed Church definitely stipulated that it reserved the right to develop its work on the Lupwe field along strictly Reformed lines and no one raised the

point that this might conflict with the S.U.M. ideal that there be one union church. The Board is not ready to make a final decision on this problem, but it did decide to:
a. Ask of Rev. E. H. Smith as our representative on the Field Council that he continue his work on the matter with the greatest care;
b. Ask of him to continue to keep the Board fully informed of developments;
c. Inform Synod of these developments.[14]

The Synod agreed to this; however, a year later it endorsed the policy of church union "as now in effect on our Nigerian field." It went on to say,

The term "Church Union" may raise in our minds the spectre of denominations seeking to unite organically. That is not the connotation of the term as applied to Nigeria. It refers to a rather loose organization, a spiritual fellowship with only advisory powers.
The reasons given were,
1. This is in harmony with our decision of 1939 to continue the work on the Nigerian field along indigenous lines.
2. It would do irreparable harm to the work if this policy were to be discontinued.[15]

The Synod endorsed "the policy of church union as now in effect on our Nigerian field" and in 1945 that could rightly be described as "a rather loose organization, a spiritual fellowship with only advisory powers." This fellowship involved all the local organized churches of the SUM of which there were thirty-seven, one of them being in the CRC field at Takum. A twentieth-century American restricted to living in his own country can have no conception of the depth of spiritual fellowship existing between first generation Christians emerging from an animistic background. In America Christians are almost all content each with his own denomination and know little beyond it. In Nigeria at that time Christians knew nothing about denominations but were close friends with anyone who named the name of Christ. This common love for Jesus Christ was supreme.

In 1945 the Synod of the CRC felt that it could name the young church emerging in Nigeria the *Christian Reformed Branch of the Ekklesiya cikin Sudan*. It is not clear why this was done. It was another nine years before the church in Nigeria decided what name it would be known by and then it was not bound by a decision made by the CRC.

That same Synod offered a *suggestion* concerning the form for ordination which suggestion was well received by all the congregations of the SUM complex. The time was not too far distant when Istifanus Audu was to be ordained and the suggestion was that an additional question be asked of the candidate, viz., "Do you promise to adhere to doctrinal teachings and practices which are the common usage of this particular congregation?"[16] The thirty-seven congregations mentioned earlier followed several different denominational trends. When Audu answered this question affirmatively he was binding himself to a Reformed tradition whereas others in answering the same question would bind themselves to other traditions. All the congregations accepted the proposal and so a suggestion from a foreign church in another land met with success on a far-wider scale than had been visualized.

Missionaries' Salaries

One other agreement reached when the transfer was carried out was that the work in Nigeria should continue on indigenous lines. At the time the CRC did not practice these methods in its other mission fields. For some years the CRC Board felt that they applied to the salaries of the missionaries and so paid them according to British scales. In 1943 it realized that the wages of its own workers were not part of the indigenous scheme and set the matter straight. When it did this it did two things which differed from the general practice of missions in Nigeria and of that to which the CRC missionaries there had been accustomed. One was that the married women of the CRC mission were no longer considered to be workers but became wives only. In the British SUM where the wife had been a paid worker she had to pass the same tests as any other worker in order to be acceptable and had to fill the role given to her by the mission. This is not so in the CRC. It does not mean that wives may not work; many of them do so and some of them become very much involved in mission activities but this involvement is a labor of love and one which is a blessing to the giver. The people appreciate it very much when a missionary's wife takes a share in the ministry and it encourages them to be active for Christ. Mrs. Smith had been recognized as a missionary since 1930 and her church congregation in the United States petitioned the CRC Synod concerning her status. It was pleased to "instruct the Board to recognize the status of Mrs. E. H. Smith as that of an officially appointed full-time missionary."[17]

The other difference which became apparent when the wage scale was changed was that workers were no longer to be paid a common salary. Instead the CRC Board paid each according to the particular work in which he or she was engaged bearing in mind the training which each had received. The change was not the choice of the workers who, in February 1943 wrote, "The only request which we had was that salaries be equally arranged regardless of attainment or office." A fundamental principle was involved. The CRC choice was to send a person as a nurse, teacher, doctor, or preacher and pay him or her for the job which they did and so the primary emphasis on all workers being missionaries was lost. Fortunately those who were affected and much disturbed by this action were few in number, and those who were employed after the change had been made did not notice it so much. Even so on one occasion many years later the Field Conference of the SUM (CRC) did petition the Board to again consider paying the workers a common wage as missionaries. The request met with no response.

Notes

1. The Evangelical Brethren Church of North America later became a part of the Evangelical United Brethren Church. Still later another merger was effected and it became part of the United Methodist Church.
2. SUM American committee, minute 8, September 14, 1940, (CRC-London file).
3. SUM American committee, minute VI, January 18, 1940, (CRC-London file).
4. Henry Beets correspondence, March 31, 1937.
5. Acts of Synod, Article 121, 1937.
6. CRC Board committee report, May 17, 1938.
7. Acts of Synod, Article 95, IV, 1938.
8. CRC Board minutes, pp. 16 f, June 7, 1939.
9. Board report, Acts of Synod, Article 98, 1939.
10. CRC-London correspondence, De Korne to Dawson, July 7, 1939.
11. CRC-Smith correspondence, September 11, 1939.
12. *The Banner*, editorials, September 8 and 15, 1938.
13. Board's copy of Acts of Synod, 1939, between pp. 88 and 89.
14. Acts of Synod, 1944, Supplement 5, Section 4, D, 2, a, b, and c.
15. Acts of Synod, 1945, Article 56, VI, B, C, 1.
16. Acts of Synod, 1945, Article 56, VI, d, 1.
17. Acts of Synod, 1946, Article 118.

7

Some Signs of a Developing Church

Witnessing Near Home

As in other walks of life there is considerable pleasure in missionary service when something significant is done for the first time. This pleasure is even more satisfying when the new innovation passes the experimental stage and becomes part of a fixed pattern. In the early 1940s there were several firsts. In many places worship services were held for the first time. Women from the various Christian centers gathered for their first general conference. The missionaries held their first properly organized business meeting. The church held its first election of officers and appointed its first Nigerian treasurer. These and other beginnings were encouraging signs of growth.

The emphasis was on witnessing to others about Jesus Christ. Anyone who showed the beginnings of trusting the Lord was encouraged to tell others about it. This related to individuals nearby but also meant reaching out to others in neighboring hamlets and villages. As growth continued a group of potential believers would meet regularly to encourage each other and to pray and study the Bible. Among other things they would develop a consciousness of the need of the people living at another place and they would send one or two to tell them about Christ. When there seemed to be an interest they would ask the chief of the place to allow them to speak to any of his people who cared to gather. The climate was tropical and on any but the wettest days an outdoor meeting in front of the chief's home was always possible. These intermittent and irregular gatherings often cultivated an interest on the part of some of the residents who would beg their friends to come regularly. In this way a Sunday service would be started. It would be disorderly and frequently interrupted, but it would include singing, praying, Scripture reading, and a talk.

So in 1942 Kwambai Christians began conducting a regular service at Jenuwa Babba, three miles away. Fikyu believers went across the Gamana River to Kpambo Puri; Lupwe sent men six miles away behind the mountain to Lumbu; and the one Bika group sent workers to the other part of their town two miles distant. After ups and downs and near failures, in most places the simple worship service became a regular feature of village life on Sundays. This expansion from one place to another nearby was like a ripple on a pond caused by a stone being thrown into the water, it slowly expands until the outermost limits are reached. Success was not by any means complete. For instance the seed sown at Kpambo Puri did not take root. There the animistic priests felt the advent of the gospel was evil because it coincided with an epidemic of meningitis which caused many deaths. In their view these deaths were caused by the strangers, not by germs, so a hostile atmosphere was created. Opposition was to continue for a long time and a generation was to pass before Christ was welcomed in that place.

Witnessing Far from Home

The Christians were also concerned for those living a long way from their homes. It was in 1942 that those in the Takum District decided to send a resident worker to the Ndoro tribe. No American minister had at that time responded to the call to work in Nigeria and so a public appeal was made to the confessing members for a volunteer to go from the Takum area. Bulus Kweshe, later known as Bulus Kimbu, of Kwambai, the evangelist at Fikyu for several years, responded to the call. He was a married man with several children. He had had some Bible training at Lupwe and by his consistent life had proved himself fit for such service. The church promised its financial and prayer support and Bulus became its first foreign missionary. His mission field was sixty miles from his home, reached by foot through much wild bush and forest country. All he possessed was what he and his wife and one or two friends could carry. The people he went to help were complete strangers, with an unknown language and a different culture and temperament. During the rare visits of black or white missionaries on previous occasions they had shown an interest in the gospel but none was committed to Christ.

Istifanus Audu took Bulus Kimbu to Galia and introduced him to the village chief and elders. He explained why Bulus had come and that he was sent by the Takum District Church. At first he was popular and his worship services and simple school seemed to prosper. But later the tribal priests realized that Christ would put them out of business and they made an all-out effort to drive him away. Some animistic religious practices are very evil and cruel and when they are being exercised, even a Christian indwelt by the light of God trembles at the Satanic power of darkness. Bulus experienced severe persecution. He was ostracized and cursed. His possessions, especially his farms and livestock, were destroyed. His congregation and school students left him and became his enemies. Then, like Job, God allowed sickness to come to him and death to his immediate family. Despite it all, he and his faithful wife, Fibi, endured as seeing Him who is invisible. They never gave up and after a long time they proved the truth of the saying, "We shall reap if we faint not."

This persecution did not deter other Christians and in 1943 Daniel Ndeyantso, a younger man and a fellow townsman of Bulus, offered himself to the church and was sent to be near to Bulus at the town of Ashuku. It was about eight miles away and the people were of another tribe, the Tigum. Not long after this Dawuda Mbo, a Jukun, and the first convert to Christ of Nyita, joined these two Kuteb brethren and served at Ndafiro. The three families strengthened each other in the faith and frequently went on gospel treks together. They were all missionaries of the Takum District Church which supported them in a very limited way. They served our Lord well and suffered much and it was from their faith and patience that the Word of God took root and grew among the Ndoro, Tigum, and Ichen peoples. Young adults of these tribes who believed attended the Bible school at Lupwe for five or six months of the year. Some became leaders among the Christians and a few are now ordained ministers in the church.

Fellowship of Christian Women

In June 1940 a Christian women's conference was held in Takum for two days of special meetings to study God's Word. Most of them walked long distances, some of them as many as twenty miles. They each had to carry their own food and sleeping mats and many of them had babies on their backs as well. A report written at the time says, "That a group of 140 women, nearly all Christians should meet and show such unity is a rare sign of progress. The competition for new hymns set to native tunes was great." It was wonderful that these women in small groups would make such long journeys on lonely footpaths and then mingle with others whom they had never met before. It was inevitable that a company of that size would have say, a hundred babies under two years of age, many of them fretful after a long journey made in the hot sunshine. The noise can be imagined better than described. At a Sunday service an elder can order the mother of a crying infant to leave the meeting, but that wouldn't work at a women's conference.

The fellowship was most rewarding. They met at the meetings, but were also together as they prepared their meals over campfires. They would sit and sing together under the stars and then retire to be packed like sardines in small round rooms or on the floor of a schoolroom. The Lord Jesus was the common point of understanding each other and in Him joys and sorrows were shared. It was also a time for sharing and learning new hymns set to their own tunes. These tunes suited the performance of home chores, like the grinding of grain, or of farming activities during planting and reaping seasons. As they traveled back home they would sing these new hymns over and over so as to learn them well. Arriving home they would share their experiences, tell the truths they had learned and teach the new hymns to those who had not been able to go with them.

Officers in the Church

The Takum Church had three elders in the early thirties, but two of them died and only Audu Istifanus was left. For several years no formal attempt was made to change this but by common consent two or three men joined Istifanus to discuss whatever problems arose. During those years many were added to the church so that in 1940 the first congregational election was held. The confessing members elected six men to the office of elder and from that time on consistory meeting was a lesson in church order, and new principal missionary attended the meetings and was the chairman. The bulk of the time was spent in examining applicants for baptism or for admission to the catechism classes. Discipline cases were always difficult as voluntary confession of sin was rare. For a long time each consistory meeting was a lesson in church order, and new principal decisions taken became part of their church order.

It was also in 1940 that the Takum Church elected its first treasurer. From the very beginning offerings had been a part of each worship service. They were used for the local Christian community and the general ministry carried on by evangelists and teachers. There was also the fund for Nigerian missionary outreach. The white missionary had been responsible for the safekeeping of church funds and of regularly reporting to the church. The accounts and handling of the general and missionary funds was now handed over to one of the church members. For safekeeping of the money the mission strong box was used but when they obtained their own an assistant helped the treasurer and the two were made jointly responsible for the church's money. Before the coming of Christianity distrust and deceit reigned everywhere so that when the Nigerian brethren reached this point of confidence in each other it was a big step forward in indigeneity. No one who held this position of trust in the Ekas Benue Church failed in the faithful discharge of his duties.

The Beginnings of Nigeria General Conference

Another first for 1940 was the establishment of a business committee for the mission. For ten years the missionary staff of four persons had managed without the formality of committee meetings. The interdenominational committee in America had received monthly reports of the work and it did not concern itself with detailed conduct of activities on the field. The workers had been free to do what seemed to be the right thing. On October 9, 1940, a Lupwe Conference was set up under the new CRC Home Board. All that happened at the first meeting was that the conference asked the Board for permission to build a missionary home which "might cost $600 in view of the increase of prices due to the European war." It also arranged for some minor building repairs and decided that wives of boarding school students with babies must bring baby-sitters to look after the children while the mothers were in school and so enable them to concentrate more on their studies. The next meeting only dealt with minor financial details. More than a year elapsed before the conference met again. It met four times in 1942 and then it was almost four years before it had another meeting. This is better understood if we recall that the number of missionaries varied between two and five and they all lived next door to one another and talked over their problems as they arose. The only matter of significance in those six or seven years was the formulation of a set of rules by the Home Board after consultation with the field secretary. These were accepted by the conference in 1942.

For sixteen years, from 1930 to 1946, these few people worked together undisturbed. America was remote and the war made it even more so because of difficulties and delays in communication between the field and its home base. The staff got along well together, the work prospered, and difficulties were solved by prayer and love in the light of God's Word. Details of each month's activities were sent home regularly but, in 1946, there had been no business meetings held by the Lupwe Conference for four years and no minutes affecting the Nigerian work had been received from the Home Board for sixteen months. This state of affairs ceased abruptly when a new worker arrived at Lupwe and showed the staff the new rules and regulations governing the Nigerian Mission which had been formulated by the Board in May 1946. With the arrival of these rules and regulations the older workers realized that a CRC Home Board of control was now in operation. It took some months for them to accept the change and put it into effect but eventually this was done.

8

The War Years

Living on the Country

Europe was at war from 1939 to 1945 and America became involved
at the end of 1941. Nigeria was under British rule and many Nigerians voluntarily became soldiers and served in remote parts of the
world. British citizens who were missionaries were liable to military
service but were requested by the government to stay at their work
as a steadying influence to the people. That this was necessary was
illustrated when the three missionaries at Lupwe left for their annual
month's vacation. With their departure the rumor spread that they
had fled because the enemy was coming. The result of this was that
the Takum market was deserted for three weeks and did not resume
normal activity until the missionaries came back to Lupwe.

Due to the sinking of ships mail was sometimes lost; other mail
was long delayed in transit. Food and supplies from other countries
were in short supply and prices soared. "Live on the country"
became a slogan and no less than three books were printed giving
recipes on how to do this. Before the war it was said that the
missionaries had a hard time, but by the end of it they had become
benefactors to friends in Europe by sending them peanut oil, butter
fat, and canned tropical fruits. Necessity was the mother of inven-
tion. Palm oil in a saucer with a cotton wick provided light, mixed
with caustic soda it made soap, and painted hot on the plaster of an
outside wall made the wall rainproof for years. Raw cotton twisted
into thread by hand was knitted into garments, old bicycle wheel

Electricity first came to Benue Province in the form of a generator charged by wind power. The duty of keeping it operating fell to Rev. Ed Smith. Because the tower was erected in 1942, when World War II was at its height, many of the people at Lupwe were convinced that it was a watchtower to be used for locating the enemy.

spokes being used as knitting needles. Many were the intricate patterns that the Nigerians knitted as they walked along the paths to their farms.

Traveling in war time was hazardous, full of delays and uncertainties. Tena Huizenga traveled by Italian steamer to Nigeria and providentially landed a day or two before Italy entered the war against Britain. On her way home by freighter the journey took her sixty-six days and it ended with little better than hardtack to eat. The Smiths had traveled on at least nine different ships on their many trips to the African West Coast; during the war all of these ships were sunk by enemy action. Their only misfortune was to be on a ship which rammed another ship during a blackout at night causing it to sink the following day. Jennie Stielstra was delayed for a year awaiting transport. Anita Vissia arrived in the Congo from America in December and with her colleagues obtained passages on a Russian frigate which had been captured by the Free French, its crew was Chinese, the officers were British, and the captain was a third mate. The war proved that if you wish to get somewhere you can with patience do so. God graciously preserved all from harm and danger.

New Workers

Possibly the war accounted for the almost total lack of recruits for the CRC Nigerian mission. Apart from Anita Vissia no new workers were sent to Nigeria for years. Smith's station report for 1943 says, "The mission team was well balanced except in the matter of sex. The lack of manpower is a vexing problem and being a man and a monogamist, [one] gets tired of frequently being assured by African outsiders that he has four wives." A year later a letter to the Board said, "We have looked to the homeland until our eyes weary in their quest for a helper from there."[1] But in 1946 there was a break and the Board appointed two women to the staff. Margaret Dykstra, with Reformed Bible Institute training, served in the educational field and did work among the women and girls. Elizabeth Vandenberge, of Moody Bible Institute, joined the medical workers. This additional staff enabled us to reopen Wukari as a mission station. Jennie Stielstra and Margaret Dykstra went there to live, making do with cramped and very noisy quarters next to the church on the edge of the town. It was an unpleasant location since very few homes could boast of any form of sanitation whatsoever and the long grass on the periphery of the town was used as a public latrine. Soon afterwards a better location was found on higher ground and farther away.

In 1947 the Rev. Harry R. Boer joined the staff and after a period of orientation and language study he occupied the small Takum house for most of 1948. This enabled him to get a close acquaintance with a mixed urban population. He then moved to Baissa and lived in a rough bush shelter while he supervised and helped to build the first home on the crest of the hill overlooking the town. As his knowledge of the Hausa language increased he was better able to serve the church and trekked throughout the district and over the Mambila Plateau. For relaxation he cultivated the fruit orchard and pineapples and planted new trees and gardens.

The pleasure of having Mr. Boer on the missionary staff was short-lived as he received an appointment from the Synod of the CRC to serve as professor of missions in Calvin Seminary at Grand Rapids. This chair of missions in that school was to be a new venture for the CRC and the lot fell to Boer to respond to this invitation. The Nigerian Conference said, "Should our God direct him to accept this appointment the Nigerian mission field would be the loser. After having waited eight years for its first male worker subsequent to the transfer it is a hard blow to have him called from us after only nine months of service here. Our Lord rules over all and should He direct our brother to accept this task we foresee that the church through its future ministers, and the world through the church, will profit and not least the ministry in the Sudan."[2] The best was made of a sad situation and it became true that the world would profit and "not least the ministry in the Sudan" when several years later Boer returned to Nigeria to serve in another capacity.

He did not leave Nigeria immediately but was able to serve for two years before going to the United States. The field's loss was alleviated by the arrival in 1948 of the Rev. and Mrs. Peter Ipema and the Rev. and Mrs. Peter Dekker. They studied the Hausa language in Jos for some time, then the Ipemas joined Jennie Stielstra at Wukari and the Dekkers were posted to Lupwe. Towards the end of 1949 Mr. and Mrs. Gilbert Holkeboer arrived in Nigeria to supervise the primary schools and about the same time the Rev. and Mrs. Robert Recker and Mr. and Mrs. Donald Van Reken joined the staff. So at the close of that decade the number of adults from America had risen from four to seventeen and the number of mission stations from one to four.

Notes

1. Smith-CRC correspondence, January 8, 1944.
2. Nigeria Conference minute 222, August 1948.

9

Mission Board Delegates Visit Nigeria

The Rev. H. J. Evenhouse and Dr. J. C. De Korne Go to Africa

Towards the end of 1946 the Rev. H. J. Evenhouse, president of the Christian Reformed Foreign Mission Board, and Dr. J. C. DeKorne, its secretary, went to Nigeria. This was the first visit of official Board delegates to the field and it resulted in much greater interest in the field being generated in the church in North America. The visit was remembered with considerable appreciation and admiration by the missionaries on the field. It was an encouragement, for instance, for a younger man to see an older one jump out of bed at the first tinkle of the alarm clock at five in the morning and to immediately kneel by his camp cot to dedicate his life to God for another day. It was a joy to see these visitors trekking many miles through rugged bush country on foot. Or, when toward the end of a journey, though drenched with perspiration, they could smile with appreciation because the chief and elders of a village had walked two miles in order to welcome them with fanfare of horns and beating of drums used only on the most important occasions. One recalls John De Korne shivering his way through an unusually cold night along the Acha Valley and the dismay of Henry Evenhouse when he stumbled upon a fetish seance in a secret grove in the Galia forest.

The visit was a most generous one of four months duration. Their report says in part:

> From Mkar it is eighty miles to Lupwe. Our arrival on December 2nd will ever remain a precious memory to us.

95

As we drove on to the compound, we were at once impressed with the attractiveness of the driveway, lined with lovely shrubbery and plants. As the car drew to a stop a swarm of little children surrounded us and sang most touchingly a song of welcome to us and a song of greeting to their returning "father," Mr. Smith. We met the personnel of our mission force, and were happy to find them all well. During our stay in Lupwe we went on trek three times. We made a trek of one week to see the mission stations and preaching centers in the area close to Lupwe. We made an auto trip to Wukari and Ibi, and a two-week trek into the Eastern area of our mission field to see the work and study the opportunities for expansion in this area. We have journeyed much and seen much and learned much, and we can truly say that the travels alone, in and through these mission fields, have been very rewarding in revealing to us the scope of the work and the challenge that is present before us.[1]

The arduous foot journeys which they made for nearly three hundred miles through wild bush and forest were in every way fruitful. The nationals everywhere were encouraged that the CRC and its leaders thought so much about them, and the missionaries were strengthened. The church in North America was greatly benefited by the exciting reports which the delegates brought from the field. One result was the stirring of men and women to go and tell the gospel story. The physical, mental, and spiritual demands on the delegates were very great but so were the fruits of their endeavor.

Publicly proclaimed vision and faith are of great importance from God's point of view. They are the essence of progress. When Evenhouse and De Korne reported to the Home Board they not only outlined prospects for immediate progress but they spoke of further expansion possibilities. They said:

With our limited staff at present it may seem visionary to speak of possibilities of even further expansion beyond those plans discussed above. Yet we must face the possibility of a mighty stirring of the Spirit of God among our young men and maidens so that a more adequate proportion of our people will offer themselves for missionary service than has been the case thus far. If it pleases the Lord of the harvest to answer our prayers, and our people rise to the challenge of pagan and Mohammedan Africa, we might well give consideration to an unoccupied field east of Lake Chad in French Equatorial Africa. The region is almost solidly Mohammedan, and missions among Mohammedans are among the hardest in the world. But what right has the living church to sidestep the hard fields? Our Lord demands that the gospel be brought to the Mohammedans too. Our church has not even remotely approached the limit of its missionary potentialities.[2]

The Lord did answer these prayers and the people did rise to the challenge of pagan Africa. What was not known at the time was that pagan expansion would be to the west into Tiv territory. Because of the heavy demand that this was to make upon the CRC the Muslim vision lay dormant for a time but was not forgotten, as the history of the later years will show.

Some Observations on the Benue Church

In referring to the Benue Church the Board's delegates described it as an intelligent church, a disciplined church, a self-supporting church, a singing and a joyful church, and a missionary church. On this last point they said:

We distinguish between a mission church and a missionary church. A mission church is one which has been founded by missionaries and is in an uncompleted state of development. A missionary church is one which realizes that God has placed a church on earth to be His witness and that it is the solemn responsibility of the church to make the name of the Lord Jesus Christ known everywhere.

In this respect it seems as though the Nigerian Church has come to an understanding of the genius of Christianity to a greater extent than many of our churches in this country have done. Every local group of Christians has stated times when it sends out a couple of its members to bring the gospel to . . . outlying areas and unevangelized tribes. Practically all of the new work that has been opened in recent years has been started by these natives themselves. Offerings for missionary extension are received regularly. Our one congregation at Takum of one hundred and eighty-six members has already sent out and is supporting three missionaries to the Ndoro and Tigum tribes.[3]

While the two visitors were in Nigeria they were privileged to attend the Taron Zumunta [Gathering for Fellowship] of the churches related to the SUM. They noted that this was a unique conference in that it was consultative only, and yet it was also the conference assembled to attend to the ordination and installation of Istifanus as pastor of the Takum church. This conference lasted for five days, and missionary problems common to the several fields represented were taken up for discussion. Each branch of the S.U.M. was hereby enabled to gain inspiration from fellowship and instruction from the discussions, but yet free to follow its own convictions on its own field. It was evident to your committee that the several branches of the S.U.M. are striving, notwithstanding their differences, to cultivate a unity in the African churches they are severally developing.[4]

The Ordination of Mr. Istifanus Audu

The ordination of Mr. Istifanus Audu, the first minister of the Benue Church, was also unique. It took place at the time of the Taron Zumunta Conference mentioned above, the worship service on Sunday, January 19, 1947, being entirely in the hands of the Takum congregation. Dr. J. C. De Korne gave the charge to the new minister and the Rev. H. J. Evenhouse took part in the laying on of hands. The service was unique in that the others who participated in the laying on of hands were Rev. A. J. Brink—Dutch Reformed, Rev. E. I. Engskov—Lutheran, Rev. T. L. Suffill—Baptist, Rev. D. O. V. Lot—Church of Christ in the Sudan, and Rev. E. H. Smith—CRC. The ordination was followed by the Lord's Supper. It was a wonderful day in the growth of the Benue Church. As had been suggested two years before by the Synod of the CRC, the Rev. Istifanus Audu signified in his ordination vows his adherence to the Reformed faith. At the same time the nature of the service indicated the interdenominational character of the intimate fellowship of which the Benue Church is a part.

Delegates' Assessment of the Growth of the Church

Towards the end of their report to the Board the delegates had this to say about the growth of the church in Nigeria:

It may have some value at this point to submit an analysis of the reasons, as we see them, for the rapid development of the church in Nigeria.

1. Of primary importance is the fact that our sovereign God chooses His own time for the founding and growth of

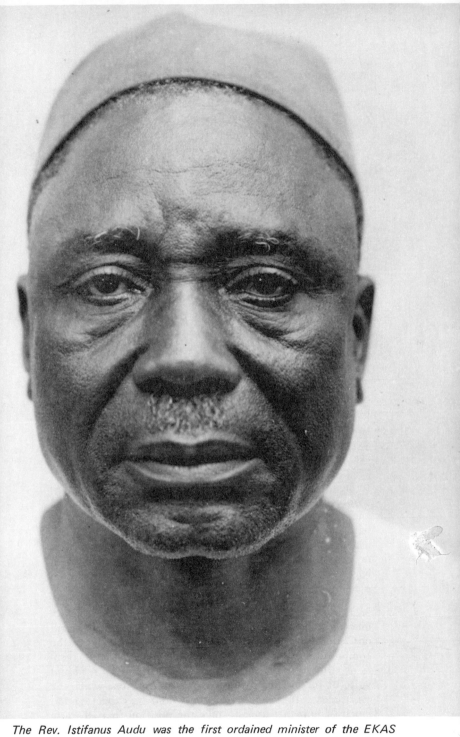

The Rev. Istifanus Audu was the first ordained minister of the EKAS Benue Church. Mr. Audu, who served in East Africa in World War I, was converted in the early 1920s and was ordained in January 1947. He continues to serve the church into the 1970s.

His church in definite areas. When His Spirit begins to work, no man can stay His hand. This seems to be God's hour for Nigeria. We are not forgetting that God uses means and that He holds His children responsible for the way they use or neglect those means, but the most important thing to remember is that while Paul may plant and Apollos may water, it is only God who gives the increase. It is with a deep feeling of thanksgiving to God that we acknowledge that the Christian Reformed Church has come to the kingdom in Nigeria for such a time as this.

2. An indispensable link in the chain of events is the faithfulness and efficiency of the missionary. We say indispensable, not because God could not work without human beings, but because, as far as we know His will, He has chosen to work through human instrumentality, and it must be recorded here with great emphasis that we have a faithful and efficient group of missionaries on our Nigerian field. They are well trained for their work, they are consecrated to their task, they have hitched their wagon to a star and are permitting nothing to interfere with the carrying out of God's will in their lives.

3. Sound methods have been found for broadcasting the gospel and for developing the indigenous church. Not only is there an insistence on proclaiming the whole counsel of God, an insistence which we naturally expected from missionaries with a Reformed world and life view, but there is also a recognition of the necessity of using sound methods for carrying on that work. The missionaries refuse to use foreign money for building churches or schools (other than schools which aim to train teachers and native evangelists) and they refuse to use foreign money for the support of native pastors. This is very close to the heart of what has usually been known in mission circles as the Korean Plan or the Indigenous Church Plan. . . . Our missionaries in Nigeria are wholly committed to this indigenous church plan and are carrying it through with great efficiency.

4. In seeking to lay bare the reasons for the rapid development of the church in Nigeria we must also be realistic and not overlook the cultural value of the church for the community. At present in Nigeria, with very few exceptions, there are no opportunities for learning to read and write or for further education other than those which the missionary offers and brings. It would be expecting too much of human nature to take the position that all those who come to the missionary to learn about the gospel are

moved purely by the desire to know God; we will just have to face the fact that very likely some of them are more interested in learning to read and write and in the cultural values which Christianity brings to them than they are in spiritual truth. Yet it is also realistic to say that this situation is also within the providence of God, and if He has enabled us to face a situation where people are willing to come and listen to the gospel message, even though their motives may not be of the purest kind, the Word of God is powerful to affect those lives, to screen out their less worthy motives, and thus bring them into the fellowship of the sons of God.[5]

The visit of the officers of the Board of Missions to Nigeria was vital to the well-being of the mission. Two sessions of the Lupwe business conference were held with them present and the close fellowship over several weeks helped to dispel the tension between the missionaries and the Board. Moreover the generous amount of time spent visiting the mission stations, churches, towns, and villages, afterwards helped the president and the secretary to speak with knowledge and confidence to the Board and Synod on Nigerian matters. The missionaries and the Christians were very grateful for the visit of Evenhouse and De Korne and, because of it, they, like Paul the apostle on his way to Rome, thanked God and took courage.

Notes

1. Report of CRC Board delegates to Nigeria, 1946-7, p. 3.
2. Ibid., p. 11 (5).
3. Ibid., p. 16 G.
4. Ibid., p. 5, D.
5. Ibid., pp. 16-18.

10

The Law and the Educational and Medical Services

Geographical Boundaries

Nigeria became an entity in A.D. 1900. Before that time it was the residence of approximately four hundred distinct tribes. These differed greatly in size, ranging from small tribes of a few thousand to large ones of several millions. When the British enclosed it within a geographical boundary and called it one country the inhabitants were not consulted. As far as the western and northern boundaries were concerned the British and French decided where these should be. On the east the Germans and the British determined the line of demarcation. At one point this came within a few miles of Lupwe. These physical limits imposed by foreign nations paid no heed to tribal divisions and in numerous cases they cut tribes in two with one-half being under German or French rules, the other half under British rule. The German influence in the Cameroons ceased in the early days of World War I. Later on the League of Nations partitioned that country between the French and the British. Although the colonial control of those two nations has now ceased, nevertheless the boundaries remain between the Republic of Nigeria and the Republic of the Cameroons. The tribes along the boundary are still divided.

The British spoke of the Colony and Protectorate of Nigeria. The coastal town of Lagos became the capital. For the first forty years the development of law and order was very slow. In the local situation much use was made of the traditional forms of government but British ideas were imposed on higher levels. As telegraph, road, and railway communications improved law could be implemented more effectively. In the 1940s educational and medical laws were more clearly defined and there was a steady tightening of control. New laws were not always immediately enforced everywhere throughout the land. The coastal peoples who had been in touch with civilization for a much greater length of time felt the weight of authority earlier than those living in the interior.

Primary Schools

In 1944 Miss Stielstra wrote, "If pollywogs are frogs then Classes of Religious Instruction (CRIs) are schools. Of course pollywogs don't have legs and lungs as do their grown-ups, but if given a chance they will have these some day." At that time four of the CRIs in our area had become schools. In a CRI it was permissible to teach the Bible, reading, writing, and how to count up to 100. To teach more than this simple curriculum in a CRI would be contrary to the law. The religious class would have to be upgraded to become a primary school. To be recognized by the authorities a primary school had to teach at least grades one to four, the teachers needed to be qualified, and the building had to be satisfactory. In the early years these requirements were set at a low level and teaching was permitted in the vernacular or the Hausa *lingua franca*. Later English was introduced as a subject and still later it became the only medium of instruction from grade one onwards; that was hard for tiny children who on entering school for the first time didn't know a word of English. It also affected the low level teachers who lost their certificates because they also didn't know the English language. All of this is quickly written but it covers many years of headache, heartache, and lengthy discussion to raise the standard of education in the community. Fortunately the humble, vernacular, CRI has never been forbidden by law and it continues to thrive, helping thousands of illiterates to become literate.

Concerning the development of education Mr. W. M. Bristow said the following in 1942,

> Africa is in the act "of changing into high" and "stepping on the gas." . . . These changes are so stupendous that the whole future of the Mission will be altered whether we like it or not. By no manner of means can the thing be stopped or retarded. There are only two alternatives, either we must learn to understand and drive the "1942 model" and its still more complicated successors, or else sit on the

roadside watching the cloud of dust disappearing over the horizon.[1]

The betterment of the educational system meant an increase in governmental control. Ultimately teachers and schools serving agencies such as missions and churches would be taken over entirely by the government. As early as 1942 government financial subsidies for schools were talked about. The CRC mission board decided at that time that "on the basis of such information as we now have, we would advise our Sudan missionaries to keep clear of government subsidies in education if that is possible. It might be possible for us to accept government aid, if there is no interference with the religious quality of the instruction given and that we retain the right to dismiss teachers who are unsatisfactory from our point of view."[2] At first this fear was common to most missions in the north but by 1948 practically all of them had changed their earlier attitude and indicated their intention to accept the offer made by the government to pay the major portion of the teachers' wages. At that time most of the schools in our area were owned and operated by the Benue Church and it decided to accept government aid. The church's record shows the following resolution was passed: "Our schools are Christian schools and we resolve to maintain their Christian standards. We will accept government aid only if it does not endanger the Christian character of our schools. Every effort will be made to be sure that all pupils attend the classes for specifically religious subjects and exceptions will only be made with the consent of the manager."[3] At that meeting of the church the teachers accepted a contract drawn up by the church. It indicated that the teacher was a servant of the church, he could be transferred to any school, he would be subject to the manager, and in addition to his teaching duties would serve the church in other ways. Every effort was made to keep the teachers in the same relationship with the church as that of other workers. For some years this succeeded but later the relationship cooled and they acted as servants of the government even though they were sponsored and controlled by the church and mission.

Government subsidies meant that it fixed the teachers' salaries and their pay was considerably higher than that of any other paid workers in the area. Indeed at that time they were receiving ten times as much as the best paid church workers. In the main these high salaries came out of the Nigerian taxpayer's pocket so they could be considered as indigenous, but the disparity between the salaries of the teachers and other church workers created problems. At that time the records show that all the church could do was to increase the CRI leader's pay by four cents a week.

Religion and the Schools

When the new education ordinance went into effect it soon became apparent that whether a nongovernment agency received financial aid or not the requirements of the law were still applied. No new school could be started without permission, buildings had to meet certain specified requirements, and the teacher must have a proper certificate. One of the clauses of the Ordinance of 1948 said, "No pupil shall receive any religious education objected to by the parents or guardians of such pupil or be present when such instruction is given." The three Protestant representatives on the Northern Board of Education tried hard to get this wording altered but did not succeed. History was to prove that it made no difference to the character of the Christian schools. The fears expressed proved to be groundless.

Another vital aspect of the ordinance was very useful to Christians and the spread of the gospel. Religion was included in the curriculum of all schools. In other than Christian schools this opened the way for the children to be taught the Christian religion. Where there were Christian teachers in such schools they would teach the Bible. Where there were none, able and qualified Christians from the community who were willing had the privilege of teaching the periods for religion. In the early years of this program Margaret Dykstra was very active in this way and in the years that have followed many missionaries and missionary wives have served the schools. It is frequently and continually acknowledged by the Nigerian government that the country has profited greatly from the educational activities of Christian missions. Because this is true the government has shaped and implemented its laws so as to be helpful to missions and churches.

For the first twenty years it was good that authority in eduation on the local level was left with the mission and the emerging church. They were formative years and a Christian quality was imparted to the schools and through them to the community. The spiritual and moral character of the teachers was a most important factor. Therefore, should a teacher fail in his conduct, discipline could be applied in conformity with the character of the school. For instance in a Christian institution it might be necessary to dismiss a teacher for committing adultery, bigamy, or for drunkenness in order to uphold the Christian nature of the school. In public schools discipline for such offenses would not be considered necessary except on rare occasions.

In a land so big and so well populated as Nigeria the implementation of any new law had to take note of degrees of development which varied throughout the country. Coastal areas were ahead of the interior, cities were better off than rural communities. The ordinance set the pattern for progress. As levels of education rose and better qualified teachers and better facilities became available the demands of the law were more rigorously applied. The upward trend continues to the present but there is still a long way to go before education for all between the ages of six and fourteen is made compulsory.

Teacher and Other Leadership Training at Lupwe

We note these phases of the CRC mission teaching program in the 1940s. Teaching young adults for six months of the year to better understand the Bible continued at Lupwe and was begun at Wukari and Baissa. To this was added a two-year course in 1942 in order to produce teacher-evangelists who would conduct CRIs or teach the first two grades of a primary school. In January 1949 this was upgraded to a teacher training school in line with the new requirements of the government. There were twelve students for the first term. The early efforts in this were made by Mrs. Smith helped by Mrs. Dekker and Miss Stielstra during furlough periods. Successful graduates earned government certificates and were qualified to teach in primary schools.

Meanwhile in the towns and villages numerous CRIs were opened and were manned by the successful trainees of the teacher-evangelist school. They carried the heaviest and most vital load in the growing church. Each had to teach daily for two or more hours and sometimes there were two two-hour periods, one for adults and the other for children. The leader also conducted all the religious meetings of the local community except that of the women's fellowship. It was also his job to lead in the handling of all the palavers.[4] These were many and complex when a congregation was emerging from paganism into the Christian faith. In due time the more central CRIs developed into primary schools as qualified Christian teachers became available. By 1947 the law required that a proper building also had to be erected. At that time the labor and local materials were donated by the Christians and only about ten dollars was required from the congregation's treasury. By 1950 there were ten primary schools in the area.

The summer school or refresher course conducted throughout the month of August each year was a most valuable contribution toward the growth and well-being of the church and schools. All leaders and teachers tried to attend. The fellowship with each other and with the missionary teachers for four consecutive weeks meant much for the spiritual encouragement of all. After eleven months of hard work Christ's servants felt a great need for renewal which was met by praying, studying the Word, and talking over problems together. The daily discipline of hard study with helps of many kinds offered by available missionaries prepared each for the year of work ahead. It gave valuable opportunities for newer workers to learn from the others and helped the work as a whole to maintain a single course.

Medicine and the Law

As for education, so for medicine laws were made and later applied when and where the authorities felt able to do so. Some laws were not enforced; for example, a red flag being placed at the entrance to a home where a leper resided. Knowledge gained later has shown how unnecessary it would have been. In the early days it was good that pioneers with only 10 percent of a doctor's knowledge were allowed to apply that knowledge and help the sick. A great deal of good was done and very little harm. That such days must pass was inevitable. Better treatment by more qualified people became the rule. Stricter laws were enforced concerning the dispensing of drugs and legal permits were required for this. Laws were also made to control the giving of injections. This led to the curtailment of a missionary's activity until he or she or a suitable replacement could measure up to the higher standards required by the authorities. At a slower pace the same became true concerning the activities of midwives in the birth of babies. During World War II there was an increase of nursing homes of ill repute where prostitute mothers could abort their babies and laws were necessary to stop this. However, the application of maternity laws had to take into consideration the circumstances of each location. Difficult childbirth as well as disease was commonly attributed to evil forces and not to natural causes or germs. Against this general misconception well-meaning missionaries and other foreigners had to contend and even now some Nigerians hold to this belief. After fifty years few people are convinced that boiling drinking water will kill dangerous germs and multitudes of infants die of intestinal diseases caused by their being given unboiled water to drink.

Comprehension is slowly dawning and ignorance is being overcome. Sometimes persuasion had to be used in order that whole communities could be examined and treated for such diseases as smallpox, yaws, sleeping sickness, and the like. Health is improving, the age of life expectancy continues to rise, and the number of children attaining the age of five years continues to increase. This contributes to the population explosion.

The Need for a Hospital

The missionaries in the early 1940s at first resisted any move towards building a hospital. At the same time they wished to relieve suffering humanity and slaved night and day to do so. Some of the sick, accompanied by their relatives, would stay at Lupwe for several days or weeks. They occupied tiny rooms provided for this purpose. In a crude way the sick were hospital inpatients. Then in 1947 the authorities passed a private hospitals ordinance. It became apparent that some day this law would be applied to the Lupwe medical ministry. The primitive facilities provided by the missions would have to be changed to measure up to the requirements of the law, such as providing so much cubic air space and so much window space per patient. Moreover it was necessary that a qualified doctor accept responsibility for the Lupwe work. Lupwe had no doctor and the one who accepted responsibility lived 330 miles away. He, among other things, also controlled a 100-bed hospital so he was able to visit Lupwe for only a day or two every six months. This was unrealistic and yet for some years CRC medical work continued under those conditions. For a long time the authorities looked the other way and so permitted the suffering community to get such help as was available to it. But it became necessary for the mission to decide either to abandon its medical ministry or else to obtain qualified professional aid and erect facilities in accordance with the law. Eventually it decided to do the latter.

Already in 1946 the CRC Home Board delegates had been approached by the elders of the Benue Church to request that the mission provide doctors and a hospital. It was twelve years later, in 1958, that this prayer was answered when the Takum Christian Hospital was dedicated to God. From simple beginnings such as giving aspirin tablets to relieve a headache, or lancing an infected swelling, or making a mother comfortable by the wayside after she had given birth to her child, two large CRC medical complexes have arisen.

Medical staff in the 1940 to 1950 decade was very limited in numbers. In 1941 Anita Vissia, a registered nurse, joined Tena Huizenga, and in 1946 Betty Vandenberge, first a practical nurse and later a registered nurse, joined the other two. Audu Siman was joined

A leprosy patient awaits treatment at Gidan Tamiya, a large village for lepers only on the east of the Katsina Ala River.

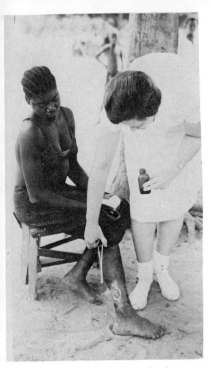

Nurse Anita Vissia joined the Lupwe staff in 1941 and is still serving there. Here she is shown treating an ulcerated leg.

Nurse Tena Huizenga began her medical ministry in 1937. She was unaided by a doctor most of the time. This picture, taken in 1943, shows patients waiting at the doors of the Lupwe clinic.

Scores of Africans have been trained to assist in the medical programs of the Benue and Tiv work. Pictured here is Siman Istifanus with his family

during the decade by Danjuma Gwamna, Siman Istifanus and Yakubu Bete. For those years these workers with whatever help Smith could give, especially in the villages, bore the brunt of the work. With the exception of Audu Siman who was taken to higher service, these Nigerians continue as faithful workers. Black and white did as much as their limited numbers permitted. Much more than ordinary duty was required of them. They were on call night and day and were often called upon to attempt more than they had been trained to do. Over three thousand patients were treated every year; the average patient's hospitalization lasted a little more than a week. The gospel of Christ was told to them each day and slowly its message was explained. The leprosy patients benefited most from the good news of Christ because they stayed for much longer periods. Many of them became Christians.

Leprosy

Despite the small number of medical workers progress was made. Since Bertha Zager's days lepers were treated on the Lupwe mission compound. When government law required that they have their own separate treatment center a place was erected along the Takum road. However this did not last long as the authorities decreed that it must not be within "shouting distance" of a main road. As segregation was to be more strictly enforced the mission asked for seven square miles of territory behind Veenstra Hill. This request was granted. A sizable donation provided the first treatment buildings and the new village became known as Gidan Tamiya [Termeer] in memory of the mother of the donors. In June 1951 the Lupwe report said, "Since January 450 leprous people have migrated into the seven square miles of territory beyond Veenstra Hill. Of these about 100 are close adherents or full church members. They have chosen leaders acceptable to the church and are building a small meeting place. Out of deference to their wishes the word 'leper' is dropped and their location [is] known as Gidan Tamiya and their disease as 'Wednesday sickness.' "[5]

This segregation village was another testimony to the indigenous method of doing missionary work. Each patient with the help of his relatives had to erect a simple home. Each was given a portion of farmland to meet his own needs. Then each patient donated two hours of labor each week to the upkeep and general appearance of the treatment section. Moreover community farms belonging to the village were worked by able patients. The fruits of these farms fed those patients who were unable to work. Work is an excellent part of the treatment of leprosy and farming suited to the strength of the patient is no hardship. Handicrafts such as weaving, knitting, and carpentry work are valuable aids and the whole contributes to the independence and dignity of the men and women concerned.

The Tamiya community has always been run by the people who live there. They have their own chief and council. The treatment center is now run by patients or expatients. In the main the general oversight and responsibility has been that of Anita Vissia, who in 1970 was the senior missionary on the field. The community begun at Tamiya in 1951 now has its own church and school. In 1952 the station report reads, "The Resident [Governor] of the Province called at Lupwe to see the . . . Segregation Village where over 500 now reside. He was very pleased at their contented attitude and reported favorably on the mission buildings. Five hundred patients is beyond the limit permissible but [in March] agreement was obtained that, providing a missionary supervises the work and providing the Native Authority will provide more land for farming, six hundred may be taken in. This is probably the largest segregation village in Northern Nigeria."[6]

Maternity Work

Despite limitations in the number of medical staff, progress was also made in the field of midwifery. For many years Lupwe was a last port of call when expectant mothers were in desperate need. Our nurses did what they could but they were presented with the worst cases. Many of these women had been in labor for many hours or even days. There was no doctor and many mothers died. Yet a reputation for good was built up. During the 1940s a four-room maternity center was built at Lupwe and near to it there were erected some cubicles for ladies in waiting. In the annual report for 1948 we read, "The maternity work very clearly demonstrates this confidence [in our nurses] for over seventy mothers came to us for the period of confinement."

The law required that nurses and midwives be registered. They were separate registers, each requiring the applicant to meet the qualifications set by the government. The nurses did not qualify as midwives. In 1949 a report was made to the CRC Mission Board from which we quote, "Dr. P. W. Barnden says he will not be content for this to go on [the operation of a maternity center] if no steps are taken by our nursing staff to get training which is acceptable to and registerable by the Nigerian Government. He said some unfortunate incident now can mean great misfortune for the nurse concerned,

113

and her probable dismissal from the country, and, in addition the blacklisting of the work we are doing here."[7] The result of this warning was that Lupwe Conference recommended that Anita Vissia take a course in maternity training, which she did in New York. Later on other nurses took similar training, some in Kentucky and others in England. Where there was a resident doctor the nurses did not need midwifery certificates, but those who had them were able to carry on when the doctor was absent.

The Synod of 1947 authorized the Board to appoint a doctor to serve on the Nigerian field as a first step towards a more stable medical ministry. Two years later the field staff made an urgent plea that this doctor be sent out and it was pointed out at the time that "a hospital will almost certainly be required if a doctor stays for any length of time. Such a hospital must comply with the government's standards."[8] As a result of this appeal the Board requested the Field Secretary to present tentative suggestions for a thirty-bed hospital which would include a maternity ward. This had to be presented within a week. It concluded by saying, "At this present time it is not unreasonable to suppose that all this might cost over $60,000." In a later chapter the account of the arrival of the first doctors in 1953 and the dedication of the hospital in 1958 will be detailed.

The lack of enthusiasm on the part of the early missionaries to establish a hospital can be understood when taken within the total mission situation at that time. The energy of the few workers was about equally divided between evangelistic, educational, and medical services. To open a fully staffed hospital with so little being done in evangelism and education would have placed too great an emphasis on the physical. However with the multiplication and application of medical laws the mission was forced to decide either to close down the existing medical work or else to develop it and eventually open a hospital. It decided on the latter course. The brave and hard-pressed African and American medical workers of the 1940s maintained and increased the ministry of sympathy and love. Christ was trusted and served at every point and the less complicated service rendered was well suited to the slow emergence of the population into a more enlightened age. The foundation principles which had been laid earlier continued to mature and towards the end of the decade one report observed, "It is possible that the Government might help the [hospital] project financially. It is not expected that the local Church would pay towards the erection of this institution but it is expected that the patients will pay fees of a sufficient nature to cover the actual costs of drugs and materials, including those used in operations, and to cover the wages of the African staff."[9] In this way independence and interdependence were both served.

Notes

1. CRC-Smith correspondence, p. 3, June 8, 1942.
2. CRC Board minute 1236, July 1942.
3. Benue Church minute pp. 156 f., December 3, 1948.
4. "Palaver" in Africa is a long and involved debate over a particular issue.
5. Lupwe Report to Board, June 1951.
6. Lupwe Annual Report to Board, 1952.
7. CRC-Smith correspondence, February 1, 1949.
8. CRC-Field Secretary correspondence, June 2, 1949.
9. Ibid.

11

Evangelism and Church Development: 1945—1950

Evangelism East of Lupwe

The conclusion of the Lupwe Annual Report for 1946 reads, "As our roots spread out and our fruitfulness increases it imposes ever greater demands on the existing staff. The addition of two ladies is encouraging. We wish to expand, and we will expand. Humanly this is not possible but we reckon on the power of our God. Though our call for helpers has been made for so long a period that it may have taken on the nature of a forlorn hope to the listener at home, yet we have confidence that it is clearly heard in heaven. In God's own time He will fulfill all His desire for this people. 'He abideth faithful; he cannot deny Himself.' With this we rest content." All of the missionary workers were active in evangelism and had had training in Bible institutes. The coming of Miss Dykstra and Miss Vandenberge made a division of our forces and the reopening of Wukari station possible. Moreover as soon as a second man was available we planned to move into the eastern area.

As early as 1939 it was said of Baissa, "Practically all of the Tigum and Ndoro people trade in Donga and the routes followed all come to a bottleneck at Baissa or just west thereof (4 miles). So that is a reasonable location. An African could reach this place and return to his own home the same day from Banti, Galia, Ndafirol, Ashuku, Gwanda, and Dida. If they came from Asha, Nama, or Tati they would need to spend the night before returning. Akwatiru, Akowe, and Batu residents would take more than a day to reach Baissa.

117

Baissa does not appear to be a place that will give a big response to Christianity," and then added, "Baissa section would probably be best for a center.... I still feel strongly that God is ready to do a work in these parts."[1]

Because Nyita was twenty-eight miles nearer to Lupwe than Baissa it was possible for the missionaries to visit it and its surrounding villages more frequently. There were rewards for those who tramped along these bush tracks from village to village but the journeys were not easy. Mrs. Smith and Miss Vissia walked the three-day journey to Nyita except that, where the path was smooth enough, a one wheeled chair was used by Mrs. Smith. This strange device pushed and pulled by two porters helped to ease the strain on arthritic joints. Miss Vissia says of the trek:

> By 4 a.m. we were up, and on our way by 5:15. Just outside Manya we crossed the Donga River in a canoe. It was lovely in the early morning coolness. Bordering the path was tall grass and since there was a heavy dew the night before, it wasn't long before we were drenched. it certainly isn't a nice feeling to have water oozing out of one's shoes and to have a wet skirt flapping about one's knees.
>
> On Tuesday night we had a storm. The hut in which we were had three doorways but no doors. You should have seen us as we scurried around trying to find coverings to keep the wind and rain out. The wind blew so hard that it blew the grass roof off the evangelist's kitchen. On Sunday afternoon we visited a little village two and a half miles from Nyita. Just shortly before our coming five men had burned their fetishes and decided to follow the Jesus way.[2]

When the accommodation for two women for as much as a week was one small room with "three doorways but no doors" and no bathroom facilities, then privacy was nonexistent and rewards had to be looked for elsewhere than in the comforts of such a place. But they were there—in the service rendered, in fellowship with the saints, and in the beauties of nature.

To visit further east took much more energy and time. Even so a steady interest by personal visits was maintained and the placement of three evangelists in that area by the Takum Church assured continual daily contact. These men were used by God to build up a body of believers and some of these would walk as much as eighty miles to attend the Bible school at Lupwe for several months of the year. One man, Maisanda, with a withered leg hopped with the aid of a staff along bush tracks for sixty miles in order to go to school. His was a prime illustration of courage and keen desire to know God's Word. These men became the backbone of the Christian ministry in their own tribes. Occasional visits by missionaries sustained the activity of three evangelists throughout the countryside, and the deepening of the knowledge of God in the new believers was a good preparation for the establishment of a mission station.

Baissa Mission Station

In January 1947, while John De Korne carved three sets of initials on a tree at Baissa, Henry Evenhouse and Ed Smith selected and marked with cairns of stones the four corners of a five acre plot of land. The Smiths went there again in June and concerning the plot of land he wrote:

> Here at Baissa we have spent six days. We have cleared much of the site of undergrowth and worthless trees. It was kneedeep in grass but the trek carriers have cleared much of that away. Now we can see the corner posts and have planned where to build. We have planted some orange trees and will add others before we leave. We are also putting in guava cuttings, mangoe tree seeds, and palm tree kernels. The view from the southern verge of the knoll is marvellous now that the dust haze has cleared. The skyline of the south is the Mambilla Plateau—perhaps twenty five miles distant and 4,000 to 6,000 feet high. Between it and us there are many ranges of mountains, but none so near as to make one feel closed in. The knoll lifts us above the heavy forest surrounding us. This site has been applied for but not yet granted. It is agreed to by the local District Officer and by the Local Chief. We have planned the building for the coming season and hope to find time to do it.[3]

The reference to a knoll which "lifts us above the heavy forest surrounding us" gives an indication that the Baissa mission is in entirely different terrain. Instead of the open bush savannah of Lupwe and Wukari there is heavy forest. The rainfall of over seventy inches per annum causes this and on little-traveled foot tracks jungle conditions were encountered. The physical change is not the only one. In placing a missionary at Baissa the mission set its seal on accepting the responsibility to bring the gospel to three more of Nigeria's tribes. These are the Ichen, Ndoro, and Tigum. God's grace was already at work among them and He was channeling it through

The Rev. Bulus (Kweshe) Kimbu
served as a lay evangelist and the
first resident missionary in the
Baissa area. He and his family suffered very much for Christ's sake.

Kuteb and Jukun believers and their white missionary colleagues. All these Christians, the givers as well as the receivers of the gospel, were becoming a single body. They would become the Ekas Benue Church.

Each one of these new tribes was quite distinct from the others and was also different from the Kuteb and Jukun. Each tribe had its own tradition and language, its own characteristics and habits. Those of these tribes who accepted Jesus Christ were brought into friendly relationships with each other by Him. The missionaries who were themselves of other tribes and traditions sought to mold these diverse groups and themselves into one manifestation of the body of Christ. For verbal communication every one had to forego his mother tongue and use the Hausa language. At first the growth of the numbers of believers was slow. It later became evident that this was a blessing from an all-wise God. First of all Jukun and Chamba Christians learned to love each other. They shared the gospel with the Kuteb, who likewise accepted and enjoyed the family bond. Then the Kuteb and Jukun shared their Savior with the Ichen, Ndoro, and Tigum, and these, through their new Master, found fellowship with each other and with their benefactors. Intermingling with it all were their few white brothers and sisters. So slowly but surely a strong Christian community was built up which crossed the barriers of tribalism.

In 1947 the Smiths made one further journey through the area. They arranged to have some beautiful mahogany trees cut down for lumber and planted more fruit trees. They trekked on through Galia, Tumbu, and Ashuku. They had had many tumbles and had skinned their knees badly so their brief five-year diary reads, "Most difficult trek ever made [by them]. Heavy forest, bad climb. Met two herds of cattle at the stream [and they had] spoiled the path. Deep mud to top of shoes. Ed went to Kararuwa—difficult path, three hills. Tummy trouble." Then the next day, "Rained all night. Off at 7:00 a.m. Rain on way. Two rivers. Boat hauled out of river, lost pole [while crossing]. Wet to middle while crossing at Baissa River. Planted twenty fruit trees." These terse notes indicate the hazards of the way and the weakness of the flesh. But the price had to be paid if the evangelists working in the villages were to be encouraged.

First Boer and Later Recker Occupy Baissa

A year later, on July 9, 1948, the Rev. Harry Boer arrived at Baissa and was the first missionary to reside there. For some months his home was one rough room of dried clay walls, an earth floor and a grass roof. In doing this he followed the pattern set at Wukari in 1906 and Lupwe in 1919. He supervised the building of a more durable home and visited the resident Nigerian evangelists in their forest homes. Among other treks he ascended and descended the heights of the Mambilla Plateau on which occasion he walked four hundred miles proclaiming the message of peace. It was at the beginning of his residence at Baissa that he received the appointment to the chair of missions at Calvin Seminary. This did not prevent him from putting in another hard year of spiritual and physical service.

He prepared the way for the long term residence of the Rev. R. R. Recker. Rev. Recker first made some preliminary investigations at Baissa and then on December 14, 1949, he and his family left Lupwe "for our home in Baissa." In his report he wrote,

> With the baby in a basket on top of the head of one of the natives, with my wife seated in the single-wheeled chair of Mrs. E. Smith, and with Paul in a chair on the back of my bike, the Lupwe staff bade us farewell on the trail alongside of Miss T. Huizenga's house. Their interested farewell touched our hearts, and caused a glow to reside there far down the trail. Soon Paul became tired because of the many bumps of the trail, and thereafter he was held by my wife most of the time. Can you picture us traveling down the trail with twenty-four carriers!
>
> At our second stop, I had the privilege of measuring a spot for the building of a church; I also spoke to them of the meaning of Christmas. Our next stop we spent the weekend in the Christian school house of Nyita; thus we had spacious lodging for a change. Once again on Sunday I preached twice to the people of Nyita. . . . We arrived at Baissa at 1:00 P.M., Tuesday, December 19 [1949]. . . . We were barely settled when on Christmas day I left my wife for a little village, Ashuku, eight miles away; here the Christians had gathered together to remember Christmas. On Christmas night I had the pleasure of speaking to two hundred followers of Christ. The next day I returned to our home in Baissa. We had spent our first Christmas in Nigeria parted by eight miles of bush, but all in all, it has been a blessed time. What a difference from former years for both of us, but God's grace is sufficient. I thank God that my wife is willing to do these things for His glory.[4]

The above excerpt from his report shows the pattern to which Recker fell heir as a pioneer missionary. Trekking by foot and bicycle, measuring a site for a church building, preaching and teaching in a new language, separation from wife and family, and so on.

The Rev. Robert Recker conducts an open air gathering in a village. From such small beginnings Christian congregations were born after years of effort.

Two years later at Christmastime the Smiths visited the Reckers and they were encouraged to find the family, especially Mrs. Recker, so contented and happy. In twelve months she had seen only two white women and had not been anywhere to visit and yet she was enjoying life to the full. God's enabling grace is amazing. At the time Smith wrote, "We greatly enjoyed meeting the Reckers and seeing what God has wrought since I first trekked into these parts fourteen years ago. Nearly five hundred [people] gathered Christmas day at the convention and it was pleasing to see nearly one hundred hold up their Bibles at the Bible quiz."[5] More will be told about Baissa later on.

Wukari Mission Reopened

Jennie Stielstra and Margaret Dykstra occupied the old mission site at Wukari in 1947. They served in Bible teaching and literacy work and Miss Stielstra was counselor to Iliya Gani and a handful of Christians. They trekked to many villages and went as far as forty miles from home. For a while lions prowled around their town "home" with its open windows, but probably the most terrifying experience was when half the town was burnt down. Strong winds carried flaming torches of grass thatch from one roof to another and in only a few minutes the devastation was wrought. The water from the mission well and the frantic efforts of a bucket brigade stopped the fire only yards from the mission home.

In December 1948 the Ipema family joined the Wukari staff after studying the Hausa language in Jos. A new site was obtained for a mission station which was located on a rise in the land a mile beyond the town limits. The Ipemas were able to transfer to this location fairly soon but the Don Van Rekens, who arrived from the United States in February 1950, held on at the town site awaiting the erection of a school and boarding quarters on a five-acre extension of the new place. When these buildings were completed Van Reken opened a school which in one form or another has been in operation ever since. He, as its first teacher, spent his first term of service in this area of the work. Later on he was transferred to Mkar.

After nearly two years of residence at Wukari the Peter Ipema family was transferred to the Tiv station at Zaki Biam twenty-eight miles to the west. Ipema had in this short time demonstrated his ability with the Hausa language and contributed much to the counseling and preaching services in the town and district. He also began to learn the Jukun language and was soon to show that he could grasp and use the Tiv tongue as well. His transfer to Zaki Biam and a little later that of Jennie Stielstra to Lupwe and the Don Van Rekens to Mkar meant that Wukari had a checkered experience during the first years after it was reopened. Yet all these workers and Margaret Dykstra were used in setting up this renewed outreach for God. The stabilizing of the Wukari ministry came with the advent of the Dekker family. The Rev. Peter Dekker had served at Lupwe for a time and had acted as executive officer there during Smith's furlough. In July 1951 he and his wife Rena with their children settled permanently at Wukari where they were to serve for many years.

Ibi Visited

Twenty-three miles to the north of Wukari lies the town of Ibi on the River Benue. The Sudan United Mission had its headquarters there when rivers were the highways of the land. During the 1940s this British mission station was often vacant but when it was occupied its personnel always included the veteran Clara Haigh. She was there when she celebrated her seventieth birthday. In the early part of the 1940s the Ibi station was run by the British SUM and Wukari was visited from there. It was also at that time and through Miss Haigh's ministry that a Tiv center at Pevikaa, which lies between Ibi and Wukari, was established. Later the Ibi station was transferred to the CRC Benue field; however, Miss Haigh remained there as missionary in charge. In earlier days she had served as friend and colleague to Johanna Veenstra for many years and when she died she was laid to rest by Miss Veenstra's side at Vom.

As a result of the transfer the CRC mission now came into vital relationship with the organized church of Ibi. Statistics show that it had always remained a small church but it did not dwindle as did some of the others. It is quite different from all other Benue churches in that it is a light surrounded entirely by the darkness of Islam, not of animism. Ibi is a town of Hausa-Muslim traders. The mission is situated outside its boundaries on the south side. For a long time a church building was not permitted within the town. In 1928, however, for the first time in the town's history a new chief was appointed, a member of the Jukun tribe, and he was not a Muslim. He gave a plot of land for a church building within the town and the native administration confirmed the arrangement in February 1929. It was good that without delay a church was built there, as the Jukun chief did not remain in office for long. In 1932 the Muslims took over again. They have tried to oust the Christians many times. From time to time the interior has been defiled with human excreta and in recent years deep trenches were dug along the walls to

Traditionally the king of the Jukun people is considered by his people to be a god. Here, in compliance with a centuries old practice, the corpse of the former king (in ceremonial garments) is being escorted on horseback to Matan Fula. When the escort returns to Wukari town his successor will be wearing the religious robe and hat.

Family devotions are a common innovation after a father has become a Christian and has learned to read.

cause the building to fall down. But the believers have persisted in their faith and worship and since 1960 the Christian community has grown very much. Each of the larger towns in the Benue and Tiv areas has a Hausa-Muslim community living alongside pagans and Christians but it is only in Ibi and Chinkai that they comprise almost the entire population. Opposition to Christians is only sporadic and most often relationships are peaceful though cool.

The Divine King of the Jukun People

In the Wukari-Akwana sector of the Benue Province the strongest anti-Christian pressure came from the Jukun people. The religion of practically all of the tribes in the CRC is animistic. The public manifestation of the Jukun religion is in their paramount chief, the Aku Uka, who to them is god incarnate. The four men known to the writer who held the chieftancy were all well disciplined, equable, and courteous. The Aku Uka exercises authority over his people but is himself under the close scrutiny and direction of the elders or priests of the tribe. In the nineteenth century and the early part of the twentieth his influence was vast and affected hundreds of thousands beyond his own tribal people. It was generally believed that he became a deity at his installation into the office and from that point on he no longer needed food, drink, or sleep and was not subject to sickness or death. Great care and measureless self-control are necessary to keep up this make-believe and to convince a whole nation. Ripley, the cartoonist, once depicted him as being about to cough but he dared not because two youths were watching him round the corner of the door. The cartoon was titled "The king that cannot cough." From time to time the Aku Uka did die but this was never admitted. Several weeks after his decease, and when his successor was to be installed, his fully dressed and mummified corpse would leave the city riding on a horse, accompanied by his successor. He was seen by many thousands of people as he returned to the land of the gods.

This pretense of continuing life has always caused much fear and mystery. It was not until 1970 that death was publicly admitted by the tribal heads. Never has an autopsy been permitted by the tribe and for this reason it was secretly rumored that death was occasioned by other than natural causes. In December, 1945, a resident wrote, "The cause of his death seems mysterious. He was in his usual robust health that morning. . . . He was in the office when he appeared unwell and the D. O. [District Officer—a government administrator] advised him to go home and rest. He staggered out of the door and with difficulty reached home. Speech was impossible. He died about

127

four p.m." This death was not publicized. His next public appearance was in early 1946 when, royally dressed and riding a horse, he kept his successor company to the secret place of his final departure. Fear of a like sudden and violent death effectively shuts the mouths of inquisitive individuals. A pagan religion with a divine king is not easily displaced.

Even Jukun Nigeria must keep pace with the changing world of which it is a part. The life and death of the Aku is now a matter of more than casual interest to the nation as a whole. Can a political leader suddenly disappear from the national scene and no questions be asked? The answer is obvious and so a modernization process is at work. In 1960 Aku Uka Asumanu Adibyewi took office. His request was granted that he take his oath as a second class chief on the Christian's Bible. He had made a profession of Christianity earlier in life and had been principal of Katsina Ala Secondary School for several years. At the time of his installation certain Jukun religious artifacts were exposed to the public view for a few minutes. There was even more publicity given in 1970 when Aku Uka Awudumanu Abe Ali took office. However, at both the 1960 and the 1970 ceremonies which lasted three days, there was one point when secret religious procedures took place. But in 1970 as far as the public knows the body of Adibyewi was not taken back to the ancestral burial grounds.

It is fiction and not fact that each Jukun Aku Uka is killed after reigning for seven years. The writer knew four of the Akus and they reigned for thirteen, four, fourteen, and ten years respectively. The cause of death is a matter of speculation. That death does occur has now been admitted in the official and traditional brochure published by the Jukun tribe in June, 1970. In this brochure we read in the past tense that, "The Aku acted or was regarded as an intermediary between the numerous spirits and man. He was also the source of national existence. He had supreme power over everything. He had the power of life and death." The establishment of a strong and progressive Christian community of Jukun people is cause for thanksgiving since it thrives in the midst of this deep-rooted religious system of the tribe.

A Wider Ministry

In the later 1940s besides the increase in numbers of missionaries the staffing of our Nigerian field was affected in another way. The Rev. Edgar Smith was invited to be the secretary of the Field Council for all the branches of the SUM working in Nigeria. H. G. Farrant of

Britain had held this position for thirty years and was soon to retire from the field. In speaking of the nomination Mr. Farrant wrote:

The nomination has two important elements. The first is that it is a recognition of Mr. Smith's qualifications for the office. They are his success in his own area both as an evangelist and in the administration and building up of the Church: his grip of the nature of the African Church that is being built up and the relation of missionaries and Branches to it: his understanding of the environment in which the Church has to grow. The second element is that Mr. Smith belongs to a Branch other than the British Branch and by holding the office he will inaugurate the change of constitution. In the second aspect the Branch is more important than the man for he is representative of it and of its contribution to the African Church. The Branches reach a focus in the Church. When their work is done they will leave behind them a closely knit African community to the glory of God. The Field Secretary of S.U.M., then, is a servant of all Branches in their journey towards their common goal of a single Church. The substance of the thing hoped for lives in his heart by faith. His position is greatly strengthened by being at the same time the administrative officer of his own Branch. He brings its weight into Council.

A still greater thing is attached at present to the office of Field Secretary. For more than twenty years I have been Secretary for the co-ordinating work among all the seven Missions in Northern Nigeria. It is the hope of S.U.M. that the African Church will include the fruit of other Missions. Also, there are things in which Missions must speak with a common voice and a Secretary is a necessary spokesman. This Secretary is chosen by the Missions and the choice need not necessarily fall on an S.U.M. man. Yet the S.U.M., by its special character, is naturally associated with this harmonising work and I am of the opinion that one of our men will be chosen if he has the qualifications. Mr. Smith has them.[6]

The Board of Missions and the Synod of the CRC were happy that their missionary was honored in this way but for a considerable length of time the Board hoped that he would not accept the invitation. This was due to a misunderstanding. It was felt that should he accept, he would cease to serve the CRC. After considerable correspondence of which the letter referred to above was a

129

part, it became clear that the CRC was and always had been a Branch of the SUM. Our Branch always had at least one official and voting member on the Nigerian Field Council of the SUM. In looking round for a successor to Mr. Farrant the Council's choice had fallen on one of its members, who was also the member for the CRC.

The Board granted permission for Smith to do this work which meant that he might be absent from his own field of labor for as much as three months in a year and to that extent be unable to give his attention to the local ministry. The Board and the CRC staff were willing to loan Smith; consequently, he was able to serve as secretary to his own mission and also as field secretary to the SUM.

The SUM Constitution

Early in this new service the constitution of the SUM was revised and the revision required ratification by all the participating members. This meant that the CRC had to consider whether it would agree to the new constitution or not. When the matter was discussed it brought to light the difference of opinion as to whether the CRC was part of the SUM or not. And yet, in the report of our Board given to the CRC Synod in 1939 it says, "As the field council [of SUM] is administrative in character and advisory in emergencies, we think wisdom will dictate that, in the event we take over the field, our mission personnel be represented on this field council." In 1945 the Synod adopted the recommendation that "we shall continue to have a missionary representative on the Field Council."[7] This membership on the Field Council of the SUM upon which the CRC Synod insisted implied that it was agreeable to the constitution of the council. When changes in the constitution required ratification by all the council's members including those of the CRC, it took quite a long time for the CRC to reach a conclusion. In its report to the Synod of 1951 the CRC Board said:

> For several years there has been among us an unsolved problem on the question of the official relationship of our board to the Sudan United Mission. At the annual board meeting of 1951 a motion prevailed to approve the constitution of the Sudan United Mission with a clarifying statement of Rev. Harry R. Boer. Here follow, first the Constitution of the SUM, next the clarifying statement:

Sudan United Mission Constitution

1. *Name.* The name of the Mission is the Sudan United Mission.

2. *Definition and Object.* The Sudan United Mission, founded in Great Britain, is composed of its various Branches with their respective Home Boards. Its object is to give the Gospel to the various peoples in the Sudan not yet adequately reached, and to take its part in fostering the growth of an African Church, self-governing, self-propagating and self-supporting.

3. *Doctrinal Basis.* The doctrinal basis of the Mission remains as at the inception of the Mission, namely:

The Divine inspiration, authority and sufficiency of the Holy Scriptures.

The right and duty of private judgment in the interpretation of the Holy Scriptures.

The Unity of the Godhead, and the Trinity of Persons therein.

The utter depravity of human nature in consequence of the fall.

The incarnation of the Son of God, His work of atonement for sinners of mankind, and His mediatorial intercession and reign.

The justification of the sinner by faith alone.

The work of the Holy Spirit in the conversion and sanctification of the sinner.

The immortality of the soul, the resurrection of the body, the judgment of the world by our Lord Jesus Christ, with the eternal blessedness of the righteous, and the eternal punishment of the wicked.

The Divine institution of the Christian ministry, and the obligation and perpetuity of the ordinances of Baptism and the Lord's Supper.

4. *Government.* Each Branch shall be governed in accordance with its own By-Laws and Regulations, and shall be responsible for the appointment, sending forth, maintenance and supervision of its own missionaries; and for the conduct and maintenance of the work which it undertakes on the Field.

5. *Field Administration.* Each Branch shall administer its own work on the Field. Where two or more Branches of the Mission work in neighbouring areas of the Sudan, there shall be a regional Field Council composed of representatives of these Branches to consider all questions relating to the work of the Mission as a whole in that region.

There shall be a general Field Council composed of representatives of the Regional Field Councils, to consider all questions relating to the work in the Sudan as a whole.

These Councils shall have advisory powers only and shall

report and refer all decisions or suggestions to the Field Authorities of the various constituent parts.

A Secretary shall be appointed by each Council. He will hold office for three years and be eligible for re-election. 6. *International Committee.* An International Committee shall be formed for the purpose of securing uniformity of policy and co-ordination of action in the Mission, and shall consist of one member nominated by each Branch together with the Secretary of the British Executive Committee, who shall be convener of the International Committee. Each Branch shall have the power of referring to the International Committee questions relating to the policy of the Mission, interpretation of the Constitution, or suggested amendments to the Constitution. Findings of the International Committee shall not be binding on the Sudan United Mission until they have been approved by the Branches. The International Committee shall meet when necessity arises.

Clarifying Declaration

The Sudan United Mission whose revised Constitution we are asked to endorse is a federation of missionary agencies active in the Sudan and each of which is autonomous on its field and independent of control by the others. Of this Sudan United Mission we are an integral part and constituent member. I avail myself of the word "integral" advisedly so that there may be no doubt in the mind of our African mission staff or in the mind of the British Branch from whom we took over the field that we consider ourselves as much and as fully a part of the S.U.M. as does any other branch on the field.

The Sudan United Mission as described above is to be distinguished from the British Branch of it which is also known as the Sudan United Mission. This branch, the largest of all the member branches, is the founder of the federated S.U.M. of which we are a constituent member. It has no voice in the affairs of the other member branches, and these have no voice in its affairs.

We are one of five branches working in Nigeria. These five together constitute the Nigerian Field Council of the S.U.M. Of this Council the Rev. Mr. E. H. Smith is field secretary. Member branches of the S.U.M. are also active in French Equatorial Africa and in the Anglo-Egyptian Sudan.

The five branches working in Nigeria are represented on the Field Council in proportion to the number of workers in each branch. The Field Council is an advisory body. It has no authority in the affairs of any of the branches. It is not responsible to any one branch, but each branch is responsible to its home board for any action in which it may engage in pursuance of Field Council decisions or recommendations.[8]

The above quotation is given in full in order to make it clear that the CRC mission work in Nigeria is rightly named the "Sudan United Mission." Moreover it is only by this name that it is recognized by the Nigerian government.

As a member of the Field Council of the SUM and before becoming its Secretary, Smith was well known to the member bodies. In 1942 he was active in helping to relieve a crisis over the question of baptism which threatened to divide the branches into two camps. The crisis passed and the mission remains one while its branches practice either one or other form of baptism. Then in 1944 and the years following he took a leading part in compiling a guide for the conduct of the churches. This was an aid for all workers, especially new ones so that missionaries might know the character and habits of the various congregations arising within the SUM.

In 1945, when he became Field Secretary he was the SUM's liaison with the Nigerian government and had to represent the mission in person whenever necessary. The Protestant missions were prospering in the central zone of Nigeria and through them the term "Middle Belt" first came into use. As political pressure increased and the emergence of an independent Nigeria began to be talked about, the need was felt for a human rights clause in any constitution that might be drawn up. Both missions and churches were active in promoting the inclusion of the clause. The need for this was accentuated when there were a few incidents in the Adamawa Province which led to the imprisonment of many Nigerian Middle Belt Christians on trumped-up charges and the expulsion of two SUM families from their homes for no truthful reasons at all. It was the field secretary's duty to lodge complaints with the highest levels of government on such issues.

These experiences were not without their value to the CRC Branch of the SUM. Smith's liaison not only with the rest of the SUM but also with other missions and churches of the North, drew the CRC missionary staff and the Benue Church into intimate bonds of fellowship with them. They were dependent upon the others in cases of sickness, the birth of missionary babies, rest homes when weary, and learning the Hausa language. One of the rich blessings of being a missionary abroad is to be cast so much upon the goodness and help of other Christians. The CRC on the field also profited from Smith's position as field secretary for he was one of three Protestant representatives on the Northern Board of Education, and also represented the Protestants of the North on the Central Board of Education. By this means the CRC was able to contribute to the formation of educational policy and work at the highest levels to protect the interests of the Christians. Smith also represented the SUM on the Christian Council of Nigeria of which he was to become vice-president and then president. But the most valuable and rewarding service the office could render was to maintain and promote harmony between the diverse branches of the SUM and to encourage the cause of the Gathering for Fellowship (Taron Zumunta) of the African churches. In time this was to lead to the formation of the Fellowship of the Churches of Christ in the Sudan (TEKAS).

Trials and Victories of the Takum Church

Concerning the Benue work of the 1940s mention has been made of the effect of the law on the medical and educational ministries. We have also spoken of the development of the Wukari and Baissa sectors of the work after there were sufficient workers to man those places. Takum-Lupwe was the main hub of the mission and progress was greatest among the Kuteb people. In 1940 a fine new church building was dedicated in Takum town. It was built and paid for by the people. It was the first building to have arched windows. However during a Sunday school hour early in 1943 a heavy storm threatened and the leader dismissed all classes before the lesson was given. Only minutes after all had left, the two main walls, sixty feet long and fifteen inches thick, were blown down. It was a great mercy that so many lives were spared. Two earlier churches on the site had been razed by fire and now that this had happened there was no spirit to build again and for years the congregation managed with a grass-roofed shelter with mats surrounding the whole. Even this was to disappear when enemies of the Christians maliciously set fire to it.

In November 1946 the church council started to make fresh plans for a central church building which would serve the Christians within a radius of thirty miles on special occasions such as annual conventions and quarterly celebrations of the Lord's Supper. All the village groups pledged their help, but to get anything done when so many volunteers lived far away without benefit of transport laid a heavy burden on the local leaders and missionary. Seventy thousand bricks had to be made and carried to the site, scores of palm trees had to be felled, split into lengths of twenty feet and carried many miles by head porterage. Rocks had to be dug from hillsides and hauled in springless carts. But by January 1949 the cruciform-shaped building was complete. At the time Peter Dekker wrote, "This church is not just another building, but has an architecture which suits it for worship and communion. The architect and superintendent in the construction of this church was none other than Rev. E. H. Smith whose heart just overflowed with joy as he saw thirteen hundred people coming from far and wide to worship and rejoice with us at our big annual meeting in January. And we all could say 'The Lord hath done great things for us.' "[9]

Of the dedication service we are told, "The five doors were all closed and in an expectant hush, the service commenced by reading Psalm 122, followed by that hymn of adoration, 'Holy, Holy, Holy, Lord God Almighty,' and the invocation. It was a sight which, we believe, even the angels rejoiced to see. One orderly mass of over a thousand people, men and women, neatly dressed in their best, rising and worshiping God together. Words of welcome were spoken and four churches, one of them of the great Tiv tribe, responded. . . . The sense of our Lord's presence in the ordered quietness was most manifest. One and another of the leading Africans—men who are not given to cheap emotionalism—confessed afterwards that they were moved to tears as they saw what God had wrought and how that from many different tribes and tongues, from villages near and from villages as far as a hundred miles away, this great gathering was made possible, because of the salvation our Lord hath wrought and because of the love He has shed abroad in our hearts. Surely the gospel is the power of God unto salvation."[10]

In the forties and fifties a large central church was common to most groups of Christians throughout the Middle Belt. It was natural for believers to get together once a quarter or once a month in order to fellowship around the Bible and the Lord's Supper. It became a tradition and in some areas even when numbers became far too great there was a reluctance to form sister churches. Part of this was caused by fear on the part of the leaders who felt that they would lose power and financial backing if the number of churches was multiplied.

Church Order and Liturgical Forms

The Ekas Benue Church's rule that members must be monogamous and allowing no bigamous or polygamous persons to be church members was often criticized by missionaries and American church leaders. Where women were concerned this began some months after the Takum Church elders accepted into its membership the second wife of a polygamist. Years before her husband, a communicant church member, had been excommunicated because he had married her and thus become a bigamist. Some time after her marriage to him she became a Christian and was then accepted as a communicant member. Thereupon the excommunicated husband asked for reinstatement believing that since she was acceptable he must be acceptable too. The elders felt that they had erred and in 1942 decided, "no second or subsequent wife of a polygamist shall' be received into . . . the church. If, said they [the elders], we discipline a Christian when he becomes a polygamist [bigamist] why should we after a time accept his wife as a believer, the woman who consorts with him in sin?"[11]

The church sought to encourage faithfulness in married life and so it required believers to make vows to God at the time of their marriage. It even encouraged couples who had been married before becoming Christians to publicly declare their intention of lifelong fidelity to each other. Only to Western eyes was it strange to see a couple stand before the congregation with one or two small children clinging to the mother during a ceremony for the confirmation of a marriage. Well into the fifties the church retained the custom of teaching converts for two or more years so that they might know the basic elements of the faith before they became communicant members. This included learning to read, and the study involved and the ability to read made for a more intelligent membership. Church or Christian community visitation was also instituted in the forties; two Christian leaders would visit every village which had a Christian community in order to help the believers as a community and to explain the requirements of organizing a church congregation.

These requirements included liturgical forms and their correct use. In 1944 these forms were submitted to the CRC Synod and a thorough study of them was ordered. The forms for the burial of Christians and the dedication of infants were set aside by the CRC. However, though they were considered unnecessary in America both were valuable in an infant church in Africa. The ritual surrounding death in an animistic society could not be practiced by Christians; therefore, when one of them died they needed some form of procedure to replace the pagan custom of the tribe. Burial had to take place within a few hours of death; it could not await the arrival of better informed Christians from a distance. It was good, therefore, to have a simple form for use by the local Christians. During this long period when new converts were being instructed in the faith, new babies were sometimes born to them and they wished to give thanks to God and offer Him their child. Since the parents were not yet baptized it wasn't reasonable to baptize the child; at the same time it was not possible to refuse a person the privilege of dedicating his offspring to the Lord. Hence a form for dedication was needed. When both parents were baptized the child or children could then be baptized also.

The ratification of liturgical forms for use in Nigeria by the CRC Synod eventually fell by the wayside. This is understandable. The forms of service used by an organized church are the prerogative of that church. The Ekas Benue Church is a Reformed church but it is not a Christian Reformed Church and so its forms of service did not require the approval of the CRC Synod.

Preliminary Steps Toward Church Organization

By 1950 there was a considerable increase in the number of places interested in the gospel as there also was in the number of confessing members. Since there were ordained men from the United States, talks began on the eventual organization of a denomination. *Ibi* was a congregation which we had adopted. A congregation had been established at *Nyita* to serve the eastern area. In April 1951 the groups at Wukari and Donga were reconstituted as one congregation under the name *Immanuel*. In July the Takum district sent Pastor Istifanus and others to visit the southern circuit and they installed elders and formed the congregations of *Trinity* (Kwambai, Kwambo, and Jenuwa Gida), *Jenuwa* (Jenuwa Acha, Jenuwa Kogi, and Bete), and *Lupwe* (Lupwe, Lumbu, Atsafo, two Bikas, and Gidan Tamiya). A short time after this a congregation was established at *Fikyu* (Fikyu, Nyipu, and Kpakya). Up to that time these congregations of the southern circuit had been part of Takum. The *Takum* congregation now comprised those believers living in the town itself. As time passed many of these divisions were again subdivided to form yet more congregations.

On July 25, 1951, Pastor Istifanus, the missionary pastors Dekker, Recker, and Smith, and two elders from each organized congregation met at Ibi, presented their letters of authority from their local congregations and so constituted the first meeting of the Regional Church Council. All congregations were represented except that of Fikyu. It joined at a later date. In the beginning this council was referred to as the East Benue Classis but this was dropped in 1954 when a more formal organization took place with a different name.

Notes

1. Lupwe Monthly Report, August 1939.
2. *Missionary Monthly,* May 1944.
3. CRC-Smith correspondence, June 5, 1947.
4. Recker report, fourth quarter, 1950.
5. Annual report to Board, December 1951.
6. Farrant-Dawson SUM correspondence, pp 1, 2, October 13, 1947.
7. Acts of Synod, Art. 56, C, 3, 1945.
8. Acts of Synod, p. 300, D to p. 303.
9. Dekker report, January 1949.
10. CRC-Smith correspondence, January 30, 1949.
11. Report to Home Board, May 1942.

12

East of the Katsina Ala River

DRCM Developments

The majestic Benue River which rises in the Chad and Cameroon republics flows for hundreds of miles in a westerly direction until it joins the Niger River. South of it there is a vast plain of savannah country which continues until it merges with the Cameroon foothills and mountains. There are a number of large rivers which intersect this plain as they flow northward into the Benue River. One of these is the Katsina Ala River on both sides of which the Tiv are located, occupying thousands of square miles of territory.

As has been related in chapter 3 the Dutch Reformed Church Mission (DRCM), whose missionaries had for several years served as part of the SUM, started work as an independent body in 1916 but continued to work with the Tiv people. There were comity arrangements between all Protestant missions of the north and in those arrangements the Tiv area had been given to the South African Branch of the SUM. When the DRCM took over it was agreed that the Tiv become their area of influence so that from the very beginning during the early days of George Botha, there has been a Reformed emphasis in the Christian ministry to the people of the Tiv tribe. The comity arrangement was intended to refer to a defined geographical sphere. However the migratory nature of the Tiv and the ease with which good farmland could be obtained to the north and east created a problem. With the continuance of peace under British rule and the hunger for more productive farm land, the Tiv moved into and also through to the other side of tribal lands bordering them to the east and north. Where the Tiv migrants went the Dutch missionaries and the Tiv Christians followed them with the gospel. Sometimes a center for worship was started in territory which had not been allotted to the DRCM. This was natural, especially so because they were the ones who knew the Tiv language. Problems arose when the Tiv believers in these peripheral areas would not integrate with the Christians of various tribes who were already there. This has continued to be a problem.

During the next thirty-five years after 1916 there was a slow penetration of the Tiv tribe with the gospel. Simple schools were opened and medical assistance was given, both serving as evangelistic agencies in an attempt to win the people to Christ. Fruit in the way of lasting conversions was scanty. However mission activity increased so that by 1950 there were seven mission stations and twenty-nine South African workers. Eleven of the missionaries were married and most of the wives, though not listed as workers, were very active in the work. Seven of the workers were mainly concerned with evangelism, six with education, eleven with medicine, and five with building and administration.

Too Much Work to Do

As the years progressed the DRCM became more and more aware that bringing Christ to all of the Tiv people was too great a task for them to handle alone. In the translation of E. N. Casaleggio's book we read:

> In 1931 the Mission Board enquired of the field whether it thought it desirable to hand over the unoccupied part of Tivland to another society in case it became impossible for us to occupy it. . . . The [Field] Council, however, informed the Board that such a step would be undesirable.
>
> The matter was again discussed by the Council in 1934. . . . The Council again confirmed their sacred conviction, "It was under God's special guidance and disposal that this Mission had its origin, and that our Church took over the work from the Sudan United Mission. . . . The workers on the field express their earnest hope that our Church will never have to abandon this work. In case, however, in the providence of God it should become necessary to hand over the work to another mission society for complete, or part control, it is the opinion of the Council that it should be handed over to the Christian Reformed Church of America."[1]

In 1934, a year after Miss Veenstra died, the home representative of the DRCM asked Nelle Breen whether it would be possible for the CRC to take over the work in Tivland. She replied that no thought could be given to it at that time. The incident shows that the possibility of involving the CRC was already there. Sixteen years later it came to partial fruition. In those years and especially during World War II the Tiv people moved about a great deal. They were good soldiers and by volunteering to serve in the British army they not only got to see distant parts of the world but they brought the influence of their experiences back home with them. Other Tiv, while not venturing so far afield, served in the tin mines of Nigeria as a special wartime labor force. For many of the Tiv this ended in disaster. The mines were on the higher and colder plateau, causing many to die of pneumonia. The rest were sent home as quickly as possible. Others migrated into the Wukari Division from the Tiv Division and in a 1948 report we read, "A problem to be faced is the steady infiltration of the Tiv tribe into the Wukari Division. It is a large tribe, and if its migrations remain unchecked, one can foresee that it will inundate the lesser and tiny tribes for which we cater."[2] At that time, though unknown to the SUM (CRC) the Chairman of the DRCM wrote to his home board about the movement of the Tiv into the CRC area and indicated that another sphere of work would have to be established for them. He said that the DRCM did not have enough missionaries for that and inquired, "Should we not leave the work beyond the border to the other friendly Society?"[3] This was certainly a reference to the CRC.

At the time the CRC mission was itself only beginning to properly occupy its own territory. Its second, third, and fourth male workers had only recently arrived in Nigeria for the first time. Nevertheless in 1949 the field conference resolved "to ask the Rev. Smith to approach the Board (with a view to possible discussion at Synod) regarding the possibility of opening a new mission field in Africa, this investigation to be governed by the desirability of locating this field as closely as possible to our present field compatible with the demands of a good field."[4] At this point there was no thought of the Tiv becoming a CRC mission field. It is noteworthy that the missionary personnel had vision and were looking to the future. The request was carried to the Board but it drew no action from the Synod that year.

Eastern Tivland Transferred to SUM(CRC)

In November 1949 the Chairman of the DRCM wrote to the CRC Field Secretary while he was in the United States and said:

The Rev. and Mrs. A. J. Brink of South Africa served as missionaries in Nigeria for over forty years, first for the SUM and then for the DRCM of which he was chairman for many years. It was his foresight which prepared the way for the CRC to take over the DRCM.

For some time it has been worrying me that our field of work gets bigger and bigger (our people moving into your field of labour) and our staff getting rather smaller than bigger. The Lord led me to pray about it and at a convenient time I discussed it in our Field Council where the reaction was quite favourable. I wrote to our Home Secretary privately and he agreed with my views. So a resolution was passed in our Field Council meeting on the 22nd of October. It reads as follows:

"**Transfer of Part of Tiv Country East of the Katsina Ala River to the Christian Reformed Church of America working in the Wukari Division.** We heard that the C.R. Church who is doing mission work next door to us and who has the same creed as we have, is looking out for a new mission field. The question therefore arose whether it is not now the time to offer a part of our enormously big field to them, for instance the part east of the Katsina Ala river. They can therefore help us financially and we can help them with teachers and evangelists and also with some of our European staff that we may be able to spare and who may be willing to help during the transition stage. We can also help them with the training of native staff, not withstanding such a division. The thought is that the church may remain as one under the Tiv. By such a transfer the burden of our limited staff and the financial burden on our Home Commission may be appreciably relieved and we will also have the opportunity to do more justice to the great areas of the Tiv country that are still barely reached. Our European staff is asked to give this matter our prayerful attention. We propose that the question be brought up in January 1950 at our Council of Congregations and the Field Council. This recommendation will be laid before Mr. Smith, the Field Secretary of the C. R. Church working in and around Lupwe, by his return from leave."[5]

A month later the Nigeria Conference of CRC regarded this offer enthusiastically and appointed a committee which sent a report to the Board in January, and in April 1950 told its committee "to arrange details of the transfer of the Tiv field should this materialize." The following month the Synod of the DRC in South Africa and in June the Synod of the CRC in America had agreed to transfer part of the DRCM Tiv field to the CRC. The Tiv Church, which had not been ignored in the discussions, was agreeable to the proposal but was not enthusiastic about it. The first mention of a transfer had been made only eight months before and everything had happened suddenly. On July 11, 1950, Brink, Orffer, and Gerryts in behalf of the DRCM and Dekker and Smith in behalf of CRC signed a transfer agreement in the vestry of Mkar Church. The Nigeria Conference endorsed it in August and forwarded it to the Board for its ratification.

After a preamble the agreement reads, " . . . it is hereby agreed to transfer as a sphere of missionary endeavour that part of the Tiv tribe living east of the Katsina Ala River and those Tiv living north of the Benue River but not resident in the Tiv Division, to the care of the Sudan Mission of the Christian Reformed Church from that of the Dutch Reformed Church Mission before July 1, 1953. . . ."[6] There followed ten conditions.

Zaki Biam was the main mission station in the transferred area and, partly for the sake of the Tiv Christians resident in the area, a simple ceremony was held at that station on September 14, 1950, ratifying the transfer. The Rev. W. D. Gerryts remained in charge of Zaki Biam and the Rev. Peter Ipema and his family joined him there on October 17. The CRC had accepted responsibility to make Christ known to 150,000 more people.

Effect of the Transfer on the People

The transfer of eastern Tivland was agreeable to the South African and American churches. The CRC missionaries were enthusiastic about it but the DRC missionaries agreed to the proposal with reservations and the Tiv Church Council agreed reluctantly. It was essential that the Tiv concur. One of the conditions was "that the present unity of the Tiv church situated on both sides of the Katsina Ala River is recognized and it is agreed that this unity be maintained as long as the Tiv Christians so desire, providing it does not conflict with Reformed principles."[7] It was also agreed that the Tiv General Church Council was to continue to be the ruling body of the Tiv church for both areas. American pastors placed in charge of districts were to be members of the Tiv GCC and a CRC missionary was to be a member of that council's executive committee.

The conditions made one reference to the non-Tiv churches of the Wukari Division when they said, "It is agreed that the fellowship between Tiv churches and the others be developed as far as possible." The first CRC committee report made some months earlier spoke of the Tiv east of the Katsina Ala River joining with all the other Christians of that area to form one Reformed Church. They wrote, "It [the transfer] would mean that the whole vast area stretching from the Katsina Ala River to the French Cameroons in the East would become our missionary responsibility. One envisions the several tribes of this area as coming to the unity of the faith in one Reformed Church. As that Church grows and the mission decreases the eventual union of the Tiv Church to the West of the [Katsina Ala] river with the Church now emerging in our area may be looked forward to."[8] This did not materialize. Tiv Christians in the transferred territory continued under the jurisdiction of the Tiv GCC which always met west of the river.

From the point of view of the gospel witness the Eastern Tiv was not untouched territory. To the contrary it had been served by the DRCM since the beginning of that mission. The first mission station was at Sai. It was later closed, but Zaki Biam twenty-eight miles west of Wukari and Sevav still farther west near the Katsina Ala River were serving that area when the CRC became interested. Apart from foreign riverside traders the South African missionaries were the only resident expatriate influence there for a great many years. It was into their shoes that the CRC was to step. The fruit of the gospel influence is indicated in an early report made by Mr. Ipema. He says that there were sixty-three places where worship services were held regularly every Sunday and in thirty-eight of these daily Bible instruction was given and reading was taught. Moreover there were forty-eight Nigerian Christian workers centered in this station and 185 confessing members were eligible to partake of the Lord's Supper.[9]

All of this makes it plain that the CRC was not beginning a new work among an untouched people but it was building on a foundation which another church had laid. True, there was not a formally organized Tiv church denomination. There was a local congregation centered at Zaki Biam and another at Sevav and these church groups were joined with others in the meetings of a general Council. In 1950 this Council was predominantly influenced by the missionaries attending it. Even in 1953 it was the DRCM in consultation with the CRC which prepared and circulated a tentative constitution for a Tiv church. However at that same time the CRC missionaries attended the Tiv Church Councils and discovered that the Tiv leaders were firmly asserting themselves in the business of the churches. In 1953 Ipema wrote:

> From my attendance at this Council meeting and two subsequent meetings of its executive committee I received one persisting impression. The leaders of the Tiv Reformed Church seem to consider that they have attained their majority. They desire that the Tiv Church be no longer considered a growing child of the mission, but rather a full fledged partner in the business of the propagation of the

Gospel and work of the Church. This puts a Church mission in a position which makes future cooperation a delicate matter to be undertaken with Christian, loving, diplomacy and patience. As an instance; the pastor's training class was initiated by the D.R.C.M. But this mission desires that now this project shall be fully sponsored and adopted by the Tiv Church. The leaders however politely made it clear that since they were not consulted on the project at its inception the mission should just carry on now. The Church would send occasional financial tokens of its interest, but would not underwrite the project.

On the local scene here at Zaki Biam I meet the same tendency. There is a definite reluctance to allow me the position and functions of chairman of the consistory. In March, a matter was brought before the consistory over my protest that it flagrantly disregarded the order of procedure set forth by Christ in Matthew 18. On other matters in which they have no previous experience to fall back on, my counsel was overruled. One such matter was their insistence that deacons should be paid employees of the Church just as are the evangelists. Some time later my strictures seem to have gone in home to them for they rescinded their previous decision. Our working relationships are on the whole good, but the prevailing winds of nationalism are inhaled also by Christians.[10]

In this same vein Ralph Baker commented, "I had a sermon prepared for Zaki Biam but the elders felt I had too much work to do without preaching. They do this to Ipema oftentimes."[11] As there were no ordained Tiv ministers at the time this indicates that the elders kept the "preaching" in their own hands. From the beginning of the CRC occupation of the Eastern Tiv the church made it plain that it did not consider our missionaries in authority and control. They did submit to the authority of the DRCM since it had under God brought the church into being. They felt that the same respect was not due to the newcomers and this puzzled and sometimes frustrated the missionaries. It is true that Tiv correspondence to the mission or missionary often includes the question "Are you not our father and our mother?" but almost invariably this refers to practical help which is needed and not to filial obedience.

Early Missionaries in Eastern Tivland

Missionaries appointed to serve this new field had to learn the Tiv language and culture. They had to adjust to a Tiv Christian community which was functioning according to a set pattern and had already laid down some basic principles by which it was governed. Moreover they had to live in harmony with white missionaries from a nation other than their own who also had their own distinct culture. The South African Dutch culture had very definite ideas as to relationships with black people. However, there was this which the two missions had in common: they both had Dutch origins and the theology of both was Reformed so that no changes in basic teaching were necessary.

The Rev. Peter Ipema was the first CRC missionary to settle in Tiv country. He had already served at Wukari for two years and had learned the Hausa language. He, his wife Jean, and their son Billy moved to Zaki Biam on October 17, 1950, and of this he wrote, "We loaded our worldly possessions on two African lorries, filled our little station car with family, houseboys, cook, cats, chickens, turkey and left Wukari to take up residence in a school house at Zaki Biam. Settling in and adjusting this building to our needs, providing a dwelling for our egg factories (vital), our cook and his pots and pans and stove, these things took many weeks to complete but we gave only one full work day to arranging things. On the second day . . . we were being taught the Tiv language by Rev. Gerryts." He added, "One particular Sunday stands out as a Lord's Day in a fellowship of gratitude, repentance and blessing with our Tiv Christians. We witnessed the baptism of twenty-two Tiv men and women, the consecration of twelve elders to their responsible office and then partook of communion together."[12] Thus the CRC was on its way to a great ministry for Christ among the people of one of Nigeria's large tribes.

The South African missionary in charge at Zaki Biam in 1950 was the Rev. W. D. Gerryts. He and his wife did all they could to help Ipema with his second African language. He proved to be an apt pupil and within two years was so far advanced as to be able to teach his new colleagues the grammar of the Tiv language. He also benefited from Mr. Gerryts' long experience when attending church councils with him and trekking widely through the district. The Fred Volkema family joined the Ipemas in September 1952. He was the educational supervisor for the CRC mission. The Ray Grissen family arrived there early the next year in order to build a home and other facilities for the staff. For a time the staff also included Betty Vandenberge who was transferred from Wukari. She also had to learn a second African tongue. She was a nurse and did a good work in the Zaki Biam health treatment center. Later she worked at Mkar Hospital and at the large medical center at Kunav.

Another medical worker who came in 1952 was Aleda Vander

Vaart. She and the Dr. Herman Gray family, who arrived the following year, went directly to Mkar, Miss Vander Vaart serving as nurse at the hospital and the Grays joining the staff at the Benue Leprosy Settlement. Dr. Gray had made a special study of leprosy and had served the American government in this field for some time. Another layworker who came at this time was Geraldine Vanden Berg. At first she served the Tiv women and girls and in time became a very valuable member of the mission's educational staff. The Rev. Ralph Baker and his family arrived in Nigeria in 1953. The Rev. Gerard Terpstra family arrived soon afterward. Both of these served in Eastern Tivland.

In time Ipema took over from Gerryts at Zaki Biam and also served as counselor to the Sevav congregation. Later on this congregation was ministered to by the Rev. Gerard Terpstra. The CRC opened a new mission station at Harga in Eastern Tivland south of Zaki Biam. In May 1954 the Baker family moved to Harga and the two southern districts of the Zaki Biam congregation became his responsibility in consultation with the church. One of his first responsibilities, with the help of Lupwe and Mkar colleagues, was to meet the spiritual needs of Protestant students and teachers at the Katsina Ala government secondary school. The school and town were twenty-four miles west of Harga on the Katsina Ala River.

Differences in Church Practice

With the emergence of new national churches differences arose between the missionaries and the churches; some of these problems could not be resolved. We learn of one of these from a missionary's report sent to the Board of Missions in early 1953:

> . . . should the present practice of accepting other than the first wife of a polygamist by baptism into the Church continue? Some DRC missionaries, but all of the Tiv delegates, unanimously believe that under present Tiv social circumstances such a Tiv woman may not be denied baptism and communion, for she is not yet really a free agent in deciding her marital affairs. Mr. Brink and I took emphatic exception, for we do not feel that God's law nor the purity of Christ's body on earth may be compromised by circumstances of any given social order. But the practice of baptizing any of the plural wives of a man continues another year while the church "prays to know and to do God's will." I took the occasion to declare there that I shall not be able so to prostitute the Bride of Christ

and cannot baptize any such women living in adultery. I write this for your interest but also that you may determine our Church's missionary policy on the matter of the sacraments and plural wives. How will you advise your representatives?[13]

What happens when the autonomous church decides that such a woman is acceptable to it but the missionary declares, "I cannot baptize any such women living in adultery"? The CRC did not make a pronouncement. The situation was eased when Tiv men were ordained and accepted the responsibility. The practice continues until now.

The instance quoted here will also serve as an example of differences between one national church and another. The Benue Church does not accept such women into confessing membership but the Tiv Church does. Such differences as this one need not prevent fellowship between two churches but if they were to seek total union the differences would have to be resolved. In the 1950s the friendship between the Benue and Tiv churches was often demonstrated. At the organization of the Benue Church there were Tiv leaders present and at several General Church Council gatherings each church entertained official delegates from the others. Quite often annual conventions were addressed by speakers from the other group. All of this promoted better understanding between the Christians. One big problem affecting union was due to the fact that the Benue Church was multi-tribal whereas the Tiv was uni-tribal. The brighter hopes for union of the 1950s faded during the following decade.

In September 1952 the DRCM held a service at Mkar to inaugurate the first course for training pastors. Two of the men chosen to be students were from Eastern Tivland. In 1953 the office of deacon was established and there was pressure encouraging the local congregations to form into classes. So the churches were led towards ecclesiastical independence, a goal which some missionaries were keen to attain quickly; others, however, were reluctant to promote it.

But in the early fifties the primary task was still that of evangelism. One report says:

> Only a small part of our congregation is accessible by motor road. For the rest, the area is subdivided by multitudes of small footpaths which wind in and out of every nook and cranny of the inhabited countryside. I believe Tiv country, seen from the air, would appear to be crawling with innumerable snakes, (i.e.) if these bush paths, often scarcely visible from the dizzy height of a bicycle seat, could be seen from an airplane. At every juncture

An outdoor village class for religious instruction is being taught by graduate of Benue Bible Institute.

Miss Laura Beelen teaches sewing to women students at the Benue Bible Institute.

gospel meeting is held in a Tiv compound. Mat weaving and smoking
ntinue uninterrupted as the evangelist tells his story.

he Tiv Christians introduced the use of simple musical instruments into
eir worship services about 1960. This Africanized and greatly enhanced
e services.

where two or three snakes cross over each other, there seems to be a Tiv village. Even the path-wise native of the country is frequently puzzled as to which path to take out of a village to reach his destination and must ask an old grandad or grandmother of the village for direction. The paths are worn by the constant foot tread of the populace and are dug deeper and more ragged by the pounding torrents which send small rivers down the slightest decline. Loose sand, exposed tree roots, numerous boulders, high grass and the deep streams that intercept paths, make them difficult to negotiate by cycle.

It is very tiring repeatedly to dismount, push a cycle through dense undergrowth or sand, and finally mount and ride again. All this is made the more unpleasant in early morning by a dew bath, and later in the day by a sun bath. No, travel is not easy in the bush, and the lodging is not commendable either to one accustomed to hotels or motels with their hard floors, clean beds, attractive airy rooms; and plumbing facilities leave much to be desired. It becomes annually more difficult to obtain the services of men to carry the 100-150 pound gear for such expeditions. The preaching in the hamlets done by the missionaries is in a very strange, foreign kind of Tiv, understood only with considerable concentration by the hearers. The results are hardly perceivable. Now, do you wonder why it takes some considerable self-discipline for the missionary to compel himself to take to the trails to go in search of these sheep of Jesus? But the evangelists of the Tiv Church who can do the work more effectively, are too few, and they experience these same travel trials in a lesser degree. They have become less active than they should be in this work. Inspiring them by words is not enough. They are encouraged, as are the scattered witnesses in the outlying district, more by the evangelistic love and deeds of the missionary evangelist. So, let us go to the other villages also (Luke 4:43).[14]

On one of his first bushland treks with the Rev. W. Gerryts, Ipema covered 250 miles. In this itinerant ministry he was joined by Baker and Terpstra and later Rev. Harold De Groot joined them. Only by going on foot or bicycle from home to home and staying overnight with the farmers could the missionaries really get to know the people and realize the size and urgency of the task that was theirs. Although it was costly in terms of endurance, it was done out of love and this endeared our missionaries to thousands of humble farmers and their families. Moreover it was this example that caused many Nigerian Christians to go and do likewise.

At the end of the CRC's first five years in the eastern Tiv field Rev. Baker wrote, "This December [1954] there were fifty adults baptized. About fifty were added in 1953 also, as also in 1952. This means that the adult membership has doubled in the last three years. Or to put it more graphically, from 1911 to 1951 the membership slowly grew to about 150. In the last three years [1952-1954], the membership has grown to nearly 300. Looking for God's harvest in the future, there appears to be a large Tiv church in the making."[15]

Benue Bible Institute

With reference to Tivland as distinct from Ekas Benue we are told that "[1933] marks the beginning of the bush Bible schools. These simple Bible classes were begun by the people spontaneously all over Tivland. They heard the call to worship, to read the Book, to be people of God, to call Jesus the Savior. No longer a foreign influence, this was their own real thing."[16] By 1945 these Bible-literacy classes numbered 100, and ten years later there were 400. However little or nothing had been done to train the leaders of these classes for their work. They were able to read and many of them may have had as much as a grade four education in a primary school. In 1955 the DRCM wrote to the SUM(CRC) "[Our] Field Council realized that something should be done to make our Classes for Religious Instruction . . . a more successful means of evangelization. We concluded that more attention should be given to the teachers of CRIs . . . that more regular religious instruction classes should be organized for the teachers of the CRIs."[17] At the time the CRC missionaries were surprised to hear this. For more than twenty-five years they and their predecessors had carried on seven-month courses at Lupwe each year to train laymen to be leaders of CRIs. When Wukari and Baissa stations were manned they also had their Christian Leaders Training Schools and later one was opened at Serti. Evidently in Tivland nothing special had been done to train CRI leaders.

Later in 1955 the Rev. R. Baker said, "Many schools [CRIs] start up spontaneously—the teacher may know books, but not God. Would it be wrong for the Mission to take a more active part in training suitable Bible School teachers? . . . Should we then ignore these schools whose teachers are questionable in their faith?"[18] He also said, "The CRI, I believe, is the distinguishing feature of the evangelistic advance in Tiv country. Here is where the Bible is taught day by day, and services are held every Sunday. . . . It is from these classes, I believe, that most converts come."[19] It was four years later, and after he had served in Nigeria for six years, that Baker was fully convinced of the need of training Tiv men to become CRI leaders and he succeeded in persuading NGC to recommend to the Board that a Tiv central Bible training school be opened. It was begun at Zaki Biam in temporary quarters in 1960. At that time a special gift fund was opened in North America for $33,000 with which to build an institute at Harga. By 1963 this sum had been increased to $60,000 and of this amount the Tiv Church was asked to contribute $560. It was the solicitation of this large sum of money and the very small participation of the Tiv Church which caused a misunderstanding among the missionaries on the field. The training of non-Tiv peoples had been going on for decades in modest facilities which had cost the mission very little indeed but which had, by comparison, cost the Benue Church and its Christian students a very great deal. The proposal that the CRC help the Tiv Church so lavishly was felt by some missionaries to be unfair.

However, in April 1964, NGC recommended that a complex be built at Harga to include nine dormitory buildings, two classroom blocks, a chapel, and two homes.[20] The Board approved of this the following year and while it was meeting the first classes were held at Harga, for, anticipating approval, building had been going on for some time. By 1970 the total building was complete and Mr. Baker had the joy of seeing the whole dedicated to the service of God and His church ten years after the first classes began at Zaki Biam. It is largely due to Baker's steady determination that the project has succeeded so well.

He has been the principal of the Institute from the beginning and Laura Beelen has been teaching throughout the years. Mrs. Baker took a large share in the work, more than commensurate with her home duties which included caring for six children. Nancy Chapel also made a fine contribution. The Rev. Paul Agba, a graduate of the Theological College of Northern Nigeria, taught in the school for five years and served as chaplain. His salary support came from the Tiv Church. The church is sole proprietor of the school but there are a minority of missionaries on the board of governors. A fresh class of students is accepted each year and in 1967 there were 175 applicants of which number 32 were selected for the 1968 class. The school has a three-year course. For many years the students had to do a year or two of village ministry at a CRI between each year of training. That has changed and training is now given for three consecutive years. By 1969, 100 students had completed three years at the Institute and by 1972 it is expected that that number will be doubled. The number of CRIs in Tivland is about 900 with 30,000 children in attendance.[21]

Benue Bible Institute (BBI) has been the name of the school for the last few years and its constitution speaks of six things that the Institute aims to do. Briefly they are: the personal development of students and staff in Christian faith and practice; the strengthening of the Christian home and family (all married students bring their families to the institute); the training of church leaders; the preparation of wives of students for an active part in the work of the church; the encouragement of agricultural development; and the encouragement of a wide Christian cultural concern. Practical application of the teaching includes preaching in the villages, teaching Sunday school and catechism classes, and evangelizing near and far. For a week or two each year the students go out in pairs to bring the gospel to an area where there is a real need. One report speaks of twenty-six teams, each of which concentrated on a village or restricted area for seven days. At the end of that time 317 persons indicated their desire to follow Christ and to receive instruction in the Christian faith.

Rev. Baker says that about 75 percent of the graduates have remained in the work even though the support they receive is very low indeed. Their responsibilities include teaching catechism, Sunday school and literacy-Bible classes, preaching, serving as elders and deacons, and teaching Bible in primary schools. Several have gone on to further training in the Tiv vernacular to become pastors and others acquired enough English to gain entrance to the TCNN. The improved agricultural methods acquired at BBI are of great value to the graduate since he lives in a farming community and depends on his farm for a living. He also imparts his knowledge to the community. In 1971 Baker said, "I remain convinced that the church needs such a training school for laymen." This conviction is endorsed by most missionaries.

Notes

1. E. N. Casaleggio, *The Land Shall Yield Its Fruit*, p. 107.
2. Annual report to CRC, 1948.
3. E. N. Casaleggio, *The Land Shall Yield Its Fruit*, p. 109.
4. Nigeria Conference minute 315, b, April 1949.
5. Nigeria Conference minute 396, b, and letter November 21, 1949.
6. Nigeria Conference minute 434, p. 5, August 1950.
7. Ibid., p. 5, item 7.
8. Acts of Synod, p. 300, D to p. 303.
9. Zaki Biam Annual Report, 1952.
10. Ipema, First Quarter Report, 1953.
11. Baker, report, December 1954.
12. Ipema Fourth Quarter Report, 1950.
13. Ipema First Quarter Report, 1953.
14. Ipema Second Quarter Report, 1953.
15. Baker, report, December 1954.

16. *The Banner*, p. 14, January 29, 1971.
17. NGC minute 1510, May 1955.
18. Baker, report, July 1955.
19. Baker, report, October 1955.
20. NGC minute 4803, April 1964.
21. Baker, report, June 1968.

13

Negotiations for Further Transfer of the DRCM to the CRC

Preliminary Exploration

It was Dr. Henry Beets who initiated the steps in America for the transfer of the Lupwe-Takum field to the CRC from the SUM, but it was Dr. J. C. De Korne who brought the transfer to completion. Likewise it was Dr. De Korne who set the ball rolling for the acquisition by the CRC of the greater Tiv ministry and it was the Rev. H. J. Evenhouse who brought it to fruition. In accordance with the Mission Board's decision of February 1951 to seek further Nigerian expansion De Korne inquired of the DRCM regarding the possibilities in their field. On December 9 of that year De Korne was suddenly called into the presence of His Master. He had served Christ and his church well for over thirty years. He had served faithfully as a missionary in China and a short time after that field was closed he became successor to Dr. Beets as secretary of missions for the CRC. From the very limited facilities located above a store on Eastern Avenue in Grand Rapids, with his loyal aides Reta De Boer and Harry Boersma, and his wise counselors Henry Denkema and Henry Hekman he propelled the CRC forward into a burgeoning mission ministry which his successor was to see circle the globe. It was providential that a few brief days before his home call he was photographed and his voice was recorded in the missionary film, "Bread upon the Waters." For that reason especially and also because of the record that this movie gives in sound and pictures of pioneer days in Nigeria, it has been preserved in the denominational archives.

De Korne wrote to the DRCM Chairman and told of the Board's decision " . . . to explore the possibility of opening new fields and sending more men into Nigeria."[1] Two months later the Rev. A. J. Brink replied, "When your church has occupied your present field [Eastern Tivland] to the satisfaction of your Board and your staff on the field, do not look for a new field anywhere else, but tell us."[2] The CRC Field Secretary knew of this and in a letter to De Korne explained that the proviso was reasonable since the CRC, which had accepted responsibility for Eastern Tivland about a year earlier had, at that point, sent out no workers for it. He also added, "Mr. Brink does not think that it [the full transfer] could be accomplished in less than fifteen years."[3] The following year Brink modified the time by saying, "It will take eight, ten or even more years to take over the whole field so as not to cause a shock"[4] and added that the transfer should be done "very gradually, without hurry."

In November 1952 the DRCM chairman wrote to the CRC Field Secretary in America saying, "I received a letter from our General Mission Secretary saying that a special committee has been appointed to go into the matter of a possible transfer of our whole Sudan Field to another Mission, meaning of course your Mission, and what our opinion is on the matter. To let any other Mission have it will cause too great a shock and disturbance." He added, "Will you discuss this matter with your Home Board and let me know their views on it?"[5]

The Officers Committee of the Board considered the matter and asked Edgar H. Smith to write to the DRCM. He was to suggest the need for a formal request being made to the CRC relative to a possible transfer of the western or remaining portion of the Tiv field and the reasons for it. In his letter to Brink, Smith said, "It [the CRC] will not wish to make promises relative to your Western Field without doing so in direct committal to God himself and it must therefore be clearly guided as to God's will in this matter. . . . in the past God did not err in placing our two fields of Reformed persuasion in such close proximity to each other."[6]

In answer to its request the following description of what was involved was given by Smith to the CRC's Officers Committee:

The Sudan Mission Field of the Dutch Reformed Church Mission of South Africa

The territory. The Tiv Division of the Benue Province of Northern Nigeria as it is found west of the Katsina Ala River. This may be as much as one hundred miles by eighty miles in extent.

The people. The Tiv [people] are the main people in this area. Together with those living adjacent to but outside the borders mentioned above they probably number 800,000. This is by far the largest pagan (as opposed to Moslem) tribe in the Northern Provinces. With some not-too-difficult dialectical differences these all speak one language. These people do not live in large towns or even villages but, for the most part, live in small farm hamlets of two or three households. There are communal centers where the leading men meet periodically and the area is divided into clans with their clan heads. They are nearly all farmers and are a virile as well as a fertile people.

The Mission. Protestant missionary work has been conducted among them entirely by the Dutch Reformed Church of South Africa until 1950 when the CRC took over a part. Work was commenced about 1912 with one or two workers and has increased gradually. Never has the number of workers exceeded 40. At present there are some 35 workers on the active list. Roman Catholics are very active in this tribe.

Mission Posts. Besides Zaki Biam and Sevav, now being taken over by us, there are five Mission Posts. They, with the activities they carry on, are as follows:

Mkar. Organized Church; Evangelistic; Full Hospital and Maternity; Teacher Training; Full Primary (Grade) School; Leprosy Settlement (large); Workshops; Includes some 18 residences, an excellent Church, hospital with operating theatre etc. and a large number of other buildings.

Shangev. Organized Church; evangelistic; out patient medical; grade school.

Turan. As above.

Kunav. As above with large medical work and nearby leprosy clinic.

Makurdi. Business center. Large house with stores. Organized Church about 6 miles away.

Mission Staff. The present staff includes eight ordained men, eleven teachers and school workers, three medical doctors, eight nurses and medical workers, five business and industrial [workers]. Many of the workers are new to the work, but a few have been there for over twenty-five years.

Church Congregations. Each post is the center for an organized congregation and they with the two in our new Eastern Area form a General Church Council. The number of communicants is unknown to the writer. The New Testament is already printed in the Tiv language. The Old has been translated and is being revised.

Methods. The indigenous system is the method employed. As far as possible and in every department use is made of

Africans—many of them trained and certificated as teachers or nurses and midwives.

Considerations.

1. The opportunity is unique and a challenge to the faith of the Christian Reformed Church. It must always be considered as only the providence of God which placed our fields in such close juxtaposition in the first case so that such a transfer would be reasonably possible. Moreover in all Africa today it would be exceedingly difficult to find such an offer as that of 800,000 people all speaking one language.

2. The task is a big one. Given gradual transition it should prove possible. Certainly 10 years is not too great a time to accomplish such a change.

3. The greatest care must be taken where the resident Tiv are concerned. These are mature people. Nationalism is rampant. To prevent a break away from all missionary counsel and advice spiritual diplomacy must be employed continually. This difficulty is not lessened by the fact that most of our men will be new and, like most new people, apt to err on occasion. Such errors when adopting another's work could prove fatal.

4. Undoubtedly not less than 35 workers will be needed. To obtain further and urgently needed development even more will be required. This can be worked out as to costs.

5. Should we adopt this new work care must be taken not to belittle or set into a baser place the work which alone was ours [the CRC's] until a year or two ago. The tendency will be for the greater to overshadow the lesser. This will be natural but if not carefully handled will react on the East Benue Churches and Christians in an adverse way. E.G. These people have long set their heart on a doctor. Now one is coming to them. Will he be switched to this new field? The attitude to the Mission could be gravely affected were this to be done.[7]

At the end of 1952 Brink said that there were eight organized congregations, 1132 baptized members and 1040 adult catechumens. These figures referred to the entire Tiv tribe including those living to the east of the Katsina Ala River.

Some Misgivings Expressed

The Rev. P. Ipema, acting secretary in Nigeria, wrote to the CRC Board, "It is true we would, by taking complete control be put in the way of a great challenge and opportunity, but it is also true that we would fall heir to a host of unsolved and insoluble problems and difficulties, for the work is far developed and may never be considered as approaching a new and virgin field. Is it not possible that the work has developed almost far enough so as to be nearly self-sufficient?"[8] It was his feeling, which was by no means unwarranted even at that time, that the Tiv Church had progressed so far and was so self-sufficient that there was doubt whether a mission was needed anymore.

Another problem was that of relationship of the Tiv to the rest of the Benue peoples. In the report above it was proposed that "care must be taken not to belittle or set into a baser place the work which alone was ours until a year or two ago. . . . If not carefully handled [this] will react on the East Benue Churches and Christians in an adverse way." Unfortunately this anxiety was to be abundantly justified in later years. Both of these misgivings expressed as a prelude to Western Tiv transfer showed the looming disagreements between the Nigerian churches and the mission.

There was also the question as to what the DRCM missionaries thought about any further transfer of this work out of their hands. Not a few of them had made a total commitment of their lives to God to serve Him in Nigeria and they would have to leave their life work if the proposition went through. It was pointed out to De Korne in 1951, "Nor is it to be taken for granted that everybody in the DRCM will welcome a further transfer, for the opposite is the case." Two years later there were CRC representatives at the DRCM Field Council and in their report to our Board they said, " . . . as far as the staff of the field was concerned they felt that they should continue to man the stations on the west of the river which they now have and serve the districts where they were situated."[9] The Chairman of the DRCM on the other hand felt strongly for transferring the whole field and exercised the prerogatives which pertained to his office; but he did not carry the missionaries with him—they were not in favor of this transfer. This made it much more difficult and required empathy and much patience on the part of DRC and CRC missionaries. The whole operation bristled with difficulties for the CRC and DRC workers and for the Benue and Tiv churches. However, up to the present time the changeover continues to bear fruit, very much of it pleasant and only a little of it not so.

Basic Agreement for the Transfer of Western Tivland

On January 4, 1954, a joint meeting of representatives of the DRCM and the SUM(CRC) with members of their Home Boards was held at

Mkar. Professor G. B. A. Gerdener and Professor A. C. van Wyk came from South Africa and the Rev. H. J. Evenhouse and Mr. J. Daverman were present from America. There were four DRC and three CRC missionaries officially representing their field conferences. The record of the meeting shows the DRC representatives were unanimous in their desire that the CRC of America be asked to take over this field:

> "Granted we obtain the consent of the Government and of the Tiv General Church Council (Raad van Gemeentes) and we have the assurance of one Tiv Reformed Church ultimately, we are prepared to hand over all our work in due time to the Christian Reformed Church. We feel that the work should be handed over as soon as and as far as the CRC have effectively occupied it to our mutual satisfaction. . . ." [Professor van Wyk].
>
> The CRC representatives acknowledged the honor done to their Church and Sudan Mission in this request being made. They were unanimous in agreeing to recommend to their Home Board, providing consultation with the Mission's Field Conference proved favourable, that the Christian Reformed Church take over the Tiv Field west of the Katsina Ala River,[10] that this be done gradually and as God shall enable them. Each step shall be completed adequately to the mutual satisfaction of both Missions before another is taken. . . .
>
> It was agreed that the emphasis will always be placed on the spread of the Gospel and the development of a single Tiv Reformed Church. Apart from this it was conceded that each phase of the work would be examined on its own merits and in the light of the overall policy before deciding whether to continue, to modify, or to discontinue as the case may be. . . .
>
> The DRC representatives made it clear that their welcome to the CRC is wholehearted indeed and involves no vital question of finance.
>
> All present felt the guidance and manifest grace of God in the foregoing proposals, and we express our united belief that the problems which are bound to arise will yield to His wisdom, love and patience. We believe that His Name will continue to be glorified and the ministry of Christ fulfilled amongst the Tiv people of Nigeria.[11]

There were a few less important matters discussed at the same meeting and they with the items quoted above became the basis on which the transfer of the Tiv field from the DRC to the CRC was conducted. On April 6, 1954, official representatives of the two field mission executives signed the document and sent it to their respective Home Boards. In June of that year the Synod of the CRC authorized, "the Christian Reformed Board of Missions to take over responsibility for the Tiv field west of the Katsina Ala River, providing that it be understood that the emphasis will always be placed on the spread of the gospel, and the development of a single Tiv Reformed Church, and this be done gradually and as God shall enable us."[12] In South Africa the Particular Synod of the DRC concerned agreed. However ratification was also required from the General Synod which did not meet until 1957 when it also agreed to the proposal.

The two missions on the field set up a collaboration committee on which both were represented. It met at irregular intervals to discuss the current problems related to the transfer. All business discussed which required action was referred back to the two mission executive committees. The agreement stated, " . . . each phase of the work would be examined on its own merits and in the light of overall policy before deciding whether to continue, to modify, or to discontinue as the case may be." Naturally South African and North American missionaries differed in their policies on some issues. Where education and the orphanage were concerned, efforts to reach agreement continued for years and exercised the patience of both missions. However, the writer was present at most of the committee meetings and can testify to the blessing of the grace of God upon all, enabling us in a quiet spirit and in due time to reach workable agreements.

In the Western Tiv area in 1952 there were five mission stations. Four of these—Shangev, Turan, Kunav, and Makurdi—were centers of evangelistic work, and each conducted primary schools. The first three had a medical center; that of Kunav was very large. Makurdi was the capital of Benue Province and so had many government offices. It also had a large railway center and the only rail and road bridge across the Benue River. Related to all four stations were organized local church congregations.

Mkar was at that time and continues to be the hub of the mission's activity. The Rev. and Mrs. A. J. Brink began the work at Mkar in March 1923. Casaleggio writes,

> The village head showed them an old hut which had previously been his pigsty. First of all the dirty soil had to be cleaned out and a new earth floor provided. It was an open hut, a roof on poles, known by the Tiv as an "ate,"

so they had to surround it with grass mats to have some privacy. After everything was ready there was room for two small camp beds, a small table, two chairs and a few chop boxes containing their provisions. This was their dining room, sitting room, bedroom, bathroom and store room for the next few months until a bungalow could be built. This was the humble beginning of the headquarters of Mkar.

By 1952 the station had become the center of a wide evangelistic ministry and there was an organized congregation using a fine church building. There was a hospital with a maternity section and not far away a settlement for over one thousand resident leprosy patients. There was a full primary school of seven grades and the small beginnings of a training college for teachers. It was the mission's administrative center, and the maintenance workshops were there.

To carry on the activities of the five stations South Africa employed eight ordained men, three medical doctors, eight nurses and other medical workers, eleven teachers, and five people engaged in business and industrial work. Many of these were married and about half of them lived at Mkar. Each phase of this.work would be considered by the CRC and it would become responsible for it when it was convinced that it was necessary.

In 1953 Evenhouse wrote to the field about "the great question" of Tiv expansion and said, "We may be sure that the kingdom of our Lord will never go forward on a highway of convenience but will always be a challenge of faith. May God give us much of the spirit of Caleb . . . and we may have to say with Caleb, 'Now, therefore, give us this mountain.' "[14] About a year later the Synod of the CRC had accepted the challenge of the Tiv "mountain." After it had done so one missionary wrote home and said, "As one who is told by —————[an observer at Synod] that the greater Tiv expansion was accepted in a few minutes flat I cannot but tremble. Is the Church aware of the enormous task which it has decided to handle?" Other correspondence shows that the trembling was accentuated because that Synod, which a year or two before had accepted responsibility for work in India, now rejected it and withdrew its workers. There was fear lest having accepted responsibility for work in Nigeria it might withdraw from that also. This was not to be. The faith spoken of by Evenhouse was expressed by the missionaries on the field and was then pressed forward by the Board so that the Synod and church took this step of faith which God so abundantly honored throughout the years.

It was the divine foresight and vision of the Rev. A. J. Brink that set in motion the machinery to bring about this change of missions in Tivland. This is much more remarkable when we know that he had served for over forty years in that country and he might have held on to the Tiv work as though it were his, but he did not. Moreover he persisted in planning the transfer in the face of the reluctance and unwillingness of his colleagues to proceed. He did not live to see the completion of the task but history reveals how very wise and timely were his decisions. His colleagues were very loyal to him and did not embarrass their new CRC neighbors with the differences which existed in their own mission.

Notes

1. CRC Board minute 5263, February 1951.
2. DRCM-CRC correspondence, April 27, 1951.
3. Nigeria Conference-CRC correspondence, April 19, 1951.
4. Brink-Smith letter, November 12, 1952.
5. Ibid.
6. Smith-Brink letter, November 27, 1952.
7. CRC officers' committee minutes, November 1952.
8. Ipema-Home Board letter, January 28, 1953.
9. Smith-Board letter, August 1, 1953.
10. When ratifying the agreement this location was described as "The Sudan Mission field of the DRCM."
11. Basic agreement for Western Tiv transfer, January 4, 1954.
12. CRC Acts of Synod, 1954, p 68, V, B.
13. E. Casaleggio, *The Land Shall Yield Its Fruit*, p. 29.
14. CRC-Smith letter, March 23, 1953.

14

A Brief Survey of the Bush Mission Stations

The Stations at Turan and Kunav

In a few short pages we will dispose of a number of places in the Middle Belt of Nigeria. Before we do so may it be said that each place already mentioned or yet to be mentioned represents people; real, live, warm-hearted people; men and women, boys and girls; black, white, brown people; laughing and crying, hungry and well-fed people; undressed and over-dressed people; South African, American, Jukun, Tiv, Juteb, Ndoro, and people called by different names. This record does not easily reveal this. The record is matter of fact and tries to be precise. This is inevitable but let us from time to time remember that the facts and figures refer to loveable, likeable people. All are precious because God made them and some are even more precious, because, like you and me, Christ redeemed them and His Spirit lives in them. This indwelling of man by God made possible the progress and steady increase of the gospel of Christ in the Benue Province throughout the twentieth century.

At the outset of SUM(CRC) interest in Western Tiv there already was a doctor, a nurse, and a teacher working with the DRCM. Dr. Herman Gray and his wife were working at the Benue Leprosy Settlement assisted by three South Africans. Aleda Vander Vaart was a member of the Mkar Hospital staff and Don Van Reken served the Teacher Training College of Mkar and bore much of the burden of it in its early stages of development. These three were already living with their new Tiv and South African neighbors and trying to adjust their lives to new cultures and languages.

The mission station of *Turan* was a few miles inland from the Muslim-Jukun settlement of Jato Aka situated on the left bank of the Katsina Ala River. Here the DRCM carried on evangelistic, medical, and primary school ministries and the Rev. E. N. Casaleggio was the minister in charge. In November 1955 he was joined by the Rev. R. Tadema and his family. For one year Casaleggio and Tadema worked together; then Casaleggio left to work at another post. After one full term of service the Tademas returned to America and another newcomer of the CRC, the Rev. George Spee with his family, took over.

The Turan location was very difficult of access during the wet weather when two rivers cut it off from the rest of the mission field. The government authorities remedied this situation by the erection of permanent bridges and better roads which helped Spee in his work. He was also helped by the ordination into the ministry of the Rev. Shinyi Ugo who was installed by the Turan congregation to be its minister. Shinyi was one of the first four Tiv to be ordained and of them we read, "Mr. Gerryts expressed his firm conviction that the present pastors are well able to entirely manage a local church with the aid of their elders and without the aid of others."[1]

Mrs. Jean Spee did a fine work with the women and girls of Turan in addition to caring for her own family. She helped to calm the community when alone during the riots of the early sixties. Nurse Frances Vander Zwaag carried on the medical work of the area for several years. Spee and Shinyi worked the district together until 1966. Since that time missionaries of the CRC were no longer posted to Turan; the facilities were handed over to the Tiv church, and Pastor Shinyi, with the help of trained Nigerian medical assistants and primary school teachers, took full control.

Turan is situated southeast of Mkar and is near to the periphery of the Tiv Division. Immediately south of Mkar and about forty miles from it is the mission station of *Kunav*. A not-too-distant neighbor and a prosperous center is Adikpo. The DRCM had a station at Adikpo for a very short time but later closed it and concentrated on developing Kunav. However Adikpo without resident missionaries has always prospered in a spiritual sense and has a flourishing church.

Kunav was the next DRCM station to be adopted by the SUM. In 1957 it was served by the Rev. and Mrs. J. Orffer. At that time they had already served for thirty-eight years in Nigeria. Orffer was engaged in the translation of the Old Testament into the Tiv language, a task he shared with other DRCM colleagues. At this point the Rev. and Mrs. Harold De Groot joined them as the CRC's first contribution to that area. De Groot said of the Orffers, "Especially remarkable was their intense prayer life and their devotion and consecration to God." This remark was true of many of the other South African workers as well. The Orffers left Kunav after the CRC officially took over that station and district on July 1, 1957. De Groot took all of the ministerial and most of the other responsibilities. At the time he reckoned that the district had a population of three hundred thousand people. The Kunav records show that of these ten thousand were attending Sunday morning worship. By 1962, five years later, this number had risen to thirty thousand and ten thousand of these had been added in the last year. De Groot believed that much of this was indirectly due to the serious riots which took place at that time. He wrote, "In September 1960 the Tiv rioted and much property was burned and otherwise destroyed. We had several tense days and at that time wondered *why* this had to be so. We soon saw the reason . . . the attendance at the church services increased dramatically. Men and women seeking comfort and peace came to the church."[2]

De Groot, who was to serve for seven or eight years at Kunav, saw steady growth and rich blessing on the church work there. One of his first privileges was to hear the confession of faith of eighty adults. He and the Kunav church elders were able to promote the establishment of six daughter churches in addition to Ikyave which had been transferred to another classis. In early 1963, when the church was growing rapidly, he witnessed the ordination of five Tiv pastors who joined him and one other ministerial Nigerian colleague in the work.

De Groot enjoyed good health; as a consequence he was able to make extensive treks in his district. He said, "I like to go out each Sunday to a different place, and during the week treks are made from village to village preaching and selling books." During 1960 ten mass-evangelism campaigns were held in different centers and twenty-seven thousand pieces of literature were sold. Distribution of tracts and the sale of Christian literature was fostered by him and in the end he left Kunav to give all his weekday attention to the literature distribution program of the mission.

As early as 1960 the Kunav report to the Board said with emphasis, "*The number one arm of evangelism is the Bible school [class for religious instruction—CRI].*" Ten years later this continued to be true—some statistics distributed by De Groot showed that out of 1000 adults examined by him at the time of confession of faith no less than 487 said that they had come to Christ through the ministry of the CRIs. It is also well to note the very strong influence of

Delegates to the Reformed Ecumenical Synod in 1963 are (left to right) Rev. J. E. I. Sai (NKST), Rev. Daniel Anakaa (NKST), David P. Ashu (Benue), and Rev. Daniel Ndeyantso (Benue).

Shimrumun Yakobu was ordained in September 1969. He studied at TCNN and Calvin College. His father, also a minister, is to the left of Rev. G. Spee (dark glasses).

personal witnessing. When the elderly Tar Shande was ordained into the ministry many believers had been asked the question, "Through whom did you have your first contact with Christianity?" and the answer of over 30 percent was, "Through Tar Shande." Undoubtedly well over 90 percent of Nigerians get their first introduction to Jesus Christ from their fellow countrymen.

At the Kunav mission station there was a very large medical ministry which still continues. Because of this and since the heaviest density of Tiv population is in this area there were serious thoughts for a time of transferring the Mkar Hospital to Kunav. Among others Betty Vanden Berge, Angie Hoolsema, and later, Frances Vander Zwaag rendered excellent service as nurses assisted by Nigerians. The residence of Dr. and Mrs. Gray was a rich blessing for soul and body for patients attending the main treatment center or village clinics. They were visited regularly by the doctor or a nurse. At home and on trek the gospel was faithfully told and lived by all the workers. Much was done to teach the elements of maternity care and midwifery to female students to enable them to serve expectant mothers living far away from more qualified aid. In time the multiplication of village medical clinics required the services of a full-time administrator and A. Reberg was appointed to this job with his headquarters at Kunav.

As the DRCM vacated its mission stations one by one, they handed over the property and their right to occupy areas of land to others. The churches and schools built by that mission were generally transferred to the Tiv Church when it had been legally established. The rest of the property and land was assigned to the SUM and the power of attorney was held by the Field Secretary of the CRC. A token payment of one Nigerian pound ($2.80) was made on each plot for legal purposes except that two thousand pounds ($5,600) was given for the stations at Zaki Biam and Sevav. The intention of the DRCM was that this would be used by it for buildings at Uavande. It was a great help to the CRC to have suitable facilities at each station which it occupied. These included homes, medical treatment buildings, sleeping accommodation for patients, and sometimes school buildings.

Makurdi

To the northwest of Mkar and about sixty miles from it is *Makurdi*. Makurdi is a large town. It began during the 1920s when the railway first reached the River Benue from Port Harcourt, an ocean port nearly three hundred miles to the south. As the railway continued northward the trains were ferried across the wide river. In 1932 a fine bridge was opened there for rail and road traffic and for a time it was the longest bridge on the African continent. This rail and road junction makes Makurdi an important center. It is the capital of the Benue Province and its population from the very beginning consisted of many different tribes. It is in Tiv territory but until this last decade the Tiv preferred to live outside the town.

The DRCM opened a mission station at Makurdi in 1931. From the point of view of business, for government contacts, and as an aid to numerous transient missionaries who passed through it by rail, road, and river, it was excellent. For the spread of the gospel in earlier years it was not too good. The mission station had to be built in the European reservation so it was far away from the Nigerian people. Though the response to the gospel in the immediate area was poor it was much better at *Apir,* which was eight miles away on the road to the south. The first church congregation in the area was organized at Apir and it was there that the Rev. J. E. I. Sai was ordained on January 26, 1957. There was a small mission station in Apir but it was never occupied by the SUM(CRC). It was given to the Tiv Church.

After World War II the Tiv people pressed beyond their traditional borders and many from Kunav country moved to Makurdi and as far as Lafia, sixty miles to the north of the river. From among these migrants some settled in the town of Makurdi and became the base of the city congregation.

Casaleggio, who handed over Turan station to Tadema in 1956 was in charge at Makurdi until 1961. The following year he handed over Makurdi to De Groot. The mission continues to be of great use to transients. The nearby public swimming pool is an attraction not to be resisted by those who live in the almost perpetual climatic combination of high temperatures and high humidity. For the resident pastors there was always much work to do. Sunday was a very full day with worship services, many in the Tiv language and some in English and Hausa. There were also services in the hospital, prison, and crafts school. During the 1967-1969 conflict there were many prisoners, thousands of them, and De Groot served them as well as the soldiers who encamped around his home on their way to and from the battlefront. All of this extra labor has passed away. Makurdi is now cared for by Bauke Lodewyk and two Nigerian pastors, one of whom lives at Apir.

Literature

In 1962 Makurdi became the head office for the literature ministry. The production and distribution of books, pamphlets, and tracts has always been a significant contribution to the cause of Christ in

172

Religious literature in the vernacular has become very popular. The small tracts are given away but everything else is sold, for this makes the recipient prize it very highly. The Rev. H. De Groot played an important role in this aspect of Nigerian mission growth.

Nigeria. Hymn books in Hausa, Jukun, and Tiv are very popular. Some of them include the Heidelberg Catechism in the vernacular and forms of service for special occasions. A number of catechism books have been produced in these Nigerian tongues for children, for preconfession classes and for more detailed teaching. Primers and school books have also been produced in great numbers. The same is true of Bible helps, tracts, and Christian booklets to promote faith in Christ.

After the first year in Makurdi it was reported that "no less than 70,800 Bibles, New Testaments, and single books of the Bible [were sold]. The number of religious tracts distributed exceeded half a million."[3] By 1966 De Groot reported that the number had risen to 150,000 pieces sold annually. When the Civil War came this number dropped to 125,000 and has remained at that level since. It is pointed out that formerly many thousands of penny booklets in the Tiv language were sold and the decrease is largely in this area, whereas booklets costing thirty to fifty cents a piece are being sold in much greater numbers. The number of pieces has declined but the size and quality of the material now being produced has increased. To produce such masses of material demanded the minds and pens of many writers and translators. Of these, special mention is made of the Rev. Gerard Terpstra who long served this work in Nigeria and continued to do so when he again settled in the United States. Other contributors have been the Rev. R. Recker, catechism materials; Mrs. Nelle Smith, catechism materials and many books of lessons for Sunday schools and women's meetings; Margaret Dykstra, school materials. Ralph Baker, Timothy Monsma, Cornelius Persenaire, and others have also made many contributions. When Terpstra returned home Gosough Ikpa of the Tiv church became responsible for all Tiv writing and translation. He examines the material produced by the missionaries and, after he has corrected their work, Baker examines the material to assure its theological soundness. Hausa and Jukun work is examined by other Nigerians. In 1968 one of the mission's evangelism goals was to "train nationals either in Nigeria or abroad for the purpose of translation, writing, publication, and distribution of literature with a view to eventually placing into the hands of the Church the literature program."[4] In part Gosough Ikpa is meeting this need.

To distribute the literature when it was produced or bought took much time and patience of many ministers and other missionaries. Where there is little or no appetite for reading material it requires much prodding to get the people to send their money for it. In 1971 De Groot reported, "All twenty-six of our bookshops are now in the hands of Nigerians. As far as I know they now have all been transferred to Nigerian proprietorship . . . all the shops are owned and operated by Nigerians."[5] The same letter tells us,

When the war began and they took prisoners of war to Makurdi and Gboko I worked to lay my hands on all the Ibo literature available in the North and Western Nigeria . . . [the missions] all sent their Ibo literature and Bibles to me in Makurdi. I was able to provide Bibles and literature for all the prisoners being kept in Benue Province. This was really a blessing to them, I believe. Also we were able to conduct services with the prisoners. Also through the Army chaplains . . . who had contact constantly with the front lines I was able to give and sell thousands of Bibles/booklets/tracts to the soldiers as well as the prisoners of war in Enugu. After the war through the rehabilitation efforts and CRWRC money we again distributed thousands of Ibo, Efik, English Bibles and Ogoni New Testaments. We bought all the stock the Nigerian Bible Society had in Lagos. . . . When the troop trains would come through town I would pass out Gospels of John to each soldier—about 1500 each load. Since they were heading for the front lines, they seemed happy to take them.

Throughout the sixties the CRC literature program gained the reputation of being the best in the country. It was a job well done.

Bible correspondence courses were established and in 1969 no less than two thousand Tiv were studying in this way. In addition, about five hundred Nigerians, Ghanaians, and members of other tribes were studying in English under Mrs. De Groot.

Distribution of literature includes the sale of very cheap phonographs and records. These are produced by Gospel Recordings Incorporated of California, a nonprofit venture of faith. Anne Sherwood and her companion worked tirelessly, ably, and patiently to produce phonograph records of gospel messages in some ten languages spoken in the CRC field. These records are made and distributed free of charge by her mission and their spiritual value cannot be overestimated. They are understood, each by the people of the language concerned, and it is delightful to see the comprehension and wonder on their faces as they listen to the story of Christ in their mother tongue. The only cost to the evangelist is payment for a simple hand-operated phonograph and the customs charges on the records. This ministry by Gospel Recordings is worldwide and in Nigeria alone they have produced gospel records in no less than 410 different languages. Assuming that the impact is the same as that of the ten languages in the Benue-Tiv area, the influence to the glory of Christ must be very great.

Shangev

A DRCM station not yet mentioned is *Shangev*. It is situated to the southwest of Mkar and south of Makurdi. In the early 1930s the DRCM missionaries felt strongly that there should be a station at this place but their Home Board could not meet the financial costs of building a new station at that time. However, the workers on the field "decided to take the financial responsibility for the opening and the upkeep of the station upon themselves for the first three years."[6] By 1935 the station was built and occupied. The usual activities of a bush mission station were carried on there. In 1956 during the missionary's absence the home was burnt down. It had to be replaced, for at that same time the DRCM was looking for extra homes where those who were translating the Bible into the Tiv language could live. So the burnt home was replaced, others were added, and all were occupied until the end of 1960.

After this the station was transferred to the SUM(CRC). But by this time the Tiv church was well established, so it was not necessary to use Shangev to any great extent as a missionary base for evangelistic outreach. It was used as a training center for new missionaries where they could study the Tiv language and culture. Another factor which had a side effect on the Shangev ministry was the opening of a girls' boarding school at Uavande. By a circuitous road there was a considerable distance between it and Shangev but by foot or bicycle across country to the northwest this was not so and the church ministries from the two locations overlapped.

Uavande

For many years the DRCM had a great concern for the welfare of Tiv women and girls. Brink often said that the tribe would not advance beyond the point reached by its women and mothers. Although the women held some significant roles in the culture of the tribe, in general they were considered to be on a lower level than that of the men. The DRCM wished to enhance the prestige of women. Much work was done for them by missionaries' wives and single women and for a long time there had been special training for Tiv girls at the Sevav mission station. The girls were drawn from all parts of Tivland. When Eastern Tivland including Sevav was transferred to the CRC, the DRCM set its heart on establishing a school for girls in the western section of the Tiv tribe. (At that time there was no thought of Western Tiv being transferred.)

In the beginning the Nigerian government was not happy that the mission wished to open such a school, but by 1954 it had changed its mind and offered the mission $15,400 with which to build it. In all, the Northern Nigerian education authorities gave $75,600 for the buildings at Uavande. The school was dedicated on October 30, 1957, and "there in between the green of Tivland's grassy fields are the white buildings of Uavande, a beacon for the emancipation and elevation of the Tiv women. Here the foundations are being laid for the Christian home in Tivland."[7]

Uavande was unique. It was the full flower of that which had only been a bud at Sevav. It was a primary school for girls only and nearly all of them were boarders. They were gathered from every part of Tivland and were all Tiv. They were served by a devoted staff of South Africans, Americans, and Nigerians. The only activity not related to the school was that of a white missionary who, at rare intervals, served the adjacent district as a pastor. Most of the missionaries were women; among these was Geraldine Vanden Berg of the CRC who had worked at Sevav but joined the Uavande staff soon after the school commenced. In 1960 Nancy Chapel was added by the CRC mission and continued there until the school closed in December 1966.

This was the first school with which the CRC was connected that was run by a Board of Governors. Financially the government had established the school and it required that it be controlled by a board of governors. On the board were representatives of the government, the local native authority, the Tiv Church, and the two missions. At first the proprietor was the DRCM. In 1962 the proprietorship was handed to the CRC and it in turn handed it to the NKST (the Tiv church) in 1964. After 1966 the government education department felt unable to meet the recurrent financial needs of the school. The NKST was also unable to meet them and the school had to be closed. This had been anticipated for some time, fresh classes had not been taken in and at the end of 1966 there remained one class which still had a year to go before graduation. This class was transferred to Mkar.

The Tiv Church did not relinquish its desire to have a separate school for girls and after several years of striving reopened Uavande as a girls' secondary (high) school in 1971. In the meantime the facilities were used for training Tiv pastors in the vernacular.

The erection by the DRCM of the Uavande school and the building of a number of homes at Shangev during the 1950s shows that the DRCM continued to be vitally interested in the expansion of the Christian witness in Tivland. Their missionaries were ardently serving their Lord and by no means idly watching the clock awaiting the time of their departure. They were most anxious that work be developed in the country west of a line drawn from Makurdi to Shangev.

Asukunya, Isherev, and Ityoshin

One reason for the lack of Christian development in the area mentioned was clan consciousness within the Tiv tribe. They are a single ethnic group with a common language, but there are within the tribe many clans. Some clans do not get on well with others and at times this disharmony amounts to enmity. This could mean that a Christian witness wishing to settle in another clan might not do so because of fear. On the other hand, since a foreign missionary was not a Tiv he could influence a number of clans from a suitable mission post. When God blessed his efforts and people of a new and hitherto unresponsive clan became Christians they would in their turn help neighbors of their own clan to believe on the Lord Jesus Christ.

The CRC missionaries caught the vision of the untouched Tiv farther to the west. This pleased the DRCM and its chairman had already been assured by our Field Secretary that it was our intention to evangelize the Tiv tribe in its entirety. He said, "This will be worked out as quickly and as fully as God shall enable us. It will also take into fullest account the existing Tiv church and will wish to cooperate with it and will look to it to take an ever increasing responsibility towards its own people. There will be no contentment or rest with us while parts of this field remain fallow and untouched."[8]

This reference to the responsibility of the Church of Christ in the Sudan among the Tiv (NKST) was timely. The collaboration committee of the two missions wrote to the NKST at this time, "We feel, and we would like your church to feel also, that it [NKST] has been created by God with the special purpose of evangelizing to the full your own people, the Tiv tribe. . . . Let us add that to reach your own people is both natural and spiritual but, in addition, there is also the rest of Africa and the world awaiting your efforts to bring them the Gospel also."[9] The Church's heartening response was recorded in April of the next year with the church saying, " . . . the new station north of Makurdi [will] be considered part of Apir classis. The whole Tiv church will send an evangelist. The Taraku station will also be part of Apir classis. The whole church will send an evangelist and the eleven congregations will each send and support a Bible school [CRI] worker who will be responsible to the Apir classis."[10] This was promising that the NKST as a whole would send two evangelists, who are next to pastors in rank, and each of the eleven organized congregations would send a gospel witness into the Western Tiv area.

"The new station north of Makurdi" mentioned above was the second of three new mission stations which the CRC built in Western Tivland. The first of these was *Asukunya* which is located on the motor road half way between Mkar and Makurdi. It relieved Mkar of some of its evangelistic work. The Rev. Rolf Veenstra was prominent in its early days of development and he had the joy of seeing a congregation organized at Wanune nearby before he returned to America. Afterwards the need of an ordained CRC missionary for field work was not so great and the station was mainly used as the center for promoting Bible correspondence courses for the Tiv people.

The mission station built on the motor road and about twenty miles north of Makurdi was known as *Isherev*. It was strategic in reaching Tiv clans which were largely untouched and had been unresponsive when help had been offered hitherto. At first the station was an evangelistic center and had a medical clinic for outpatients. Later a school was added. The Rev. C. Persenaire did the resident pioneer work of this area. During his retirement for a few years to the United States the Rev. L. Van Essen took charge. Later Persenaire returned to Isherev and afterwards took up vernacular pastors' training work elsewhere. The evangelistic ministry from this station was an important contribution of the CRC toward bringing the gospel to the Tiv of the far northwest.

Another contribution of the same sort was made further south when the *Ityoshin* mission station was established. For a long time the DRCM wanted to locate a station at Taraku, a town on the main road running south from Makurdi, but in the end Ityoshin was chosen. It was on a smaller side road further to the west. This was well suited to meeting the needs of another portion of the Tiv tribe not yet evangelized. For the short duration of its occupation by a CRC missionary the Rev. T. Monsma was in charge. As the Tiv Church was growing so rapidly and there was a greater willingness on its part to send workers into the needy areas of its own tribe, the need for foreign missionaries to serve as footslogging, hamlet-to-hamlet evangelists slowly died out. The Nigerian mission workers were always encouraged when a white brother paid them a visit from time to time and fellowshipped with them in the furtherance of the gospel. This did not, however, require the full-time residence of a missionary at a bush station.

The stations of Asukunya, Isherev, and Ityoshin, which were a useful gesture to encourage the Tiv church to evangelize their people far to the west, are no longer occupied. The same is true of Apir, Turan, and Shangev in Western Tiv and of Zaki Biam and Sevav in Eastern Tiv. *Zaki Biam,* the first Eastern Tiv station to be transferred from the DRCM to the CRC, served as a base and bridgehead for our staff members who were to serve the Tiv people. Many of them had their introduction to the Tiv language and culture here and had the saintly pastor, the Rev. Yakobu Amachigh, as their Tiv host in that district. However as early as 1952 our missionaries became aware of the independence of the Tiv Church and in the sixties the evangelistic and ecclesiastical service the missionaries could render in the local areas became minimal. Zaki Biam was vacated in 1970.

Sevav station was occupied by the Rev. G. Terpstra in 1954, his predecessor being the Rev. J. Orffer of the DRCM. In addition to his evangelistic treks and station duties use was soon made of Terpstra's aptitude for the Tiv language. In one report he spoke of having taught thirty-three members of staff. To do this he used existing materials but also produced a grammar and dictionary for the use of his students. It was a tragedy when his thatch roofed home burnt to the ground. In 1958 the Rev. E. Rubingh took over at Sevav and he was in charge until the station was handed to the Tiv Church in 1963.

Sevav is near to the Katsina Ala River and Terpstra and Rubingh knew the difficulties of counseling a consistory which had as a fund-raising project, a motor ferry to help paying passengers and their goods cross the river. It was a large canoe propelled by an outboard motor. Much time was spent monthly in consistorial argument concerning the disposition of funds raised by this project.

In 1956 the Rev. R. Baker conceived what he called "the intensive-extensive family group approach" with the gospel. This was different from the well-known method of witnessing of Christ once or twice in as many homes and hamlets as possible and over as wide an area as possible. Gene Rubingh tried this at Sevav in 1962. He wrote:

> The first phase of our newly adopted village evangelism program was completed. This program attempts to use family ties and communal bonds, which are so strong in African societies, rather than widespread trekking and random sowing. An extended-family group was selected from

which no one had yet been baptized at all. This group is the smallest clan division and comprises about ten compounds (in this case about two hundred adults). For fourteen weeks Christians went out to preach and witness in each of these compounds. Each Christian was given an outline for each message, so that the entire group received the same exposition of the way of salvation.

At the end of this period an evangelistic conference was held in the compound of the family head for three days. At the final meeting an invitation to profess conversion from the fetishes to Christ was extended. How we rejoiced when twenty-eight stood up, one by one, each with his own story of the light that had come to him. Now each Sunday services are held in the compound of the family head for the entire group, and catechism classes are conducted regularly there for the new converts. The effort has done much for the Christians who took part in the campaign—and has given them a personal interest in evangelizing their neighbors.[11]

Rubingh left Sevav soon after this experiment and took up a teaching ministry. The mission conference recorded "its gratitude to God for the blessings poured out upon the missionaries and their work during the 40 years of missionary occupation of the station. NGC now confidently commits the work into the hands of the Church and Christian community which the Lord has raised up at Sevav."[12]

Ibi and Serti

In this circuitous tour of bush mission stations we have briefly considered those which the CRC adopted and built in Western Tiv and have spoken a bit more about Zaki Biam and Sevav in the eastern sector. The station of *Ibi* served a Hausa community. After Clara Haigh left this station it was not occupied by missionaries but was handed over to the Benue Church. There is one other bush station which lies east-northeast of Takum and, as the crow flies, is about ninety miles away. On evangelistic treks from Baissa the Rev. Robert Recker was convinced that a mission station should be planted to the northeast of that station. A site was chosen near to the village of *Serti* which was in the area reckoned by the comity agreement of missions to belong to the Danish Branch of the SUM. An agreement was reached whereby the SUM(CRC) took the territory on the left bank of the Taraba River and the SUM(Danish) cared for all on the right bank. In a direct line between Baissa and Serti the country was mountainous and sparsely populated. By air the journey could be made with ease in a few minutes but by road one had to take a wide detour and it was long and most difficult. The Gilbert Holkeboers accepted responsibility for the new work and opened the station there in 1963. Locally the people were Muslims and the adverse influence of Islam towards Christians in Adamawa Province was to be felt from time to time. Serti, as a border control post adjacent to the Republic of the Cameroons, has a customs office. Smuggling was common in the area. From the beginning Nurse Margaret Kooiman carried on medical work with a special emphasis on a maternity clinic. The Holkeboers were followed by the William Van Tols who carried on the simple Bible school and a wide and energetic ministry of bush evangelism.

Of the mission stations which have Lupwe-Takum or Mkar-Gboko as their center we note that Turan, Shangev, and Apir of the DRCM are no longer occupied by missionaries and have been or are being handed over to the church. The stations of Asukunya, Isherev, and Ityoshin were opened by the CRC for a short time but, apart from some Bible correspondence work at Asukunya, are no longer used by the mission. Ibi of the SUM(British) has been given to the church as was the town site in Wukari. In all of these places the Nigerians continue a flourishing and growing Christian witness and each is an important center for either the Benue or Tiv churches. God has so greatly blessed His gospel in the hearts of the Nigerian people that now they are well able to carry on the testimony of Christ and no longer depend on missionaries from North America.

There are still missionaries residing at Wukari, Baissa, Serti, Harga, Kunav, Makurdi, and Uavande. Most of them are engaged in teaching or healing ministries. A bush mission station is no longer what it used to be. It used to be a base from which the vast and difficult hinterland could be visited with the gospel message. The workers, including nurses and teachers, would spend two, three, or four months of the year walking from place to place and living with the people in their hamlets or villages. This ministry, so costly in physical health and spiritual exhaustion, had to be done and it was produc- tive. At first slowly, so very slowly, but later with steadily increasing momentum, souls believed on the Lord Jesus Christ and became His children. Some of them were lost by the wayside and many were the tears shed over wayward ones. But God has gathered to Himself a glorious church. The churches, instead of the mission, are now the center. Where South African and American missionaries pioneered for Christ, there the Nigerian Christian now spreads the testimony far and wide that "Jesus saves." The foreign missionary continues to be the bearer of glad tidings but he now does so in relationship with the established national churches.

Notes

1. DRCM transfer correspondence, CRC file, May 3, 1957.
2. De Groot, report, Nov 30, 1961.
3. NGC minute 4401, 1963.
4. CRC Evangelism Department minutes, 1968, appendix, recommendation 6.
5. De Groot-Smith letter, March 15, 1971.
6. E. N. Casaleggio, *The Land Shall Yield Its Fruit*, p. 76.
7. Ibid., p. 82.
8. SUM-DRCM correspondence, September 20, 1957.
9. Collaboration Committee minute 144, letter August 27, 1957.
10. Ibid., minute 190, April 1958.
11. E. Rubingh, report, July 4, 1962.
12. NGC minute 4204, November 1962.

Death overtakes Dawuda Kwancha, whose unfaltering faith in God caused a great revival in Donga and created a thriving indigenous church there. The missionary is the Rev. Peter Dekker.

The New Life For All movement ("SRDK" in Hausa) for men and women has proved to be a great blessing to the Benue Church since 1965.

15

Lupwe-Takum Development

Activities at Lupwe

Lupwe used to be a walled town. In 1916 its occupants moved four miles to the north and became a part of the town of Takum. Three years later the SUM decided to build a mission station within the walls of the old town. It was located by a good spring of water. Unfortunately it proved to be the warmest and most humid of all the mission stations apart from Donga—it was *not* a health resort! The nearest habitations to Lupwe were about a mile away. In the twenties nothing remained of the old "town" except parts of the surrounding wall, the rest had been covered over with wild tropical growth. There were some lovely locust bean trees and these, or their successors, lend a parklike appearance to the place. Now there are added orchards of citrus and other fruit trees and many beautiful flowering trees and shrubs.

The faithful planting of the gospel by the early missionaries saw a real breakthrough for Christ in the 1930s, and because of this Lupwe, rather than Wukari or Donga, became the main center of our work. Here the mission's administration was carried on but ecclesiastically Takum was the pivotal point. Bicycle trips took the missionaries to Takum three or four times a week and the gradual organization of the church and consistory took place there. When people who lived in the surrounding villages became believers they joined the town congregation. The Lord's Supper was served in the town church and some communicants had to walk from five to as many as twenty miles in order to be present. Takum was the market town for these villagers and the journey would be made with the purposes of trade in mind as well as attending the church on Sunday. Most of the elders lived in Takum and the church business was conducted in the town church. Although the missionary pastor would be present to guide, this arrangement led to a greater stress on indigeneity than would otherwise have been the case.

Training Christian Leaders

Lupwe always had a Bible training ministry and the trainees were boarders. Many of them were married men and they brought their families with them. The women who prepared food for the un-married lads as well as for their own families also got as much schooling as their mental abilities would permit. In the forties pri-mary [grade] school education was introduced for children, and toward the end of that decade this led to the training of teachers to man these schools. Then during the 1950s there was a special three-year course conducted in the Hausa language for the benefit of evangelists of long standing. These students were chosen by the church and were the responsibility of the church. The Smiths, Miss Dykstra, Recker, and Dekker all took part in this training program. Ten men were trained and after graduation they were all ordained into the ministry of the church.

During the 1960s the Lupwe facilities were used to prepare men to attend the theological college. Likely students, who had to support themselves, were given a two-year course at the Johanna Veenstra Junior Seminary. Special emphasis was given to obtaining a better knowledge of the English language and a clearer understanding of the Reformed doctrines. Gilbert Holkeboer did much to get this started and he was followed by Cornelius Korhorn, a Calvin Seminary graduate, and later the Rev. L. Van Essen. In the light of other happenings in these later years it was and is a very good thing that this preseminary course serves students from both the Tiv and Benue churches. The Benue Church considers this their school; nevertheless, it is glad to have Tiv students. The mixing of students from so many tribes is a helpful thing for better understanding between them. In 1968 a higher level preparatory course was added and served better-educated students.

Grade school teachers for the Benue schools were first trained at Lupwe. Later they attended the teachers' college at Mkar. A second-ary (high) school began at Lupwe, but it was known at the time that it would be transferred to the Tivland location at Gboko. Subsequent

186

courses for the training of pastors in the Hausa language were not held at Lupwe.

The facilities used for these training projects were very simple indeed. Each new project made do with existing buildings which were no longer needed for their original purposes. This seems to have worked—it was economical and threw some of the burden onto the Benue Church. As the primary school grew, the *Ekas Benue Church* added its own new buildings on land supplied by the local authority. The girls' boarding quarters were near to, but separate from, the mission station and were handed over by the mission to the church. Then the *church* built the Christian Training Institute half a mile away and to it the CRC contributed a classroom. Later the Takum classis of the church opened a Bible school for the training of village leaders at Lupwe and some financial aid was granted by the mission. When the secondary school was opened in temporary quarters at Lupwe the carpenter's shop was converted into a classroom and use was made of the boarding quarters which were unoccupied at the time. These same facilities were then used for the first junior seminary students. As this preparatory seminary grew larger, use was made of the vacated medical quarters for classroom, library, and dormitories. This minimal financial outlay by the mission for the training of men should not be a measure of the quality of the work which went on within the buildings. It does mean that the CRC churchgoer was saved something on his annual mission quota.

Medical Growth, Physical Danger, and Tropical Disease

Early in 1953 Dr. Roy Davis and his family arrived at Lupwe and later that year Dr. Joyce Branderhorst joined the staff. With their advent the possibility of establishing a hospital became a reality, the more so because Mr. Ray Grissen, who was a builder, was already on the field. However the erection of a hospital did not get under way for some years. This was due in part to poor health and accidents. The Davis family had to return to America after a few months of service because of illness and toward the end of their first term the Grissens also had to leave. Mrs. Grissen had overspent herself in serving others in their need making it necessary for them to return to the United States. It was during her first term of service that Dr. Branderhorst was burnt when her home was destroyed by fire following a refrigerator explosion in December 1954. Fortunately Ralph Baker and Bob Recker were able to rescue her from death. We thank God for His mercy in this and that He enabled Dr. Branderhorst to carry on until her term was completed. We had hoped that she and

187

her fiancé, Dr. Raymond De Haan, would be able to serve in Nigeria, but this was not possible. Apart from things of lesser value the Takum Hospital venture was costly in traumatic experiences to human lives, lives of those immediately concerned, and of other colleagues who were also indirectly involved.

It is well to note, however, that in the thirty years of the CRC's Nigerian endeavor, it has lost only eleven-year-old Brian Scholten and the De Vries baby by death. There have been illnesses and many accidents but only those two were fatal. Many have been struck, thrown about, and knocked unconscious by lightning but none injured or killed. Cars have turned turtle, sideswiped trees, and fallen into rivers but no one has been killed or permanently injured. Dangerous river currents threatened the lives of others but deliverance was granted. Electricity has poked at some with its powerful finger and others have been in danger from wild animals but all have been saved. It is true that on occasion the poisonous but not deadly scorpion has made life very miserable for those bitten by it but, as far as the writer knows, not one worker, wife, or child has been bitten by a snake. Were all the near encounters with snakes recorded, a thousand stories could be told and from them all God has been pleased to deliver His children. The same cannot be said about attacks by rabid dogs and many a person has gone through the painful but necessary treatment; yet all lives have been spared. Within Nigeria and beyond it, by plane and by ocean vessel, through wild storms and hazards of war, millions of miles have been traveled between the Nigerian or North American homes and no lives have been lost. Had God deemed otherwise or should He do so in the future His lovingkindness would not be one whit the less, but it is cause for the profoundest gratitude that the Almighty Lord has so pleased to deal with His children.

Nigerians and missionaries are prone to the diseases common in North America. In addition there is a wide range of diseases—some of them peculiar to the tropics, others due to lack of sanitation and other health safeguards. For the country as a whole the mosquito is Enemy Number One because it carries malaria and other diseases from one person to another. Medicines for the prevention or cure of malaria fever have multiplied and for the greater part the white man is now free of its ravages. Sleeping sickness (*trypanosamiasis Nigeriense*) left its mark on one worker and poliomyelitis took its toll from another. Both missionaries made sufficient recovery to carry on their work on the field for many years. Medical treatment has made tremendous strides in the last generation and those living in the tropics have benefited greatly. The hot and humid areas of West

Africa, once called "the white man's grave," are no longer the danger that they used to be. Children, adults, and even the very old from colder climates can now enjoy, instead of endure, living in the tropics.

Takum Christian Hospital

The Takum Christian Hospital is five miles from Lupwe and stands on a hillside a mile west of Takum town and the mission's airstrip. It is near enough to the town to be easily available and it is far enough away to be free of the noise and bustle of a crowded community. It is also open to the prevailing westerly winds and has a commanding view of Mount Markham (Mba Likam) to the top of which mission-aries used to retire for vacations in the early days of the SUM.

The hospital was officially opened on November 12, 1958, al-though the treatment of patients began there in July. Dr. L. Van Ieperen and Dr. H. Gray helped to fill in the gap created in the Lupwe area when Dr. J. Branderhorst returned to America. Dr. Larry Den Besten took over from Gray and put the hospital into business. Fortunately Ray Browneye had been on the field since 1955. He was a builder and he with J. Tanko Yusufu, overseer and contractor, supervised the building of the hospital. Their efforts resulted in a neat and well-planned institution. In 1961 three members of the Christian Medical Society of the United States visited Takum towards the end of a six-weeks tour of hospitals in Africa. "They stated that the hospital at Takum seemed to be the best organized of any that they had seen, both large and small, and also seemed to fulfill the task of a mission hospital more completely."[1]

After the conception of Takum Hospital and before its completion the adoption by the CRC of Mkar Hospital became a factor with .which the Mission Board had to reckon. Because of it some feelers were put out as to abandoning the Takum project but it was decided to carry on. About that time Dr. Den Besten wrote, "I realize that some of you are genuinely concerned about the extent to which the mission will become involved in medical work. I share this concern with you and have therefore committed myself unequivocally to a limited program. This program is encompassed by the potential of the hospital which is now being constructed. In conference with the Rev. Evenhouse and the Recruiting Committee I have repeatedly stated that the mission should never allow itself to become com-mitted to solving the medical problem of Nigeria, or even that of Benue Province for which our mission is responsible spiritually."[2]

The hospital began with a modest 40 beds and the expectation

189

In this aerial view of Takum Christian Hospital complex, the hospital is on the right, the residences on the left. An orchard lies between the two.

Some of the senior staff at the Takum Hospital, 1965.

that maternity and other specialized needs would be met later. But after Dr. Den Besten left the field in 1960 building continued steadily until 1962, by which time there were 122 beds. Some private wards were added in 1966 and by the end of 1970 we learn that the number of beds had risen to 179 with, in addition, a village for chronic tuberculosis patients where an average of 40 more patients lived. The wards, but not the expectant-mother and tuberculosis villages, are all connected by a wide concrete walk. The medical, surgical, maternity, and dental facilities are complete with laboratory and X-ray departments. There is a very large outpatient facility with its own dispensary and medical supplies and an adequate administration block. The water supply, drawn from wells which were located by two Nigerians independently using the dowser system, is sufficient. Electricity is supplied by diesel-driven generators. In other words, Takum Hospital, like Mkar, is a health unit serving a wide community. It is complete in itself except that relatives and not the hospital staff feed the patients, and biopsy specimens are sent elsewhere for diagnosis.

From time to time doctors and interns have served for periods of a few months in the Takum and Mkar hospitals. Some donated their services and all of them made valuable contributions to the work. More important still, eighteen doctors have served in Nigeria for longer terms. Some were at Mkar, others at Takum, and a few worked in both places. Ten of these served the mission for a full term of two-and-a-half years and four gave eight or more years of their time. One of the medical aides especially helped by Dr. Ed Stehouwer for several summer vacations was Nuhu Ndeyaba. He is a Christian Kuteb of Kwambai who studied for his medical degree at Ibadan University and helped our hospital whenever he could. He and we hoped that he could join the Takum staff as one of the doctors after graduation. However he was indebted to the Nigerian government for his training and it required his services. Dr. N. Ndeyaba has since become chief medical officer over all the private and public medical work being carried on in Benue-Plateau State.

While only two CRC doctors served on the Nigerian field for more than ten years (including other mission fields Dr. J. Vroon also served over ten years abroad), the nurses gave much longer terms of service. No less than thirty nurses, administrators, radiologists, and laboratory technicians from North America and elsewhere have been employed by the CRC in Nigeria. Eight of these were on the field for only a single term whereas fifteen have given ten or more years to the medical ministry. Twelve of these are still at work, Miss Vissia being the senior with twenty-nine years of foreign service to her credit.

Harold Padding has served at Takum ever since the opening of the hospital. Of him the medical superintendent wrote, "Harold has succeeded in developing a really good lab where parisitology, most bacteriology, most blood chemistries and other general laboratory procedures are done. Besides that he takes care of blood transfusions, prepares all intravenous solutions for ourselves and Mkar Hospital, takes care of the compound, and manages the pharmacy as to inventory, issuing of drugs, and most drug ordering. With the installation of the X–ray unit he assumed the added function of X–ray technician. Needless to say he is much too busy, and we are anxious for the day when he will have a Business Secretary who will be able to assume many of these ancillary duties."[4] In the office Mrs. Vi Padding did a great deal to help the administration.

Like people, institutions slowly mature and take on their own individual character. The Stehouwers (Mrs. Stehouwer is also a doctor) and Paddings with Bena Kok and Mae Jerene Mast did much to form this character where the missionaries were concerned. In 1970 of the 105 workers, 96 were Nigerians, and 3 of these, Siman Istifanus, Yakubu Bete, and Danjuma Gwamna, had each served over thirty years in the Takum area medical ministry. It was their influence and that of some of their colleagues, as much as that of the foreign missionaries, that gave quality to the place. From the spiritual point of view there is no doubt that the chaplain, the Rev. Jonathan Wamada, did more than anyone else. In all there were 10 Nigerians who had gained their certificates from the government to practice as nurses or midwives. Out of many items we quote the following: "Two of the outstanding N.R.N.'s [Nigeria Registered Nurses] alternate months as operating theater supervisor which is a difficult job; we American doctors are quite demanding in the pace we set in the theater and there is much surgery to do. These men are really doing a good job. In addition I am training them to be anesthetists and they show real promise here too. This has already proved valuable to us. I feel strongly toward training our national workers to do as much as possible."[5]

Let a few statistics for the year 1970 suffice to give one indication of the value of the hospital to the community. In that year 4,623 people were admitted as inpatients and each stayed an average of seventeen days. The number of people who were treated as outpatients was 13,585. These would stay in the villages and town nearby and on an average came for treatment six days. The number of babies born at the hospital was 1,188. There were 1,293 major and 1,541 minor operations performed. Put in another way that means one baby was born every seventh hour night and day for a year; however, they were not that regular in putting in their appearance in the world. Also if we except Saturdays and Sundays there were five major and six minor operations daily throughout the year. There were 331 deaths in 1970 at the hospital. It can be seen that the volume of work is staggering and the responsibility on the doctor(s) in charge is very great indeed. Likewise we see how much good was done.

All of the patients were people and all of them had souls! That fact was in the mind of the more experienced workers all the time even though at times the strain caused by insufficient staff and overwork was so great that the patients tended to become numbers on a card. But every effort was made to be sympathetic and to meet the spiritual needs of the sick and their many visitors. Prayer was a frequent and important part of the treatment given.

The Hospital Chaplain

The Benue Church was asked by the mission to contribute to the hospital. In the very early days it gave bricks made by members of the nearer congregations. It was proposed by the mission that it supply a chapel and this was donated by J. T. Yusufu and his fellow workmen. The Benue Church was also asked to call an ordained minister to be the hospital's chaplain, and to support him and other resident evangelists, which it did. The Rev. Jonathan Wamada responded to this call and this remarkable man had a fine influence for Christ on the staff and the patients at the hospital. He had been a Christian for a long time and had already believed on Jesus Christ before ever Miss Veenstra reached Nigeria. He served the Lord first as an evangelist during which time he once walked sixty miles to tell the missionaries that the first twelve men at Kwambai had accepted the Savior. He became a primary school teacher, and later studied for the ministry. Throughout the third year of his studies he was very ill with tuberculosis. He had this disease for the remaining ten years of his life. He was neither handsome nor strong but he was a saint of God. I once traveled with him on his first plane journey and he smilingly remarked, "Today I am a black angel flying in the sky." To many hundreds of people he and his most faithful and loyal wife, Ruth, were angels sent by God to help them.

The patients attending the hospital are drawn from a wide area, and in 1970 no less than twenty-five different language groups were recorded. Of these Tiv, Jukun, and Kuteb predominated and accounted for nearly 90 percent of those treated. About half of the people were of the Tiv tribe and since they did not know the Jukun or Hausa languages, spiritual help had to be given them in their mother tongue. From the first the spiritual work at the hospital had been entrusted to the oversight of the Benue Church. For a time there was some difficulty as to who should employ and control Tiv evangelists working there. However, the Benue Church insisted on employing and paying all spiritual Nigerian workers whether they were Tiv or not. The Benue Church has always considered that the Takum Hospital belongs to it.

Hospital Administration and Finance

In the management of the hospital's administration Nigerians have had very little to say. Efforts have been made from time to time to include Nigerians in the governing body but without lasting success. The first recommendation made by the Mission's Medical Committee at its very first meeting reads, "We recommend to Conference [NGC] that the African Christian, through the Church Councils, be invited by the Mission into partnership in its medical ministry." This was followed by four suggestions, the first of which says, "We suggest that they have representatives on the Mission Medical Committee as coopted members."[6] In October 1957 the same committee recommended to NGC "to establish a Board of Governors for Takum Hospital. We suggest its composition as follows: 4 African Christians, 1 mission minister, corresponding secretary, 1 mission teacher, 1 hospital supervisor, 1 missionary nurse, 1 senior African hospital staff member."[7] The NGC did not support this proposal to establish a board of governors and offered in its place an advisory committee.[8] The advisory committee met irregularly for a few times and then was dropped. It was in 1968, eleven years later, that the doctor in charge, Dr. Gray, again proposed a board of governors and said that the Ekas Benue Church must place members on it. This showed, at least as far as Gray was concerned, that it was time the Nigerians had a voice in the executive activity of the Mission's hospital. However, no board of governors has yet been established.

Concerning the money needed to run a hospital the CRC supplies the missionaries' salaries, travel expenses, and homes. It also supplied the permanent equipment and all buildings except the chapel at Takum Hospital from mission funds. Salaries for all Nigerian workers, medicines and expendable supplies, upkeep of the buildings, and the general running of the hospital is paid for by the fees of the patients and grants made by the Nigerian government. Harold Padding made a careful survey of the hospital's finances in 1965 and reported that the outpatient department at an average charge of 28¢ per person was kept in credit balance. Inclusive charges for surgery ranged from a maximum of $22.40 for a major operation down to a minimum of $1.40 for a minor operation. Expenses were adequately covered when the government grant of 9¢ per day per bed was included. All other departments were well covered with the exception of inpatient and maternity services. For these services charges of $1.00 per person were made for the first week and 75¢ for each week thereafter. But the actual expense involved for each bed each week was $2.60 including medicines, dressings, laundry, and continual care. By that year's end almost $6,000.00 was needed to cover the deficit. An appeal was made to the CRC to meet this need. From this we note that, omitting the expenses related to missionaries and new buildings and equipment, indigeneity was demonstrated in 1965 since the people or their government paid 90 percent of the current costs of the institution.

No patient is ever turned away for lack of money. All receive good treatment including those who can pay nothing at all. Compared with North American prices the charges are ridiculously low. The top figure in 1965 was $22.40 for everything involved in a major operation. Even so the African living on a very low wage pays out a comparatively large percentage of his earnings. Unfortunately many who do not know the economic situation in the hospital believe that the mission is making large profits. Instead, that year alone the mission paid out more than $80,000 in behalf of Takum Hospital.

Auxiliary Medical Services

In late years professional dentists have served in Nigeria. Several donated their services for varying periods of time, most of them only briefly, helping missionary families and doing what they could to relieve needy Nigerians. This has now become a full-time permanent mission appointment. Dr. Ray Prins heads the department.

Medical clinics on the mission stations preceded the Takum Hospital by many years. Some of these continue until the present time and others have been added. Those supervised from Takum are Bete, Nyita, Sai, Harga, Zaki Biam, Sevav, Jibu, and Baissa. Today only one of these belongs to the SUM(CRC), though the establishment of all arose from the influence of either the DRCM or the CRC. They are Christian community medical centers and at each a local commit- tee is responsible for the general conduct of the place. The medical and other technical aspects of the work are left to those properly trained to deal with them. Once a center is running smoothly it is financially self-supporting.

The Takum Hospital has a rural health program with an emphasis on preventive medicine. In a four-week cycle involving four or five days of each week, centers in the entire area east of the Katsina Ala River are regularly visited. The program includes the teaching of good health techniques, and prophylactic treatment is offered for such diseases as malaria fever, whooping cough, measles, smallpox, and tetanus. Ruth Vander Meulen has carried on the work for some years, traveling the dirt roads by car and sometimes by motorcycle for hundreds of miles each week. She gives a Bible message at each center and the regular contact with pastors and evangelists for fellowship and prayer makes the task very worthwhile. This mobile medical ministry and that of visits to village dispensaries by the doctors or their substitutes is manifestly improving the health of the people. This is also true in the area west of the river; we will discuss this at a later point. Hospitals and all that pertain to them are the CRC's way of obeying Christ's command to heal the sick.

Wukari Combined Secondary School

Another section of the Lupwe-Takum complex is the secondary school located about two miles east of Takum town. The school does not belong to the SUM(CRC) but a number of our missionaries live and teach there. In 1955 some members of the Takum Church formed what they called, "The Education Eight Brothers Association." Three of these were sons of Filibbus Ashu, two were sons of Istifanus Audu, one was of J. Wamada's household, and there were two others. In June of that year they asked the Benue Regional Church Council to establish a secondary school. They said it was desirable to have a Christian secondary school because it would have a religious influence upon the students, it would lead to the educational betterment of the church's ministry, and it would equip Christians to hold influential posts in the government of the country. They suggested to the council that the CRC be approached about this and that the help of a white missionary be obtained to carry on the necessary negotiations. About the same time the Tiv Church was putting out feelers to obtain post primary education for its area. The mission was advised by the Protestant education adviser that the authorities would require statistical evidence that the graduates of primary schools in the area able to cope with secondary work would be sufficient in number to insure the intake each year of a full class.

Two years earlier, in 1953, the Synod of the CRC had decided that, "Education on the mission field be limited as much as possible to a literacy program in keeping with the performance of the evangelistic task—viz. the direct oral and written transmission of the gospel, and the encouragement of native covenantal schools."[9] But when this decision was taken the mission had for years been training men as evangelists and some to become schoolteachers. This teacher-training program continued uninterrupted. However, as the quality of primary schools increased from a primary four to a senior primary seven level, the question arose as to what was to be done with the brighter students.

Both the Benue and Tiv churches wanted a secondary school and the Benue Church council agreed that one be established in conjunction with the Tiv Church. The mission was agreeable and in 1956 it decided to establish a secondary school and that it would be placed at Gboko in Tivland. Although the location was not agreeable to the Benue Church, the decision to place it there was accepted with reluctance.[10] However, the desire for a secondary school in the Wukari Division persisted as far as the church was concerned even though it was discouraged by the mission.[11] Then in June 1962 the mission decided "[to] seek the Ministry of Education's permission to open Wukari Division Secondary School as a co-educational institution."[12] There is no doubt that Mr. J. T. Yusufu, a member of the Takum Church and at the time a parliamentary secretary in the government of the region, helped to bring about this change of attitude. He had twice written to the mission urging it to take action. When this was slow in coming he called a meeting at the Government Residency in Makurdi in May 1963. He now held the position of commissioner for the Benue Province and invited members of government, mission, and church to talk over this matter.

The result of this meeting was a decision to establish the Wukari Division Combined Secondary School (WDCSS). The local authority of the Wukari Division was to contribute the money for capital expenditure, the government would be asked to pay the teachers' salaries, and the mission would be asked to supply some teachers and a missionary builder to oversee the construction work. The Ekas Benue Church was to be the proprietor and would own the school. There would be a board of governors with these various bodies represented on it. The church made only very small payments to the school and yet it was allowed to be the proprietor.

For a year or two the SUM(CRC) allowed the school to use, rent free, some facilities at Wukari mission station while the first buildings were being erected at Takum. Harold Bergsma, who had started the Gboko Secondary School, now used his ability, zeal, and faith in getting this new and unusual venture off the ground. C. Korhorn followed him as principal and other missionary and Nigerian teachers

197

served on the school staff. The CRC made a loan of $28,000 towards the costs of the building program in the expectation that the World Bank through the Nigerian government would pay it back. The Hon. J. T. Yusufu showed his vital personal interest by donating $2,800 to the institution.

While the school belongs to the Benue Church it has a place in this history because the CRC sent teachers to serve on the staff and an overseer to help with the work of building. It is also of interest because secondary school education is one of the things which created tension between the church and the mission. The Education Eight Brothers Association and the church hoped that the mission would provide a secondary school in the Wukari Division whereas instead it was placed in Tivland. Ten years had to elapse before the "Brothers" saw the fulfilment of their purpose.

Linguistic Work

The Tiv Church uses only one Nigerian language, the mother tongue of its people. But those attending the Ekas Benue Church are drawn from eight or nine different language groups. Because of this, throughout the years since 1906 a *lingua franca,* the Hausa language, has been the mainstay of the work. From it translations were made by interpreters into the lesser languages. Ever since 1880 the New Testament had been available in Hausa and in 1932 the entire Bible was published in that tongue. As Christians were gathered in from the various tribes it was convenient to conduct classical and synodical business in Hausa and this was the medium of communication for interchurch work throughout the Northern Region. The tribes in the Benue Church are not large, the greatest being about thirty thousand people.

Records show that the SUM was not indifferent to the need for translations of the Scriptures into other languages. In 1914, only eight years after he first came to Wukari, the Rev. J. L. Maxwell published St. Mark's Gospel in the Jukun language of that city. Four years later the British and Foreign Bible Society published the same Gospel in Donga Jukun and in 1927 the Society printed it in Kona Jukun. Then in 1944 J. Wamada and Audu Siman completed their first rough draft of Mark's Gospel in Takum Jukun. At the time it was felt that these four Jukun vernaculars were sufficiently diverse as to be treated as separate languages. The Takum Jukun translation never got beyond the first rough draft. Because the other translations were never best sellers, large numbers of books were never used.

The missionary staff, which still numbered only six women and

198

one man in 1946, was too busily engaged to find time for translation work. Many years later one of these, Margaret Dykstra, took up linguistic work. In 1948 three ministers had been added and the annual report for that year reads, "It is a matter for concern that during the year only twelve additions were made to the roll of full communicant members. . . . I am of the opinion that language diffi-culties are the reason for much of this and that the local languages must be tackled to remedy this regrettable position. With larger staff this is not impossible. But it also requires both ability and obstinate persistence to get anywhere. It would be idle to blame the older members of the staff when they have been working a double shift for most of their time, but now that the opportunity presents itself it is time for us to lay hold."[13]

Twelve months later another report read: "The language barrier is ever a source of hindrance to effective work. Though some of our missionaries know their Hausa very well they still complain of the barrier of the Jukun language which none of them have as yet overcome effectively. Furthermore, with a small staff it was never possible for any to really make an intensive study of Jukun. The coming of Dr. William Welmers, a linguist of great ability, offered a new avenue of approach to our problem. Given time, he promised to lay the groundwork for the learning of Jukun. And so he did. During the four months that he spent in our midst he was able to prepare a workable set of notes and helps which will make it possible for at least some of us to learn Jukun. Both Miss M. Dykstra and Rev. Peter Ipema were able to make a good beginning on this study."[14]

Had the mission concentrated on the Wukari Division alone, imme-diate use may have been made of the groundwork provided by Dr. Welmers. But attention was diverted to new work among the Tiv people. Mr. Ipema was asked to learn Tiv and not Jukun and through the 1950s most workers were assigned to the Tiv ministry. In 1955 the Benue Church asked the mission for "a white teacher to teach us the Jukun language so that he could preach and teach the Word of God to those who do not know Hausa."[15] According to a reference in the church's minutes it seems that in 1961 the CRC ". . . had agreed to send a person to University to study languages." The same minute continues, "the Church Council agreed provided that the person applied himself to various languages and not to Kuteb alone."[16] Two years later the church narrowed the field down to Jukun and Kuteb. It was in June 1965, sixteen years after Welmers had offered his suggestions, that Miss Dykstra commenced her work on the Jukun of Donga/Takum and a year afterwards that Robert

Koops began on the Kuteb language. After his marriage Mr. Koops was aided by his wife, Esther, who is also an able linguist. In 1968 W. Evenhouse took up the study of the Wapan language which used to be known as Wukari Jukun.

These linguists have been greatly helped by the Wycliffe Bible Translators. They have taken courses with WBT in America and have augmented these with seminars and consultations in Nigeria. As Scripture translations are emerging, Wycliffe has contributed the help of one of their able consultants whose knowledge of linguistics and Greek has sought to ensure a true translation. In 1969 Mark's Gospel in Donga/Takum Jukun was sent to the printer and work is steadily progressing in the other tongues. In consultation with the CRC the WBT organization has placed two workers in the CRC area to work on the Jibawa language. To reduce a language to writing, to define its grammatical construction, and to discover words which are the correct equivalent of those in Scripture takes knowledge, time, and patience.

Besides missionaries, linguistical and translation work depends a great deal on capable Nigerians whose mother tongue is that with which the missionary is working. Several of these have been translators and to their work the missionary brings his learning in order to shape a better final product. These workers are indispensable.

In Nigeria the years 1960 to 1966, the early years of national independence, saw a steady resurgence of tribalism which had effectively been held in check by the British for sixty years. It culminated in the civil strife which raged in Nigeria from 1967 to 1970. This tribalism appeared in every part of the nation, also the Benue region. Concurrently with the emphasis on tribalism the mission, by the church's request, placed a new emphasis on languages. Aggressive tribalists have made use of this in their propaganda. This is unfortunate as a multitribal church such as that of Ekas Benue can well dispense with any divisive elements which tribalism promotes.

Notes

1. Dr. H. Smit, report, March 1961.
2. Dr. L. Den Besten, report, June 1958.
3. Padding to Central Christian Pharmacy, 1970.
4. Takum Hospital Report, August 1959.
5. Dr. E. Stehouwer, report, September 1962.
6. CRC medical committee minute 2, August 1953.
7. Ibid., 177, October 1957.
8. NGC minute 2243, November 1957.
9. CRC Acts of Synod p. 86, 4, June 1953.

10. Benue Church minute 469, 1956.
11. CRC education committee minutes 181 and 252.
12. NGC minute 4103, June 1962.
13. Lupwe Annual Report, p. 6, 1948.
14. Ibid., pp. 3 f., 1949.
15. Benue Church minute 448, December 1955.
16. Ibid., 885, October 1961.

16

Growth of the EKAS Benue Church

Early Planting and Small Harvests

We have written about the mission's "bush" stations and the activities related to the Lupwe-Takum center. Before we leave the Ekas Benue area and move to Mkar let us speak at length about the Benue Church. We need to remember that mission stations and institutional activities are but aids to the mission's main task. The impartation of knowledge and the gift of physical healing are secondary to the real purpose for which the CRC is in Nigeria. Mission workers past and present are sent to Nigeria to introduce the people of that land to Jesus Christ and to proclaim His salvation to every person.

In the early years the mission stations were mainly used as lodging places and as often as opportunity and strength permitted all the mission personnel walked or cycled to the villages and visited the people in their homes to tell them the gospel story. It took many years, much energy and courage, and even more grace and patience to do this pioneer work. This continued in a decreasing measure through the years of the 1950s, and in the 1960s it was the work of only a very small percentage of the total mission staff. This long period of witnessing especially by lay missionaries was an example plainly seen and emulated by the Nigerian converts. Listeners who showed the slightest interest in the Christian message were encouraged to talk to others about Jesus. Even those who knew only a little about the Master talked about Him. People who had not yet publicly indicated their faith in Christ and those who had yet to spend years before they were baptized were glad to tell others the stories of Jesus. It was the natural thing to do and no one was forbidden to converse about Christ.

Repeated contacts with this new religion called "Christianity" led individuals to the vital and necessary personal contact with Jesus Christ Himself. Whenever this took place conversion and repentance with commitment to God almost certainly followed. By faith in Jesus Christ they had become children of God and part of His eternal Church. However, rules laid down with a sincere desire to keep the budding church organization pure led to long delays before converts were baptized and became confessing communicant members of the local church.

By 1950 four ordained men of the CRC had joined the Rev. E. Smith and the Rev. Istifanus Audu in the work. However, of these the Rev. P. Ipema was transferred to Tivland and the Rev. H. Boer left the field to take up a synodical assignment in the United States. Even so it was now possible to divide the mission work in the Wukari Division and the Rev. P. Dekker went to Wukari town to reside and became responsible for the Donga, Wukari, and Ibi congregations. About this time Takum was divided and became six congregations instead of remaining one. One of these, Nyita, was part of the Baissa area and the Rev. R. Recker became responsible for it and all evangelistic work east of the Donga River and south of Donga town. Smith and Istifanus together ministered to the other five congregations of Takum, Kwambai, Jenuwa Kogi, Lupwe, and Fikyu.

Souls born again by the Holy Spirit are the living stones which God builds into His spiritual edifice; with them He is creating the one and only true Church of the Lord Jesus Christ. His Church is comprised of the redeemed souls of men of all ages and of all tribes and nations on earth. In the Benue area between 1910 and 1920 very few of these "black diamonds," as Miss Veenstra called them, were found and in the following decade there was only a slight increase. Of their number some were baptized and enrolled as church members in the earthly organization. Others did not meet the requirements set by the missionaries and the African leaders and could not be accepted even though they were genuine believers.

The SUM had agreed that when there were eighteen or more adults who had publicly confessed their faith and been baptized, they should be encouraged to organize a church congregation. This was likely to take place when some of the members appeared to be capable of holding the office of elder. In 1931 there were four organized congregations, but those who partook of the Lord's Supper that year numbered only forty-eight. Twenty years later this number had risen to over three hundred and there were nine congregations.

In expectation of God's blessing the SUM wrote into its constitution, before there were any converts, that it was its desire "to take its part in the formation of an African Union Church."[1] In 1939 the CRC was agreeable to this intention. This church wished not only to bring Nigerians to the joy of eternal life but wished them to be joined together as believers and by congregating together to be a visible manifestation of Christ's church in Nigeria. The outworking of the word *union* mentioned above can be considered later. At this juncture we will consider the words *African Church*.

Formation of a General Church Council

Members of the nine congregations of 1950 were drawn from thirty places where worship services were held each Sunday and which met the needs of about twenty-five hundred people. Of these worshipers three hundred were communicant members. The younger congregations had emerged from older ones and all of them followed the same teaching and practices. The doctrine was of the Reformed faith as taught by the missionaries. But the practices did not exclusively follow the CRC pattern. The believers were Nigerians, not Canadians or Americans, and they represented several tribal cultures, so that the practice, while it was Scriptural, was suited to an African and not a Western setting.

The preamble of the church order book of the Benue Church reads, "The reader is asked to carefully note that before the churches of Wukari Division had united in one central church council they already followed many rules and practices. These will not be found in the pages that follow. They also, together with whatever the R.C.C. [Regional Church Council] has decided, are binding on all church members, local churches, and district church councils of Lardin Benue Church and are to be obeyed."

After discussions between one congregation and another and between the ordained missionaries and the congregations, a meeting of official delegates was called to take an important step in ecclesiastical organization. On July 25, 1951, the first Regional Church Council of the churches of the Benue Province met at Ibi. One of the churches was called "Emmanuel" and was a union of the two congregations of Wukari and Donga. This arrangement was made because each of these places had too few active communicant members to enable it to meet the minimum requirement of eighteen members. Later this situation changed and Wukari became a separate church while Donga retained the name of "Emmanuel." For the first few meetings of the council only seven churches were represented. Fikyu Church joined the council in 1952.

Representatives of the churches met in council every third or fourth month and took decisions which were binding on all and in so doing made for a well-coordinated whole. The council also communicated with similar councils related to other branches of the SUM concerning the proposed "Union Church." It also sent delegates to the Taron Zumunta (Gathering for Fellowship) which met every second year and whose member bodies were half a dozen churches in the northeast of Nigeria. They often discussed the "Union Church" and drew up a tentative draft of its constitution. On the "Union Church" question the Taron Zumunta made its final decision in 1954.

January and February of that year were special months in the history of the SUM and of the churches which arose from its ministry. The first SUM missionaries had gone to Nigeria in 1904, thus 1954 marked the Jubilee Year of that work. One of the missionaries to initiate the work was the Rev. J. L. Maxwell; he was present at the jubilee celebrations in Nigeria in 1954 as well. The triennial Fellowship of the missionaries from all parts of the Sudan was held in January and the Rev. H. J. Evenhouse, who was accompanied by Board representative Mr. J. Daverman, gave the Bible studies on that occasion. After these meetings the International Committee of the SUM, comprised of representatives from around the world and across the Sudan, was convened.

In February those who had been delegated by the churches which had arisen from the work of the SUM and the Church of the Brethren Mission (CBM) gathered at Langtang. This place was near to Wase where the mission had begun its labors fifty years before. The purpose of the meeting was to decide the form which the church was to take. A report written for the year 1953 reads:

> Where we (SUM) have differed from European denominations is that we wanted an African Church. In 1953 this is very near its completion as an organic fact. Hard work has been done for years on the preparation of constitutions suitable to the peculiar set-up of the Mission in its various regions and an overall constitution for the Fellowship of these regional churches. With eleven fully ordained African pastors and a great number of congregations with their elders and evangelists there is a fine Fellowship which, despite its diversities, instinctively recognizes its oneness and has been most insistent in all its parts that nothing shall infringe upon this unity. It is our prayerful hope that the year of Jubilee will see the formal establishment of the Ekklesiyar Kristi A Sudan in each of its six regions and the recognition by Nigeria's Government of these in the Tarayya. We believe it will be done. It is a matter for the greatest rejoicing that God should have so blessed and led us.
>
> This formation of what will come to be recognized as belonging to the Younger Churches, respectfully knit to the foreign ties which—under God—gave it birth, and yet

come of age and able to make its own decisions, is most heartening. As it increasingly handles its own affairs and manages its own finance and as it spreads both within and without it shows itself as born of God and a worthy member of the new Nigeria.[2]

Five months before the historic meeting was held at Langtang the CRC Mission Board noted: "The proposed constitution for the Ekklesiyar Kristi Chikin Sudan as a policy for church union has been endorsed by our Board (BM6686) and the constitution has been returned to the field with suggestions for a few changes. At a meeting of the Field Council [SUM], the Home Board of Denmark with its American delegation felt that at this stage it could only agree to a Federation of Churches and not a single church. Thus a second constitution was drafted, the Tarayyar Ekklesiyar Kristi A Sudan [TEKAS], to cover the fellowship of regional churches. Our Nigerian section will be a regional church."[3] This comment noted the attitude of the Lutheran Branch of the SUM. However, in February 1954 the Nigerian churches did not take it for granted that there would not be a Union Church. A full quotation from the book, *TEKAS* will best explain the situation:

The Gathering for Fellowship (Taron Zumunta) was held at Langtang in 1954. It was the hottest time of a very hot, dry season and water was most difficult to obtain. The occasion was different to any that preceded it and for three days we debated as to whether the time had come to formally organise an autonomous African Church. The delegates present represented several thousands of baptized believers. In their own areas these believers were already members of local churches and each of those areas had some sort of central organization. Now the question was considered as to whether those six areas should form a single African Church or should they form six separate Churches and be united in a Fellowship.

The aim of the S.U.M. was to form an African union church. The feeling of the Nigerians present at Langtang was that they were one and they wished to remain one. However, the fact was that the six areas had each developed along the lines which their particular missionaries were used to following in their respective countries of origin. Some followed a presbyterian form of order, others were episcopal in nature and others preferred the congregational method. Then again there were many differences where baptism was concerned.

Some believed that small children should be baptized

Takum Church, built in 1949, is cruciform in shape and can seat one thousand people.

The Rev. Daniel N yantso became Cha man of EKAS Ber Church in 1970. He the son of the Ch of Kwambai whc town accepted Christian faith masse.

Ministers of the EKAS Benue Church at Takum in 1969.

while others preferred that they be dedicated to God. Moreover modes of baptism differed widely. These and other differences had to be reckoned with when formal and binding organization was contemplated.

By the end of three days of discussion it was agreed that each area should organize its own separate Church and that the six new Churches to be formed should join together to form the Tarayyar Ekklesiyoyyin Kristi A Sudan (T.E.K.A.S.) or, in English, the Fellowship of the Churches of Christ in the Sudan. It was a most difficult decision to make but it was made by all and the spirit of Taron Zumunta remained as good as ever.

The minutes of the Taron Zumunta meeting held at Langtang in 1954, record: "We met many times to consider the matter (of one Church, or six Churches and a Fellowship); we also held separate meetings—once the Nigerian delegates met alone, once the missionaries did likewise, and once each area met separately. We recognized how very much had been done by those who had prepared for this. The difficulty was as to whether we should be one Church or one Fellowship. The choice of a name was also a real problem.

"We were very thankful to the Lord that in all the discussions there was no anger and all was done decently and in order. We experienced His great love and grace. We also thank Him that our will is to continue to be one as we have always been. Not a single person present desired that we be divided."

From these same minutes we also quote: "At the Taron Zumunta meeting held at Numan in 1952 the missionaries were requested to seek a way to fulfil this purpose. Now the delegates have the answer. Since the missionaries are from different backgrounds and since there are variations in doctrine and church government it was seen to be impossible to form a single Church named 'The Church of Christ in the Sudan' made up of all the churches (in the Fellowship). For example the Danish Branch and the Lupwe Branch have their roots and form of church government either in Denmark or America. On such points there were very long discussions. In the end it was decided to accept this name, 'The Constitution of the Fellowship of the Churches of Christ in the Sudan' (The Constitution of T.E.K.A.S.). That is to say each regional council has her own authority under the 'Fellowship of Churches.' In such a name opportunity is given to Churches which are yet outside to join, such as S.I.M., C.M.S. and others who

would also have the right to carry on the type of government and teaching of their Churches which they had learnt
from foreign sources." (The quotations above are translations of the original which was written in Hausa, Ed.)

The six areas of Tekas met again after one year. The
meeting was held at Randa from February 16-20, 1955.
On this occasion the formation of the Fellowship of
T.E.K.A.S. was ratified by the participating bodies. These
bodies were EKAS—Lardin Benue, EKAS—Dutsen Mada,
EKAS—Lardin Gabas, EKAS—Lardin Lutheran, EKAS—
Lardin Muri, and EKAS—Lardin Plateau da Bauchi na
Yamma. (It was at Numan in January 1959, that the Tiv
Church joined the Fellowship and, in 1962, the Kaduna
Church became a member body.)[4]

TEKAS Affects Reformed Churches and Mission

The formation of TEKAS, which came about after long years of
discussions by a very diverse group of Christian people, left its mark
on the churches and mission of our field. In the first place Ekas
Benue Church became a foundation member body of TEKAS, accepting its constitution and becoming involved in its development as
the years passed. Secondly, after it was organized as a church the
NKST sought and obtained permission to become a member body of
TEKAS. Thirdly the constitution which had been written originally
for the Union Church became the constitution of the Ekas Benue
Church with only one addition. This was item j under doctrine, "In
addition it [The Benue Church] teaches the Heidelberg Catechism
and those other (doctrines) which are used in the Reformed Church
as well as the Apostles' Creed."[5] The other five foundation members
of TEKAS had identical constitutions as Ekas Benue but varied the
contents of item j so that each could suit its particular emphases. So
to a very large extent the six church denominations had names and
constitutions which were almost identical and made the Tekas Fellowship a much closer and more meaningful thing than is usually the
case.

A fourth effect which the formation of TEKAS had was the
secondment by the CRC of the Rev. E. H. Smith to the secretaryship
of the Fellowship. This was not a full time job but the CRC was
willing that Smith should serve all the churches of the Tekas Fellowship in this capacity. He held this position until 1967 when a
Nigerian took over. In order to do this work he had asked some
months earlier to be relieved of the position of secretary of the CRC

Nigerian mission and as field secretary of the SUM. This he was allowed to do. Throughout the remainder of the 1950s he still carried a full load of work for the CRC mission and continued to live at Lupwe.

Formal Constitution of EKAS, Lardin Benue Church

After the Langtang meeting of February 1954 the Regional Church Council of the Benue Church met at Lupwe on July 7, 1954. Its minutes read, "Establishment of EKAS Benue. It was agreed that we had already founded our Church on 25 July 1951. This has already been done. Today we confirm that the name of our Church is *Ekklesiyar Kristi A Sudan Lardin Benue.* We also confirm that the constitution of our Church is as it is recorded in Appendix X. Moreover in order that each congregation may openly proclaim before men its agreement with the name and the constitution, and promise faithfully that it and its consistory will continue to obey the Church's councils we will meet at three places during the month of August according to plan. We also wish to unite in the Tarayya [Fellowship] with the churches which are likeminded with us."[6]

Because the church was widespread and in order to make it easier for members to attend, three different Sundays and three different places were chosen for the proclamation. Certain chosen delegates had to be present at all three gatherings, at Donga on August 8, Nyita on the 15th, and at Takum on the 22nd. Henry Bello mentions in his report that at each place the CRC ministers, the Rev. R. Recker and the Rev. E. Smith (Rev. P. Dekker was in America at the time) expressed their agreement with the constitution and promised to help the new church in accordance with the Word of God. Then the official delegates, and the elders of the nearby congregations with the communicant church members all publicly declared their allegiance to the Benue Church. The Rev. J. Orffer and M. P. Loedolff brought greetings and congratulations in behalf of the Tiv Church and the government officer in charge of the division complimented the mission on the establishment of the indigenous church.[7]

These celebrations in 1954 brought to a climax the formation of a new church which, as Mr. Orffer observed in his remarks, was able with the help of the Lord God to stand by itself. Here was the fruition of nearly fifty years of gospel ministry in the area, fifteen of them being under the official guidance of the mission of the CRC. The mission is recognized in the preamble of the Ekas Benue Church's constitution. It says: "Whereas the SUM(CRC) took over the work in 1940 and from the beginning was desirous of establishing

211

a church in Africa, and whereas Almighty God, through His Holy Spirit, called to Himself a large company of believers in Jesus Christ in Northern Nigeria by means of this Mission. . . ." The Benue Church always has recognized the vital ministry of the mission whereby the Lord saved so many souls and welded them into one membership in the body of Jesus Christ.

CRC missionaries are referred to in Article 16 of the church's constitution: "It is possible for missionaries to hold office in this Church and to be members of its Councils provided that the General Church Council agrees and they subscribe to the Church's Constitution." Ordained missionaries "who have a definite assignment in the area" had the right to attend the church councils. In 1958 on the suggestion of the missionaries the church decided that they should no longer vote, although they might take part in the discussions.[8]

When the Ekas Benue Church was given its name and accepted its constitution it was self-supporting, self-governing, and self-propagating. It had one ordained minister and was to have ten more in the near future. It had its governing elders in each congregation. It spread the faith nearby and faraway and had its own Nigerian missionaries. It supported all its own workers, and owned and maintained its church and school property. It cared for its own children and taught new believers until they became confessing members of the church. When it was necessary it disciplined its members. The formation of this church brought joy to the Trinity of God and the angels in heaven. It rejoiced in those who fostered its growth and in all those who were its members.

The following statistics are given in order that the reader may appreciate the growth of this church. Detailed records have not yet been found for the years 1949 to 1956, but complete information is available from 1957 to 1970. The following are the figures for 1957 and 1970 taken from the TEKAS annual reports:

Ekas Benue Church	1957	1970	Percent of increase
Places of worship	105	198	89
Attendance, Sunday worship	5,631	19,317	243
Organized congregations	10	36	260
Ordained pastors	1	20	
Other workers	37	107	190
Active communicant members	1,431	7,980	456
Confessions of faith	297	492	65
Children baptized	71	410	480
Offerings	$4,004	$22,111	450

212

Although census figures for Nigeria have not been made public for twenty years, yet it is probable that apart from Tiv people 13 percent of the remainder within the Benue Church area were attending church in 1970. Two out of every five persons would be confessing members. The church is located in the Wukari Division of the Benue-Plateau State and the United Hills Division of the Northeast State. Serti is farther to the east. Beyond the church's borders in every direction there are other Protestant bodies. Expansion can be among the 87 percent within the church's area who do not attend church and among the small groups of people who have moved away from Benue to other cities throughout the nation. In addition the church can open up mission fields well beyond its own borders.

Subsequent to 1954 and the naming of the Ekas Benue Church the SUM(CRC) has rendered it service in many ways. Seven ordained men of the CRC served the church directly, most of them for periods of more than five years. Many of these spent much time and energy trekking their assigned areas, preaching the gospel and helping the believers. All of them carried on a teaching ministry in line with the NGC decision stating that "a major concern of the Department of Evangelism in the future will also be the developing of the eldership of the Church, the training of ministers and leaders in the Bible Schools."[9] They were counselors to local and other church councils. Benue Church students were also helped by our missionaries at the Theological College of Northern Nigeria.

Unordained missionaries, both men and women, served the church full time. Some taught in the Christian workers' training centers, others served the women and girls, later on youth clubs were established for boys and girls in many of the churches. They also served at Veenstra Junior Seminary. Later the Christian Reformed World Relief Committee (CRWRC) sent a worker to introduce improved methods of agriculture. The linguists have already been mentioned. Indirectly the men and women who served in the medical, educational, administrative, and maintenance fields were witnesses for Christ, giving time and energy to this in addition to their particular assignments. Some felt that they were not prepared for such witnessing and said that they preferred to leave it to the ordained men. They were in the minority. Many wives, though not officially regarded as workers, were also active in the Kingdom; this activity was not only useful for the people, it was rewarding to these women as well. Since the formation of the independent Benue Church, mission personnel has continued to be useful to it in very many ways.

The Relationship Between Church and Mission

In 1953 the CRC Synod discussed the fruits of a study which it had instituted on mission principles. It decided that "the founding of congregations should take place as soon as the three marks of the church can be maintained."[10] It then added, "A church duly constituted has equal standing in dignity and law with all other churches. The sending church, recognizing this, will increasingly encourage the new church to assume her full responsibility."[11] Late in 1954 the Benue Church met and sent a letter to the CRC Board of Missions. Following is a translation of a part of that communication:

> Furthermore our General Church Council of the Lardin Benue (i.e. Benue Region) met on 6 November, 1954. It then requested that I should write to you with the desire that our request is brought to the Synod of the Christian Reformed Church. In our minutes of that date, No. 322 we said, quote "We are thankful to our God that He has brought us to this standing (as a Church) in our own right. We are thankful also for those who nurtured us and brought us to this time. Moreover, if the Christian Reformed Church agrees, we request that we may become brethren in fellowship together and that it may also be agreeable that we correspond with each other to the mutual strengthening of us all." End quote.
>
> In view of this I am sending this our request for fellowship and interchange of correspondence that might be to our mutual benefit. If your Board is agreeable we should like you to bring this request before the Synod of the Christian Reformed Church in June.
>
> Without any doubt we desire the fellowship of our Lord Jesus Christ with those who by the grace of God were instrumental in our finding the way of salvation.[12]

In June 1955 the CRC Synod expressed "its gratitude to God for the founding of this native church and request God's blessing upon it, and that Synod refer the request of this new church for fellowship and interchange of correspondence to its Committee on Ecumenicity and Interchurch Correspondence for appropriate action."[13] The following year the CRC entered into full fraternal relationship with Ekas Benue Church and expressed its "great joy in being privileged to establish full fellowship with this church."[14]

As individual people the rapport between missionaries and Benue Christians, while varying considerably, has been and continues to be cordial and praiseworthy. Officially this has not always been the case. In 1958 the mission's NGC requested the churches of Benue and NKST to send observers to the meetings of its evangelism committee. This was the first inclusion of Nigerians in an official mission business meeting, whereas on the other hand the Ekas Benue Church had always had missionaries on its councils. The same year the NGC asked its Board of Missions to request delegates from both the Benue and Tiv churches to attend the Synod of the CRC in America. This request was granted and three years later Demeghba Bajah and David Ashu attended the meetings of Synod and visited many CRC churches. It was an excellent idea and Mr. Ashu shared his experiences in a booklet which the Benue Church published. In 1963 delegates of the Tiv and Benue churches attended a meeting of the Reformed Ecumenical Synod. When the CRC Board sends representatives to Nigeria the two churches invariably invite them to meet with one or another of their official bodies.

Early in 1960 the Tekas Fellowship of Churches held long discussions on the relationship of foreign missions with Nigerian churches. It made a strong plea to its originating missions to seriously consider allowing Nigerians to attend their executive committees. It also placed equal urgency on the need for missionaries to become members of the Nigerian churches. It was felt that the acceptance of these two proposals would bring about true oneness in Christ and would reduce suspicion which abounds in the minds of Nigerians when missions exclude the churches from their business meetings. The Rev. Damina Bawado said; "It would greatly strengthen relationships if the missionaries demonstrated their faith in the national church which, under God they had created, by themselves becoming members of it during their stay in this land."

Moreover, he proposed that it would greatly lessen suspicion and also prove to be an educative process in discipleship if missions would allow national Christians to attend and share in all committees which dealt with matters concerning the African peoples.

These propositions received the unanimous support of the colored and white delegates at the Church Fellowship. By no means whatsoever was there a desire to oust and replace the missionary. The nationals feel strongly that it is desirable that we should go along together, integrated and each fully trusting the other.[15]

The NGC considered these proposals three months later and made some far-reaching decisions. It declared its "determination to work through the national churches in the field of evangelism," and added, "Thus, the mission should be on guard against the implementation of programs which have not been developed in conjunction with the desires of the national churches."[16] At the same meeting it increased the representation of each church at the meetings of the evangelism department and gave them the right to vote. It instructed each of the other mission departments to include Nigerians in their committees. The NGC went even further by recommending to the Home Board that Ekas Benue and NKST each send two voting delegates to NGC, and that the minutes of NGC be sent to the churches. This was to begin in November 1960 and it was planned that by 1961 there would also be Africans representing the educational and medical departments at NGC. All of these decisions and proposals received the Board's approval. They were a sweeping manifestation at that time that the missionaries were minded to integrate with the African churches. This was so much so that a year later proposals were under consideration for the discontinuance of the evangelism department in the expectation that it would be merged with the churches.

Missionary Status in a Nigerian Church

The thought that CRC missionaries should become members of either NKST or Ekas Benue churches was not forgotten. NGC said, ". . . present church relationships make it highly advisable and desirable that missionaries be full members of the national churches with which they are associated. At the same time the missionaries are reluctant to surrender official membership in their home churches. NGC therefore requests the Board to approach the Synod of 1960 and ask it to explore the possibilities of dual membership which NGC considers to be the answer to our problem."[17] The CRC Board and Synod did consider the problem but could not see their way clear to agree to dual membership. Instead it offered a suggestion that missionaries be associate members and later this suggestion was made a formal request. Neither church had any sympathy for such an arrangement, feeling that this was a halfway proposition and by it the missionaries would not "demonstrate their faith in the national church." The Benue Church made further appeals to the CRC but as late as 1970 an undefined *associate membership* is all that has been officially suggested.

Some of the missionaries have felt that they could not become members of a Nigerian church even though the NGC urged them to do so. They were glad to attend the services of worship, to have their babies baptized, and to partake of the Lord's Supper but they did not wish to regulate their behavior in accordance with the rules of a church other than the one they belonged to in North America. On the other hand the majority felt that they should be members and

216

indeed did become members without stressing the *associate* aspect since this was repugnant to the churches. In 1965 the Board agreed that new workers should be urged to carry letters of introduction to the church in Nigeria from their home congregations. This unresolved issue of missionaries being full members of either NKST or Ekas Benue leaves an undercurrent of tension between Africans and Americans or Canadians, especially when a CRC worker seeks no official relationship whatever with the Nigerian churches.

Transfer of Mission Property to Churches

Affecting the relationship between mission and Nigerian churches was another significant decision taken by the NGC in April 1960 (3149). It declared, "We desire to assign mission properties connected with the work of the church or Christian communities to churches or Christian communities at the appropriate time." It also decided "that steps be taken immediately to assign all lands on which church buildings have been built which are held by the mission on behalf of EKAS or NKST to them." In the early days when there were but few converts the mission had sometimes built a simple place for worship adjacent to the mission station. These were now to be transferred to the legally constituted churches. The CRC agreed to this. It also concurred with the principle that property related to the work of Christian communities would be transferred to those communities at the appropriate time. Thus a far-reaching promise was made that property worth considerable sums of money would eventually be owned by NKST or Ekas Benue.

It must be remembered that each church had been responsible for its own church and school buildings built by themselves at their own expense. In the very few instances where this was not the case the mission did transfer to the churches the buildings concerned with worship and primary education, and by 1968 only one or two such places remained in mission hands. Some mission homes and medical facilities have also been handed to the churches or Christian communities. This acquirement of property is a mixed blessing. Rules governing the lease must be obeyed and expense is involved in upkeep. Moreover great care must be taken when the transfer arrangements are made in an effort to avoid friction at a later date. Again the expectation of some day falling heir to an inheritance creates its own appetites especially when there are two *children* and each expects to be blessed equally by a common *father* or *step-father*. This is true where Ekas Benue and NKST are concerned. Each church claims the CRC as its parent and since 1960, when NGC made its decision on property, relationships between churches and mission and between church and church have been affected over matters related to mundane inheritance. Even more so relationships have been affected by the physical presence of official delegates at the meetings of NGC. This had a profound and unhappy effect on the mission and the two churches.

Request for Two Missions

From its earliest days the Ekas Benue Church had been under the influence of CRC teaching. Unofficially for twenty years and then officially for twenty-one years, the Benue Church was the only church for which the CRC had been responsible. Then in 1961 the DRCM suddenly ceased to exist as a mission in Nigeria and the SUM (CRC) fell heir to the NKST Church to the same extent as the DRCM had been serving it up to that time. Even though the climax was sudden, yet the anticipation of such a change had been there, and for nearly a decade the CRC missionaries had been cultivating fellowship with the NKST. The DRCM handed over its mission's ministries to the CRC in November 1961, and in April 1962 the NKST requested NGC that the mission become two missions. The Rev. J. E. I. Sai, speaker for NKST, pointed out that until late in 1961 each church had had its own mission; the NKST had the DRCM and the Ekas Benue had the SUM(CRC). With the withdrawal of the DRCM the Tiv Church was to be united with the SUM(CRC) and consequently pressures were brought to bear that NKST and Ekas Benue should become one church because the mission was one. The NKST had no desire for church union with Ekas Benue and had declared that it was not possible to join the two churches.[18] By way of explanation Mr. Sai said that different languages and differing ecclesiastical practices brought this about. He said that his church was satisfied that both churches had the same creed, that they could interchange speakers at conventions and that they could unite through the medium of the Tekas Fellowship of Churches. He said it was better that there be two missions as there had been in the past and that the CRC should arrange this.

The Rev. H. J. Evenhouse was present at the meeting and in reply said that he did not feel that this would be possible. As it was the desire of the NKST that there be two missions, so some years later the Ekas Benue also requested that one mission serve NKST and another Ekas Benue. However, the mission insisted that there be one mission only to serve both churches.

One reason among others which brought about the request for two

218

missions was the mission's proposal that Nigerian nurses should in the future be trained at Takum Christian Hospital. The idea that this part of the training program be taken from Mkar to Takum did not please the Tiv Church. Partly because of this decision, respected missionaries holding medical and administrative authority became unpopular, and requests were made for their removal. This was a new and unhappy experience. That it should happen sooner or later was inevitable. It continues to happen and a formula for a just and reasonable settlement of such problems has yet to be found.

In the case of the nurses' training school it was not placed at Takum but was reorganized at Mkar. This change of mind of the mission pleased the NKST but it did not please Ekas Benue. At that time the Benue Church also had its own differences with the mission. In its minutes (904) it recorded that "it wanted all the matters creating tension between the church and the mission to be plainly spoken about to one another." Two were referred to in particular. The church felt it was wrong for the mission to place a missionary at a particular station with instructions to serve only one tribe instead of all the tribes in that place. It felt that doing this would cause division. Secondly, Ekas Benue said it was distressed because the mission had transferred its headquarters from Lupwe to Mkar. It is not the purpose of this history to discuss the pros and cons of such matters but to record that tensions were building up between the mission and the churches and these tensions were even greater as there was only one mission trying to handle two churches. However, the confrontation between Tiv and Benue church delegates which continued to take place at the meetings of NGC ceased in 1968 when Nigerians were no longer asked to attend.

Subsequent to the fruitless appeal of NKST for the mission to become two in 1962, the Tiv Church sent observers only to NGC and declined the privilege of voting. In this way it kept abreast of all that was discussed, offered its comments, but by not voting took no responsibility and did not commit its church in any way. Where it felt that an action should be taken other than that taken by NGC the Tiv Church did so. Whenever it felt necessary to bring its ideas to the attention of the CRC Home Board or Synod, it did so directly.

However, Ekas Benue Church continued to allow its delegates to vote at NGC. From time to time matters pertaining directly to the church or Benue community were voted down by the conference and this discouraged the church and built up a sense of frustration. These disappointments also affected the relationships between the Benue Church and mission and between that church and the NKST.

Added to this there was during the years 1962 to 1965 a spilling over of the internal civil and political strife among the Tiv into the areas immediately surrounding Tivland. This created unhappy incidents, which, nonecclesiastical though they were, did to some extent affect all. At the same time there was an ecclesiastical factor pertaining to the holding of church membership by Tiv Christians in Benue churches. Because Ekas Benue was a multi-tribal church it had no problem in accepting Tiv converts as members. NKST, however, did not completely approve of this, although they did not forbid it. The reason for their disapproval was that while NKST required the convert to wait for a period of years before becoming a communicant member, the Ekas Benue allowed converts to confess faith and become communicant members only weeks after their conversion.

Ekas Benue Requests Two Missions

In 1954 when church organization was imminent NGC advised Ekas Benue not to place the word *Eastern* before the word *Benue* in its name. It was thought that if it was omitted it would be possible to include the Tiv Christians also without changing its name, for all lived in Benue Province.[19] Many efforts were made to deepen the fellowship between the two bodies with the hope that they might all be one church. Even after the NKST's adverse decision of 1962 hopes were still held for union by Ekas Benue but by 1965 it was convinced that it could not be. That year Ekas Benue also asked the CRC to become two missions. It said:

> In 1940 the CRC accepted responsibility for the Lord's work in Benue Province, and they sent missionaries to help with the work. But about 1952 the CRC began a relationship with the Dutch [DRCM] and ten years later took over that mission. That made two missions. However in the mission of the Benue and of the Tiv each was operating its own separate church. It was not one [church].
>
> Even though the CRC first became responsible for the Benue yet later on it preferred to pay attention to the Tiv church instead of to us. It appeared as if they rejected the firstborn to give more attention to the adopted child. The Mission by way of its various committees insists on delegates of both Benue and Tiv being brought together, which arrangement continually causes unhappiness between all concerned.
>
> Ekas Benue's opinion is that it is impossible for one mission to care for two churches because the rules governing the two churches are different. For this reason the executive committee of Ekas Benue wishes the mission to

be two, one for the Benue church and one for the Tiv church and that none of their business should overlap.[20]

This request brought back into sharp focus the need for the mission to become two missions in order to serve two separate and unrelated churches. Much time, paper, and patience was consumed in discussing and recording all that pertained to the issue. The ball was batted back and forth between mission and church, between board and mission and, as is the case with all organized bodies, the interval between each play was often drawnout and fraying to the nerves. Up to the present time (1970) no solution has been agreed upon.

After two years, in April 1967, the NGC made this minute:

> NGC decided that even though repeated attempts have been made to work out some organizational plan with a nearly complete division of the mission, it has been unable in good conscience to do so and therefore informs Ekas Benue and NKST, and the Home Board that the mission is one in purpose, function, responsibility, and above all, one in Christ and can no longer entertain the concept of split or division in terms of organization. On the other hand, NGC assures the churches of full recognition as individual churches and will make every effort to work with them as such.[21]

The next NGC minute was immediately related to the above and offered to the two churches that separate committees be set up for each of them, each committee would be composed of four missionaries and four Nigerian churchmen. No one person would serve on both committees. Each committee would deal with all business affecting the church and would be in direct correspondence with the CRC Board of Foreign Missions. However, before discussions of this offer were completed, NGC withdrew it in July 1968 and at that time requested the Mission Board to allow an eight-man, all-missionary body to replace the NGC and to run the mission. In due time the board consented to this arrangement but added a ninth missionary to the list.

The NGC's meeting of April 1967 was followed by one held by the Ekas Benue Regional Church Council (RCC) the next month. It said:

> The Regional Church Council of EKAS/LB was grieved when it saw what the NGC decided in its principles of organization minute 5892, that it will no longer entertain the concept of split or division of the mission in terms of

organization. Ekas Regional Church Council knows that the mission is one in purpose, function, responsibility, and above all, one in Christ. But if this oneness has always brought misunderstanding between the mission and the local church because the mission has failed to deal fairly with two different indigenous churches among whom she is working; and if this fact has always led to a lack of confidence and brings about problems, this oneness does not bring a blessing to the work of the Lord. RCC does not agree that the new plan passed by NGC will bring better understanding between EKAS/LB and the mission so far as it is still one missionary body operating between the two different indigenous church groups of NKST and EKAS/LB. For this reason RCC decided that EKAS/LB will not take part in the new organization plan. Grounds:

1. It is a difficult thing for one mission body to claim that it can serve two different indigenous church bodies faithfully.
2. EKAS/LB does not know of any other mission field where one missionary body serves two different groups of churches. In the case of the Navahos and Zuni in the U.S. one of the two has not yet established a church of its own.
3. The mission always compares these two different indigenous church bodies and always shows that one is better than the other (NKST better than EKAS/LB.)
4. The SUM(CRC) does not care about EKAS/LB as they should. Their attention is on NKST. This can be seen in what the mission has already done in the short period since it took over the work in the Tiv area.
5. From the time SUM(CRC) joined its field of work in the EKAS/LB area with that of the Tiv, EKAS/LB cannot in good conscience say that there has been a good relationship between her and the mission, or the NKST church. Fellowship, and the exchange of delegates at church meetings of the two indigenous churches ceased to exist.
6. Even the Tiv church does not support the idea of one mission body only working with two different indigenous church groups.
7. Now the EKAS/LB is aware that the root of the misunderstanding between her and the Tiv is always in most cases brought about by the SUM (CRC).[22]

The above was written in May 1967 quite soon after NGC had recorded both minute 5892 and also 5893. It was after further thought and because of the offer in 5893 of a church-mission committee including Nigerians that Ekas Benue continued discussions into 1968. But in July 1968 the NGC withdrew its offer and at the same time excluded Nigerians from NGC which they had formerly attended. When the secretary of NGC clearly explained this to Ekas Benue in November 1968 the church felt offended and, since it was excluded from NGC, decided not to send delegates to any mission committees. However, mission delegates were still allowed to attend church committees.

The Board of Foreign Missions upheld NGC in its decisions saying, in February 1969, "It was decided to entrust field administration for two years, in view of the present tense Nigerian civil situation, to a streamlined Nigeria General Conference composed of the . . ." naming nine positions which were to be filled by missionaries and omitting Nigerians. It also decided "to respond to the Ekas and NKST request for reorganization of two separate missions in Nigeria as follows: 'We feel strongly for the oneness of the body of Christ, the Church; therefore we are not free to divide our mission into two separate conferences. It is our prayer that the Lord may lead us all to a blessed unity, endeavoring to keep the unity of the Spirit in the bond of peace' (Eph. 4:3)."[23] To this, sixteen months later, in June 1970, the CRC Synod noted its "concern that the two church bodies consent for the present to the interim method of administration, looking toward 1971 by which time there shall have been further opportunity for mutual consultation between the mission staff, the EKAS(Benue) and NKST, and possible decision."[24]

These last few pages indicate that for some years a considerable difference of opinion persisted on a major issue between the CRC and its Nigerian mission on the one hand and the Ekas Benue and NKST churches on the other.

It is to be noted that in October 1971 the difficulties were resolved. The SUM(CRC) and the two churches agreed to and started a new form of organization. Representatives of the mission in the EKAS Benue area meet with representatives of the church and make decisions which are reported to the CRC Board of Foreign Missions. The same is done by representatives of the mission in the NKST area and representatives of that church. Business of the mission not related to either church is managed by a separate mission committee.

Notes

1. SUM constitution, Article 2.
2. Smith, *Missionary Monthly*, p.p. 143 f. May 1954.
3. CRC Board executive committee minute 7078, September 1953.
4. E. H. Smith, *TEKAS*, pp. 37-40.
5. Ekas Benue Church Constitution.
6. Ekas Benue minute 250, July 1954 (translated).
7. H. Bello, *Tarihin Ekas Lardin Benue,* pp. 11, 13.
8. Ekas Benue minute 610, May 1958.
9. NGC minute 1848, November 1956.
10. CRC Acts of Synod, p. 85, D, 2, i, June 1953.
11. CRC Acts of Synod, p. 85, D, 2, j, June 1953.
12. Quoted in CRC Acts of Synod, pp. 28, 29, June 1955.
13. CRC Acts of Synod, Article 62, VIII, B, 3, p. 28, June 1955.
14. Ibid., pp. 64, 65, June 1956.
15. Smith-CRC correspondence, January 23, 1960.
16. NGC minute 3135, April 1960.
17. Ibid., 3151, April 1960.
18. NKST minute 538, 1962.
19. NGC minute 1159, April 1954.
20. Ekas Benue minute 1238, May 1965 (translated).
21. NGC minute 5892, April 1967.
22. Ekas Benue minute 1397, May 1967.
23. Board minute 7991, February 1969.
24. CRC Acts of Synod p. 73, B, 2, b, June 1970.

17

Institutional Activities at Mkar

The DRCM Mkar Hospital

Let us now return to the center of the Tiv work at Mkar and Gboko. The Rev. and Mrs. A. J. Brink opened the mission station at Mkar in 1923. As has been said, their first temporary dwelling was a pigsty which they converted into an all-purpose living and sleeping room until something better was built. The location of the mission station is at the foot of Mkar mountain, a large outcrop of granite rock rising some six hundred feet out of the rolling plain surrounding it on all sides. It was very difficult terrain for building purposes. Its water supply was limited and the tropical heat near the hill was much greater than as little as a mile away.

Mkar became the center of the work of the DRCM. One of its institutions requiring no mission-made buildings was the Saturday market. It was wise of the DRCM to open this market as this encouraged weekly trading on the day before Sunday and did away with the distraction of a market operating on Sunday. Through the mission's influence here and in other of its centers market day every Saturday became a feature throughout Tivland and wherever there were Christians. Institutions requiring buildings set up on mission-leased property at Mkar and Gboko included a hospital, a leprosarium, an orphanage, a college for training teachers, a primary school with boarding facilities, and, a few miles away, a secondary school.

Every mission station in the pioneer days had some simple facility used for treating sick people. This was also true of Mkar. Only two years after the work started there Dr. Paul Labuschagne arrived—in May 1925. Eric Casaleggio tells us that Dr. Labuschagne began work "in a grass roof hut with earthen floor and little light." He adds, "However, this room was too dark and had to be abandoned. The veranda of the medical hut was not suitable either, seeing that the operations had to be done in public, the patient being exposed to wind, dust and even to inquisitive passers-by."[1] Up to this point and for many years beyond it, less qualified medical workers had to use simple facilities. In one important point it was not a mistake that "inquisitive passers-by" could observe the technique of an operation. There was no hocus-pocus and the onlookers could see this by watching the proceedings from beginning to end. This was valuable at the time when animistic medicine men so often depended on deceit and darkness.

However, an operation on an open veranda is not ideal and it can easily be understood that during Dr. Laubuschagne's first year in Nigeria an application was made to the government for permission to build a hospital. This was obtained and a small hospital was built. It was adjacent to the mission station and school and, like them, was on the lower slopes of the Mkar mountain. The doctor's home was above the surrounding countryside, and it with the nearby operating theater were at the edge of a sharp decline to the floor of the valley. Whenever expansion was to take place the problem of difficult terrain had to be faced. This could have been avoided by building a quarter of a mile away.

Other doctors from South Africa joined the staff at Mkar and during the thirties the hospital complex was expanded; early in that decade a special ministry for lepers was begun. In 1942 Dr. Marie Du Toit joined the staff and gave sixteen very valuable years to the medical work. To the onlooker her complete dedication to the task was emphasized by her petite physical stature which housed a never dimming flame of devotion. Among other developments she started a program for training nurses and midwives, thus she and her colleagues multiplied their usefulness throughout Tivland. She also set up a separate ward for maternity cases only which the Governor of Northern Nigeria was pleased to open. On that occasion the governor, in behalf of the Queen of England, made Dr. Du Toit a Member of the British Empire (MBE) and soon afterwards the Africa Society of Britain gave her its coveted bronze medal for outstanding service to the people of Africa.

Dr. Herman Gray of the CRC joined the Western Tiv medical work in 1953, but he did not at that time become involved in the Mkar ministry. He served as a specialist in leprosy and later went to Kunav. At Mkar, only Aleda Vander Vaart served for some years, otherwise the institution was in the hands of the DRCM with Dr. Du Toit at its head. This changed unexpectedly when Dr. Du Toit said in February 1958 that she must leave the work and return to South Africa in July of that year. Up to that point the tentative efforts that the collaboration committee of the two missions had made toward transferring the hospital to the CRC had not borne fruit. Now there was a quick transition and Dr. Gray took charge until Dr. John Vroon was able to take over the work later in 1958.

The SUM(CRC) and Mkar Hospital

In November 1958 NGC indicated that an agreement had been reached whereby all buildings and other assets and liabilities of the DRCM medical department were transferred to the SUM(CRC) and responsibility became theirs. This referred to the hospital at the center and the medical work in all other Tiv locations, but the leprosy ministry and the orphanage were not included. The Tiv Church had always exercised a proprietary interest in the medical ministry. At this time this was illustrated by the president of NKST, Pastor Nevkar, when he said that "he did not feel happy at the speed with which the hospital had been transferred without their [the church] knowing."[2] This sense of possession or ownership has always been entertained by the Tiv Church and continues at the present time. Legally and medically this is not so, nevertheless the firm belief on the part of the Tiv Christians that it is so has been a major and significant influence in the development of the medical work. All major proposals of the NGC and its medical department for capital expansion have been overruled upon the insistence of the church in the way in which it felt that development should proceed.

In November 1958 NGC "decided that after 1959 nurses training will be consolidated at Mkar." It then proposed, "in view of the fact that the hospital is not adequately housed or equipped at present to carry out the [training] program," some remodeling should be done and an addition of six new wards with ninety-two beds was to be built during the following three years. NGC concluded by saying, "This program is not an expansion but is planned to provide decent accommodations for patients now being treated under very adverse and unsatisfactory conditions."[3]

However, six months later NGC gave the medical department "permission to explore [the possibility] ... for the establishment of a combined hospital at Gboko to replace the present facilities at

This aerial view of Mkar mission station shows the hospital maternity block in the foreground. The large building just left of center is the church. The schools and hospital are largely merged with the trees.

Mkar."[4] A "combined hospital" was one which would be a joint effort by the government of the country and the mission. (The Mkar Hospital would need expensive alterations and additions and the hilly situation made such improvements very difficult to carry out.) This exploration was carried out and the November meeting of NGC approved of further negotiations with the government for a new hospital at Gboko and said, "If these negotiations are not fruitful after one or two years, NGC recommends that the mission erect a new hospital similar to the Takum Hospital."[5] This request to provide a new hospital in Gboko was made to the CRC Board of Foreign Missions in 1960 and was approved by the Synod of 1961. This was not approved by the NKST and it was around this matter and the proposed transfer of nurses' training to Takum Hospital that strong feeling developed and the Tiv Church requested the division of the mission. The objections concerning building a hospital in Gboko led the mission to rescind its decision and instead asked for $80,000 to improve Mkar Hospital. The same year, 1962, this figure was raised to $122,000.

It appears that nothing spectacular happened regarding this proposition to improve the facilities at Mkar and in November 1965 it also was rescinded. In its place we read, "NGC recommends the construction of a new hospital complex on a 28 acre plot . . . near Gboko at the cost of £119,930 [approximately $336,000]."[6] The Tiv church reacted to this decision and a translation of their minute reads: "Synod [of NKST] at one time said that the mission and NKST should join together to look for another place in the Mkar area if the place where the hospital has been built is insufficient. But afterward Synod heard that the mission chose a different place at Gboko, on their own. They failed to go with NKST. Therefore, as Synod sees that the mission has excluded the church on the matter of the hospital, the church no longer has any part in it. If the mission builds the hospital in the new place which they alone chose and for which they alone have worked, then NKST no longer has a part in it, because Synod does not agree. But Synod agrees that a hospital be built at Mkar or in the Mkar area as it has said before, but not more than two miles distant."[7] In fact Tiv church leaders *were often* consulted about the proposal so the minute must mean that the Synod had not been approached officially.

From mission correspondence we learn that this reaction of the Tiv church was considered but then NGC's executive committee reaffirmed the decision of the Hospital Planning Committee and of NGC to build a new hospital at Gboko. It also felt strongly about the matter and had no sympathy with the Tiv overture requesting that it be built at Mkar.[8]

However, when our Board met in Grand Rapids two months later it deferred action on a new hospital and said, "We do not want to enter into a plan for a new hospital building without a full spirit of harmony on the matter with the Tiv church." It then added, "It was decided to authorize NGC to make further investigation of building a hospital within the framework of the Tiv decision to build near Mkar (within two miles of the location of the present hospital). . . ."[9] The mission in Nigeria had said with some emphasis that it proposed a new hospital at Gboko, but the Tiv Church opposed such a move because it had not been officially consulted. The CRC Foreign Mission Board agreed with the Tiv Church on its choice of a location.

Following this the mission's "Medical Study Committee met with the site committee of NKST . . . to 'study a place for Mkar Christian Hospital.' The NKST Committee agreed to the Mission's renovating the Mkar Christian Hospital at its present Mkar site. Subsequently the Executive Committee of NKST has expressed its approval in its minutes, 2 June 1966."[10] The NGC recommended the improvement of Mkar Hospital, giving a figure of $198,000. The proposal for a new hospital at Gboko was not referred to again. In the next few years the new Mkar Hospital was to rise, gradually replacing the remnants of the old.

The funds for the new hospital building were completely furnished by the CRC. Nothing was given by the government, the Tiv Church, or the community. The lengthy and heated discussions so briefly outlined above inevitably had their effect on prominent individuals involved in them, and at times they and the work of the mission and church suffered. A history is not a history if it does not admit that such things happen.

Gleanings from a Recent Report

Fortunately, day by day, year by year, mercy and healing were being dispensed on a large scale while committees worried their way through technical difficulties. At the end of 1970 Dr. Paul Groen, the doctor in charge at the hospital, said, "Most of the buildings we need in the hospital proper were completed in the first six months of 1970. We still need a laundry and chapel. . . . But the wards and outpatient department and regular service units have been completed. . . . This hospital is fast becoming known as the Tiv Hospital . . . [which] is an effect we don't like, but nevertheless is a very real part of Nigerian life today."

He reports that during 1970 there were three doctors and a Nigerian superintendent, Mr. A. Bur, for the nurses. He was to become head superintendent in January 1971. There were six missionary superintendents of nurses, twenty-seven registered Nigerian nurses, and thirteen qualified Nigerian midwives. Administration offices were in the hands of missionaries with fair prospects of the Nigerians taking over. Groen also spoke of "good prospects of having Nigerian doctors, Tiv men, working here within the next three or four years."

As a daily average in 1970 the hospital served 400 outpatients, and there were from two to four major and four minor surgical operations each day. The hospital has 205 beds for acute cases. There are also facilities for 100 patients with chronic illnesses who receive somewhat limited care. There is a special clinic for children under five years of age. Twice a week an ante-natal clinic for expectant mothers is held which serves between 200 and 350 mothers each time. If we try to assess this work load we shall see what an enormous job such an institution does for a needy community.

The aspects of sympathy and religious comfort are not neglected. Two Nigerians, an evangelist and a Bible woman, head up this work and many of the staff talk regularly with the patients. The gospel is "preached" two or three times daily in the outpatient department and the messages are carried through the hospital on a public address system. Dr. Groen adds, ". . . if we look at it honestly I would say that the preponderance of staff, and especially of the qualified staff, takes a second generation view of evangelism. They do talk about it but there is not a great emphasis on this. They feel that evangelism is probably the chore of the evangelist, and not so much their own. There are some very wonderful contradictions to this generalization."

In the 1970 report we also read, "Mkar Hospital has always been deeply committed to rural health work, and this is, of course, largely born out of Herman's [Gray's] interest, and is currently in a very significant phase of getting rural health work established on a local basis. . . . we have seventeen dispensaries under Mkar Hospital, and fifteen of these are owned and operated by the local communities. . . . We anticipate that in days ahead the dispensary program will grow significantly, and probably ultimately end up to be a program managing something like fifty dispensaries. . . . Incidentally, dispensaries run at a great profit, and this is an unforeseen problem . . . in getting people to work together, since nobody wants to relinquish control over funds that they consider their own."

In 1970, for the first time, Mkar Hospital had a meeting of the board of governors. This is a significant change. The board governs the administration even though it cannot commit the mission to financial outlay. It gives the local community, the church, and the

Outpatients wait their turns in the hospital waiting room. It is not unusual for the medical staff to treat five hundred patients a day.

Nurse Neva De Vries demonstrates the use of a new piece of medical equipment to an assistant and a nurse trainee.

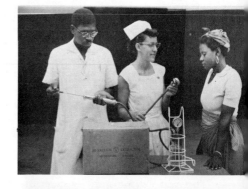

A thyroid goiter patient awaits surgery. This growth was successfully removed.

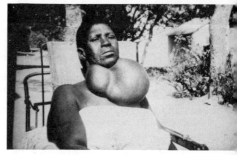

The maternity ward at Mkar Christian Hospital is almost always crowded.

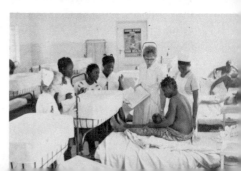

state government a say in what is going on in the hospital. The inclusion of Nigerians in the board is a step towards Nigerianization.

With the completion of the new Mkar Hospital Dr. Groen believes that it has reached a plateau of usefulness. This plateau could reasonably be stated as the performance each year of over two thousand operations and ushering into the world some three thousand babies, while 120,000 persons would receive help for their illnesses and, most important, nearly all would hear the gospel of Jesus Christ.

Funds for the buildings and the permanent equipment of the hospital came from North America but the patients and the government pay much towards the treatment of the sick. The salaries and expenses of doctors, nurses, and other CRC workers are all paid by the CRC Home Board. The payment of fees by the patients is not required in government institutions of healing and this is a point of disagreement between missions and government. Of course by way of taxation the people do pay the costs of the national hospitals but only a little of this helps missions in their activities. In some parts of Nigeria hospitals originally owned and operated by Christian missions are being taken over by state governments, but there are as yet no signs of this in the Benue-Plateau State. Were that day to come, at all events medical workers both past and present can rejoice in the Lord at the great blessing the Takum and Mkar hospitals have already been to countless thousands of people.

During 1970 there were thirty-six students in the training program at Mkar Hospital studying to be midwives; ten more were learning to become laboratory assistants and nine others were finishing a two-year course as nursing auxiliaries. In addition to this training at Mkar seventeen Tiv students were studying at accredited mission hospitals elsewhere in order to become certificated nurses recognized by the federation and another eleven were being trained in Jos to become medical workers in village clinics. In other words eighty-three persons were being trained for one or another aspect of medical work related to Mkar Hospital. Remembering Dr. Groen's hopes that there will be Tiv doctors in the not-distant future we can see that the trend toward Nigerianization is very strong in this institute also.[11]

In addition to the village dispensaries there are twenty-five first-aid stations and a large maternity center at Kunav. Francis Vander Zwaag supervises the Kunav work and from a report to the hospital board we learn that at that center eight hundred babies were born in 1970 and some twenty-five thousand patients were treated.

The Mkar Hospital board of governors conjectured that the medical income gathered within Nigeria for the year 1970 would be about $230,000. This included some $39,000 from the government and

233

$185,000 from the patients. Disregarding missionaries' salaries and capital expenditure it was believed that recurrent expenditure would be $237,000 and that the CRC would be asked to add the difference of $7,000 to its gifts for the year. When Nigerians and their country contribute to the running of the Tiv medical work, and when the CRC gives so much also, it is good that there is a board of governors which may know and disseminate this information to the people. Such a statement of accounts makes it plain that medical work is not a moneymaking proposition but is run at a loss—a loss which would be very much greater if the salaries and expenses of our doctors and other workers were not donated by the CRC.

Notes

1. E. Casaleggio, *The Land Shall Yield Its Fruit*, p. 83.
2. Correspondence, Smith to Gerryts, September 18, 1958.
3. NGC minute 2608, November 1958.
4. NGC minute 2808, April 1959.
5. NGC minute 3001, November 1959.
6. NGC minute 5346, November 1965.
7. NKST minute 858, see NGC minute 5407, December 1965.
8. CRC correspondence, December 1965.
9. Board minute 5299, A, 2 and B, February 1966.
10. NGC minutes, Appendix B, November 1966.
11. Quotations and other material for 1970, correspondence Groen to Smith, December 29, 1970.

18

Education at Mkar and Gboko

Primary Education and Religion

In the very early days when Britain took over Nigeria and before missions had made any impact on the interior, Lord Lugard recorded in his Political Memoranda "that a time shall be set aside daily for religious instruction, whether in Christian or Moslem schools, in order that the compelling power of religious sanctions may be enlisted in the formation of habits of discipline and self control. . . . Government merely recognizes, somewhat tardily, that religion is a force in the formation of character and of good citizens which cannot be ignored without disastrous results, and it avails itself of that force as a means to an end."[1] This was quoted in a White Paper of 1953 which indicated that the teaching of religious knowledge was required in schools and training centers. It said, "The private and public behaviour of the coming generation are influenced to a very great degree by good ethical and religious instruction and practice in the schools and institutions." It also added, "A greater effort should be made to give the best possible religious or ethical instruction to teachers in training, and they should also receive instruction in how to teach religion. . . ."[2] Thus as early as 1953 missions had a statement of policy from the Nigerian government which more than allowed for religious instruction—it insisted upon it. This was an open door and it remains wide open in 1970. One of the proposals made in the White Paper was that, "Prayers should be said daily in every school and training institution. In higher education institutions building plans should include suitable places of worship and grants should be paid to help defray the cost of construction."[3]

At Mkar, and contiguous to and a little to the west of the hospital, is the primary school. Like the medical work, education began in a very humble way. The schoolroom was simple with an earthen floor and mats for the adult "pupils" to sit on. Mats gave way to tree trunks and then to desks with benches. Slates and slate pencils were replaced with paper and pencils. Bible stories and teaching was the basic item on the mental menu. In addition for many years there was just reading, writing, and counting. Later a formal education up to primary (grade) two was added, followed by primary four, then five to seven were added to make the school a full primary institution. In earlier years a boarding department was included. This was located in a hidden valley leading up the mountain and was provided because of the scattered way of life of the Tiv people. After some forty years this school has become the responsibility of the government's local education authority.

The Training of Teachers

The official government pronouncement encouraging missions to redouble their efforts came in 1953 and it was at this time that the CRC had agreed to the transfer of DRCM work in Western Tivland. At about this time the DRCM was in the early stages of opening a college for the training of teachers. As in Ekas Benue, so it was with the DRCM that a less formal teacher training had been in progress. Now something better was visualized. The idea was to train Christians of primary seven standard to become primary school teachers. The DRCM had obtained a lease for a plot of land on higher ground and separated from the original Mkar mission station. Here a teachers' college was built. The CRC involvement at this stage was for it to second Don Van Reken to be a teacher there.

Also in 1953 the CRC Synod made its significant decision on education on the mission field. It said, "that education on the mission field be limited as much as possible to a literacy program in keeping with the performance of the evangelistic task—viz. the direct oral and written transmission of the Gospel, and the encouragement of native covenantal schools."[4] This decision was puzzling to the missionaries. For several years they had been training teachers of a lower grade and for two years had been under agreement with the DRCM concerning the Eastern Tiv field to assume their proportionate part of the trainee obligation of the DRCM to produce teachers, pastors, evangelists, and nurses. NGC asked the CRC Foreign Mission Board for guidance.

In June 1954 the Board replied by quoting Synod's statement (see above) and went on to decide that primary education was a basic need in order to lead up to the training of pastors and evangelists. It then decided "that advanced higher education be considered as the responsibility of the native church and the local citizenry of the Nigerian field."[5] No comment was made about the training of teachers unless that was included in the expression "advanced higher education." If this were so then at the same time it should be noted that the CRC Board had nevertheless consented to allow one of its workers to serve in training teachers. The Synod had agreed to the encouragement of covenantal schools and perhaps the Board realized that this encouragement would involve the preparation of Nigerians to become qualified to teach in such schools.

We will return to minute 7636 quoted above. For the moment let us pursue the growth of teacher training. In the late fifties a fresh class comprising twenty-four students was admitted each year to the center or, as it was later called, the college. The course of training was for three years, successful students being granted a certificate. This permitted them to teach in approved primary schools up to grade four and to draw a fixed salary which was paid by the Nigerian government. The students were boarders and it took some years to iron out the problems of such an institution. In 1955 there was a major misunderstanding between the mission and the students. The students went on strike and some three-fourths of them had to be sent home. Later on there were similar strikes over wages of nurses and builders' laborers. So student and employee problems brought their repercussions also in Nigeria.

The SUM(CRC) became proprietor of the Teachers' Training College in January of 1959. At the time the principal, Peter Bulthuis, said to the DRCM *Raad*, "What a blessing it is that this transfer may be made without changes in the aims or principles of the Institution. Our staff is extremely thankful that in the past few years we have been able to work together in the same institution without any misunderstandings arising between the members of the two missions. For this we thank our Covenant God." In behalf of the staff and the students he went on "to thank the Dutch Reformed Church who by God's grace, have been able to establish and maintain this essential institution."[6]

The students were helped and the teachers were paid by the Nigerian government, which also paid much toward the cost of the buildings of the college. For this reason the institution had to be controlled by a board of governors and on it the local and Northern Region governments had representatives. The mission paid its teachers according to its scales of pay, at the same time the government paid the mission for those same teachers at its rates of pay. The amount paid by the government was not given to the missionary teachers, nor was it sent to the Board in America. Instead, and this was agreeable to both the CRC Board of Foreign Missions and the government, the money was placed in a special account in Nigeria and used for other purposes. This was known for years as "Account 88" and as the number of teachers increased this account grew larger. It was a convenient nest egg upon which the mission on the field could call from time to time to pay for needy projects. After several years the Synod inquired into the history of "Account 88" and it was closed. CRC teachers' salaries paid by the Nigerian government are now drafted into the general funds of the CRC Board for use in Nigeria.

Although the college was placed at Mkar, nevertheless the government required that it accept students from other areas who were not of the Tiv tribe. The percentage of students who were not Tiv varied through the years. In 1959 it was as low as 11 percent, in 1961 it rose to 41 percent and in 1970 it was 20 percent of the total enrollment. In the mission's view the college met the needs of Ekas Benue as well as of NKST. In earlier years it was difficult to get enough students to meet the intake requirements for a class of twenty students, but with the great increase in the numbers attending primary schools problems arose because there were too many applicants. We learn that 359 applicants sat for the examination and 60 were accepted. These 60, who began studying in 1963, were sufficient in number to form two classes, or a double stream, as it is called in Nigeria.

About this time there was another change made when two more years of training were added and thus the school became a higher elementary teachers' college. A successful graduate of a five-year course obtained a Grade II teacher's certificate and he or she was permitted to teach up to primary class seven. In the late sixties the student body had increased to 300 as compared with 60 in the midfifties and 60 Grade II teachers were graduating every year. Many American and Canadian teachers served the college, among them Peter Bulthuis, Steve Lambers, Ralph Dik, Norman Brouwer, and Al Bierling all served as principal or acting principal. In 1969 the principalship of the college was given to John Gberkon, a member of the Tiv tribe. Several of the teachers under him were Nigerians. When Mr. Gberkon was taking over he said to the student body, "I know what you are all thinking. You are thinking, 'For the first time we have a black man for Principal, now we won't have so many silly rules and we will be able to do what we want.' I am here to tell you that *you will not!* I am going to continue the same policies and practices that Mr. Bulthuis has had. The only difference is going to be that since I am also a black man, I know all of the tricks and you will get by with less!" Mr. Bulthuis says, "He took care of in one small speech the thing which was my only worry in turning things over to him."[7] So Nigerianization continues—as Mr. Bur became matron of Mkar Christian Hospital, so Mr. Gberkon became principal of the teachers' college.

In 1970 the college had 6 blocks of classrooms, a library, a chapel, and 6 blocks for dormitories with separate dining facilities. In addition there were 12 homes for members of the staff and an administration block. Of the 17 teachers, 11 are Nigerian and of the 307 students 247 are Tiv. About half of each graduating class pass their final examination. The remainder would be able to get teaching positions in the primary schools.

From the beginning the government took most of the financial responsibility for the teachers' college and nowadays the only cash the CRC supplies is in the form of loans. The constitution provides that "the religious observance and instruction in the institution shall . . . be Christian as defined in the doctrinal statements . . ." of the NKST and Ekas Benue churches. In 1962 only 4 of the 102 students were not communicant members of the church and now it is very probable that all are church members. Mr. Bierling writes, "Academics [of the college] are primarily concerned with producing good Christian primary school teachers. So Bible and religious activities receive a great emphasis."[8] Many students conduct Sunday schools in surrounding villages and preach in the village churches while others conduct Bible classes in the Gboko prison. Total Nigerianization is not yet high on the horizon but were an emergency to arise it is probable that the transition would be as smooth and commendable as that which took place from the DRCM to the SUM(CRC) a dozen years ago.

Covenantal Schools

We now return to Board minute 7636. This refers to the Synod's decision to encourage the mission to set up covenantal schools. Christian schools and Christian school associations are highly favored by CRC people and are an important part of the CRC system. In most other churches this is not true, for the CRC emphasis upon the covenant with reference to its children is not so common elsewhere. The DRCM had no like emphasis and it ran simple schools in Nigeria as a means of evangelization. This proved to be a point of difference between the two missions for the several years that they worked together. The education department supported by the NGC aimed at setting up a Christian (covenantal) school system. The DRCM continued to believe that children and young adults would be led to faith in Christ through hearing the Word of God when at school. The classroom, especially that of the simplest school of all, the CRI, has led to the conversion of hundreds of young people.

Fortunately, despite its convictions, NGC never did restrict attendance at primary schools to covenant children but allowed others to attend also. None of the schools of either Ekas Benue or NKST became covenantal schools. However in 1954 the Ekas Benue Church formed a church-school committee to be responsible for its schools. At the time NGC said, "While parochial schools are not our ideal, this more indigenous control seems to us a step in advance over mission administration."[9] The CRC Mission Board at home agreed to this saying, ". . . it [a parochial system] probably is the necessary step towards delivering our missionaries and our mission organization from the burden of local education." It added, "We ought to move carefully in disrupting this important relationship between the mission and the educational development, even though we feel dissatisfied with the educational set-up now in operation on the Nigerian field."[10]

Throughout the sixty years of its reign in Nigeria the British government preferred to have the proprietorship of the schools in the hands of the mission. But in 1960 Nigeria became an independent nation and at that time NGC proposed transferring the proprietorship of primary schools to "a responsible Christian body which the mission feels should be a Christian parental society." However, the DRCM, whose Home Board had suffered from transferring schools in another of its mission fields to a nonchurch body, pleaded with the CRC not to take this course but hand the schools over to the churches. A year later, at the end of 1961, NGC agreed to transfer the proprietorship of all primary schools to one or the other of the two churches concerned. Official machinery of the government worked slowly but in February 1965 the Board reported, "In the area of education our mission has transferred the proprietorship of all sixty-eight primary schools to the EKAS and NKST churches. As a result our mission is no longer involved in this phase of the work except for two men on loan to the schools for a limited period of time. Tiv nationals are also beginning to teach in the secondary schools having received their A.B. degrees qualifying them for their positions."[11]

This clearly indicates that the cultivation of indigeneity in the field of education from the beginning had paid off very well indeed. The sixty-eight schools, all of them teaching the first four grades and a few of them teaching seven grades, required approximately three hundred teachers and in 1965 all of these were Nigerians with the exception of two. Ekas Benue had had a church-school committee for many years and now both it and NKST were taking the responsibility of being proprietors of their primary schools.

They were parochial schools but were heavily subsidized by the government as they had been when in the hands of the mission. Government paid almost 100 percent of the teachers' salaries and a major part of the building costs. Two or three years after the churches became proprietors the primary schools were taken over by the Nigerian government entirely and they were no longer governed by the churches. Local education authorities were established to run these schools and to be responsible to the government's central education agency. With this change the schools run much as they had done before, but under the new set-up there is no control in the constitution of the religious nature of the schools. The only hope of Christian continuity lies with the Christians of the community being sure that they are well represented on the education board of the local authority. However, all schools are open to the teaching of religious knowledge. The mission set aside workers to encourage churches, pastors, and Christian laymen to voluntarily serve as teachers of the Christian faith where the school's own teachers are unable or unwilling to do this.

Secondary School at Gboko

Another important institution owned and run by the SUM(CRC) in Nigeria is the secondary (high) school. This has been referred to earlier in connection with another secondary school which is under the proprietorship of the Ekas Benue Church. We will now consider the school built at Gboko. Although in 1954 the Board of Missions had decided "that advanced higher education be considered as the responsibility of the native church and the local citizenry of the Nigerian field,"[12] yet two years later it was considering education beyond the primary school level. By way of NGC it asked "the African church whether it can give us any assurance that within the next five years it will staff all the senior primary schools with African teachers only." It then added, "Contingent upon this the Board will favorably consider providing suitably qualified teachers for a secondary school to serve covenant youth of the churches. This will be provided that the government pays the teachers . . . and that it, with the African Church, pays the full capital costs of the school. The Board will meet any differences of salaries of missionary teachers, the costs of travel and their homes where these are not met by government grants."[13]

Two years later, in March 1958, the mission's education department recommended "that we move in the direction of establishing a secondary school if the Government is willing to give 100% capital grant." With this recommendation the mission's manager of schools said, "If we express our willingness to provide personnel we must do so with the expectation of providing their support and transport to the field and possibly housing. Government's generosity is an uncertain entity. It may provide amply for salaries, housing and other allowances. Again they may agree to helping with school buildings only. They may agree to nothing at all. Establishing a secondary school will involve us in another institution which has little hope of becoming 'indigenous' except in the very distant future. The Teacher Training Center, Uavande Girls' School and Secondary will commit us to placing staff in these institutions for many years to come. Once committed there will be no turning back short of turning the schools over to Government which might have serious repercussions in the church and community with which we work."[14]

NGC considered this statement and recommended the establishment of the secondary school. It felt that the Nigerian government would give financial assistance but pointed out "that this is not guaranteed and the Board must consider the possibility that they underwrite the project through expatriate funds, that is that Conference is asking the Board if necessary to continue paying the salaries of all teachers on the African field for a period of eight years during which time the expatriate grants will be accumulating for the capital expenditure of the school."[15]

The Board agreed to the establishment of the school saying, "It was decided to approve the building of the first complex and the effectuation of the proposed plan with the definite understanding that the Board is not responsible for capital expenditures, but that these would be taken from the Expatriate Grant Fund."[16] In the foregoing paragraph the NGC had asked the Board, if necessary, to pay the salaries of all its missionary teachers in Nigeria including those serving the secondary school. Therefore whatever the government paid for missionary teachers' salaries would go to the well-known "Account 88" and from it the secondary school could be built.

In actual fact and in due time the government paid considerable sums toward the buildings of the Gboko Secondary School. Where these were insufficient Account 88 was used. The dynamic and genial Harold Bergsma guided the school through its formative stages and early years and he prepared the first draft of the school's constitution. Since the mission wished it to serve the Benue as well as the Tiv Christians the article on religion defines *Christian* as being the doctrinal statements of NKST and Ekas Benue churches with which the school's religious practice, instruction, and observance had to conform. In 1970 there were thirteen members on the school's board of governors. Six of these were appointed by the mission (one of them being a Nigerian), three others represented the two churches and four more represented the government and community.

The school occupies a commodious site a little to the east of the town of Gboko and is about five miles from the Mkar mission station. It is named the "W. M. Bristow Secondary School." William Muckle Bristow began his work in Nigeria in 1919 when he built the first missionary home at Lupwe which was occupied by Miss Veenstra and many others who succeeded her. We are told:

> Mr. William Muckle Bristow began his work in education in Northern Nigeria in 1919, retiring from the field in 1961 after many long years of sacrificial and devoted service to the betterment of education in the Northern Region.
>
> Mr. Bristow served as Warden of the educational institutions at Gindiri from 1934-1955. He held posts as Education Secretary, supervising on behalf of the Government, the educational work of eight mission groups; he was a member of the Northern Region Scholarship Board; he was secretary of the Northern Educational Advisory Council; he was a member of the Central Board of Education, as well as the Education Superintendent of the Sudan United Mission, British Branch.
>
> Not only did he serve faithfully in these capacities, but he was recognized for his services. In 1957 he received the Bronze Medal, Royal African Society, and was honored as an Officer of the British Empire, bestowed by Her Majesty in 1957.
>
> Probably no missionary has done as much to further the cause of Christian education in Northern Nigeria, and for these reasons the Voluntary Agency, the Sudan United Mission, Christian Reformed Church Branch, in proprietorship has sought to honor Mr. William Muckle Bristow, by giving his name to this school.[17]

243

Each year seventy-five new students pass through this entrance to the W. M. Bristow Secondary School at Gboko. Those who take a two-year postgraduate course are eligible for admission to one of Nigeria's five universities.

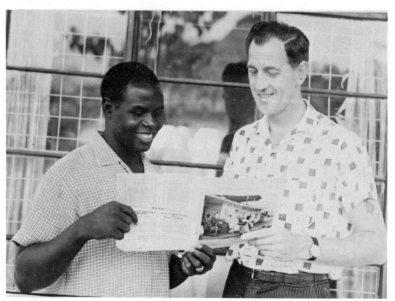

D. P. Ashu, manager of EKAS Benue primary schools and Peter Bulthuis, education secretary for SUM(CRC), 1962.

CRC's Harvey Poel had much to do with the erection of the first buildings of the school. He made every dollar count. All funds, especially Nigerian public funds, were handled very carefully. However, disgruntled subcontractors who did not land a job created trouble by spreading completely false accusations so that disquiet and distress reigned for a time as the misery of labor disputes and their aftermaths were endured.

The school began in temporary quarters at Lupwe in early 1960. By 1962 it had been transferred to its permanent location. The course was for five years and in the beginning the annual intake was 25 graduates from primary schools. In 1963, before the first students had completed their course, the mission decided to double the annual intake and to accept 50 applicants. In 1971 this was again increased and a triple stream was arranged for. In her 1970 report the principal noted that in that year the school had an enrollment of 329. She added, "Approximately 1,500 boys and girls sat for the entrance examination in March 1970. Out of this number 215 were called for interview. . . . A total number of 19 girls and 96 boys were accepted."[18] About 8 percent of the applicants were accepted, so that 92 percent of those who felt they would like to go to secondary school were unable to do so even though this was a triple stream intake.

Girls have been mentioned. The mission decided to make the institution coeducational in 1963.[19] The Tiv Church preferred that the girls' school at Uavande be upgraded to the status of a secondary school. It was by no means happy that girls and boys of high-school age should study and live together at one institution even though the boarding facilities were separated. In 1971 the desire that Uavande become a girls' secondary school was granted to the church by the government. Even so it was expected late in 1970 that the W. M. Bristow School would take in nineteen new girls the following year.

Geraldine Vanden Berg, who had served as principal at the Uavande girls' primary school, was chosen to succeed Mr. Bergsma as principal at the Gboko school. This happened when girls were first accepted there. It not only worked out well for the girls but Miss Vanden Berg proved to be a most able principal and up to the present time continues to maintain excellent rapport with the students and teachers and also with the mission and church. In African society there is much emphasis upon the supremacy of the male so that Miss Vanden Berg's success is no mean attainment. As she started her ninth year she had to get 108 first formers started and was more convinced than ever of the value of the school for the sake of the church and for society. She said "At the present time we have six ex-Bristow students serving on the teaching staff at Bristow. To help prepare these teen-agers to take their place in the new Nigeria is ever so challenging. Nigeria will need all the Christian-trained young people she can get. The educated young people will take over the rule of the nation and therefore I feel there is no better place for me to serve than in our post-primary institutions." She added "Our staff must remain Christian. Sometimes we are criticized for passing up 'good' teachers, but if they do not have a Christian testimony, they are not good for our school."[20]

Students attending the secondary school must pay fees. These are modest in comparison with other places but even so many students are unable to meet the demand. Numerous missionaries make themselves responsible for one or more students, giving them in whole or in part their secondary education. Some graduates try to take two years post-secondary work in order to qualify for entrance to one or another of Nigeria's universities.

As early as 1952 NGC decided to aid students seeking higher education. This has been continued down through the years. Help for theological students of the English language level has always been forthcoming and aid has been granted to those taking other studies. In general NGC favors students taking their university work in Nigeria rather than abroad in some foreign country. The purpose for granting scholarships was "to help students beyond the HETC Teacher Certificate or the Secondary School level to prepare in their homeland in fields which will enable them to be of greater service to their people and to become leaders in Christian service."[21]

Notes

1. Quotations, including Lord Lugard's statement, from White Paper on Religious and Moral Instruction in Training Centres and Schools of Northern Region, 1953.
2. Ibid.
3. Ibid.
4. CRC Acts of Synod, p. 86, 4, 1953.
5. Board minute 7636, p. 7, 2, June 1954.
6. Teacher's College Report to DRCM "Raad," March, 1959.
7. Correspondence, Bulthuis to Smith, February 1971.
8. Correspondence, Bierling to Smith, December 1970.
9. NGC minute 1004, November 1954.
10. Board minute 7636, June 1954.
11. Board minute 3692, February 1965.
12. Board minute 7636, June 1954.
13. Board minute 8578, February 1956.
14. Education committee minute 101 and appendix A, March 1958.

15. NGC minute 2654, November 1958.
16. Board minute 240, February 1959.
17. "Introducing W. M. Bristow Secondary School," December 1962.
18. Principal's report W. M. B. Secondary School, p. 2, November 1970.
19. NGC minute 4232, 1962.
20. Correspondence, G. Vanden Berg–Smith, January 28, 1971.
21. NGC minutes, appendix A, I, April 1961.

19

The Theological College of Northern Nigeria

Movement to Start a Seminary

Theological training and the Theological College of Northern Nigeria (TCNN) have been very much discussed both officially and unofficially in CRC circles for many years. Because of this every effort will be made to stay close to official pronouncements as they were made from time to time in Africa and America. It will not be possible to quote all that has been said on this subject in the Acts of Synod, Board reports and minutes, and in the minutes of NGC and its committees. That would produce a book in itself.

In 1954 the Foreign Mission Board developed the ideas set forth by the Synod of 1953 concerning evangelism[1] and decided "that we encourage our African staff in its plan to give regular and formal training to prospective evangelists and pastors. We believe this to be a crucial element in our mission program if there is to be a promising future for our mission service."[2] When this was said training men to be evangelists had been going on for a long time and still continues. At that time also the Ekas Benue Church had one ordained Nigerian, the Rev. Istifanus Audu and four Tiv men were about to start training to become pastors in a course set up by the DRCM.

A few months earlier the secretary of the five Nigerian branches of the SUM had written to the Rev. H. R. Boer in Amsterdam asking him whether he would consider helping Northern Nigeria toward better theological education than could be obtained by studies restricted to vernacular languages. Mr. Boer was studying for his doctorate at the time and had served two years as a missionary of the SUM (CRC) in Nigeria. His reply was encouraging and so the NGC approached the Board saying, "We wholeheartedly recommend that the Board appoint the Rev. H. Boer to the Nigerian field. We also recommend that he be placed at Gindiri for work in theological training. Conference is increasingly aware of the great need of the African Church for better trained workers and we feel that this will be a big contribution which our branch can make to this cause on a regional scale."[3] From the outset the vision of NGC was that this theological contribution was to be for all of Northern Nigeria and was to meet the need of all the branches of the SUM.

Immediately the Executive Committee of the Board decided "to recommend to the Board that the Rev. Harry R. Boer be called as a missionary to Nigeria."[4] Following this the Board decided "to ask the Synod of 1955 to authorize the expansion in placing a teacher at Gindiri for native pastor training and to inform Synod that the Board is minded to appoint Dr. Harry R. Boer to this position."[5]

Dr. Boer was installed as a missionary of the CRC in September 1955. Having become a missionary of SUM (CRC) the NGC told him " . . . [to] visit the existing theological schools in the south, (3) visit the missions and churches in the north with a view to determining attitudes toward and extent of likely participation in the proposed theological school, (4) draw up a report crystallizing his findings and proposing concrete steps for bringing the school into being. . . ."[6]

The assignment was a very wide one and involved visits to several theological schools in the south and about a dozen missions and as many churches in the north. Boer carried out this commission and made his report. This report had to be considered carefully by many bodies and this took time. Part of NGC's comment was that, "Conference heartily endorses the principle of cooperation with other evangelical mission bodies of Northern Nigeria in a united theological training school, and encourages Dr. Boer to continue work on this project."[7]

The nationwide consultation made by Boer at the request of NGC ultimately led to the limited proposal that the churches and missions of the Tekas Fellowship together with the DRCM and the NKST should establish jointly a theological college. When this was done it embraced the separate churches belonging to the Tekas Fellowship, the Fellowship itself, the NKST Church, the five branches of SUM, and the church of the Brethren Mission as foundation members. The DRCM was wholly in accord with the proposed college and made two large donations toward it when it was founded. It did not, however, become a member body because it was in process of withdrawing from Nigeria and it would soon cease to exist as a mission.

The NGC requested that our mission be represented on the college's board of governors, that it have a minister on the teaching staff and that it contribute to the cost of the college buildings.[8] The following February the CRC Mission Board decided to encourage Boer "to carry forward the plans to teach in the United Theological Seminary as originally proposed two years ago."[9]

CRC Participation

The proposal made by the Board was endorsed by the Synod of 1957 when it declared, "There is no 'compromise of our ecclesiastical principles' in the plans for theological education which were approved by the Synod of 1955 and further elaborated in the proposals submitted by the NGC to the Board." In the absence of further Board or Synodical enlightenment NGC itself assessed the comments which those bodies had made with regard to teaching at the proposed seminary and its ecclesiastical appropriateness. Even so the Conference asked the Board to declare its full participation in the program, a request that was practically unanimous. It also asked that the Board adopt the tentative constitution of the college and at the same time nominated Boer to be a teacher and the Rev. E. H. Smith to be CRC's member of the college's board of governors.[10]

The next annual meeting of the Board recommended "that Synod participate in the program for United Theological Education in Northern Nigeria." At the same time it approved the constitution, it agreed that the college be built at Bukuru, and decided that it would give not less than $12,600 toward the building program.[11]

Between this time (February 1958) and the meeting of Synod in June there was much discussion throughout the CRC and *The Banner* was used to voice the opinions of many. When the question of the CRC's participation in the TCNN came to the plenary sessions of Synod the members had no less than four reports to consider. Two were favorable to participation and were majority reports, the others were minority reports and were unfavorable. In brief, after a very long debate, it was decided that Dr. Boer should continue to teach at the college, that a nine-member committee should work on a seven-point mandate for a year and, thirdly, permission was granted for special gifts to be solicited as a help to the Benue Church which wished to be part of the college.[12]

During the twelve months that were to elapse before Synod would again consider this question of participation in the TCNN the college itself began operations. This took place in temporary quarters at Gindiri on February 9, 1959, with twenty-two students and three teachers. Some of the students were from NKST but Ekas Benue had no one ready to send at the time. The principal was Dr. Boer. The board of governors had fifteen voting members, nine of them representing churches and the Tekas Fellowship, six of them representing missions. The principal was a nonvoting member. One of the missions was the SUM (CRC) and it appointed Mr. Smith to represent it. He was elected chairman of the board.

In June 1959 the committee of nine appointed in 1958 presented Synod with a majority and a minority report. Five of the committee members were in favor of participation in the TCNN and felt there was no need "at the present time" for a distinctively Reformed seminary as an alternative to TCNN. On the other hand four members did not favor participation in the united college but desired that the CRC mission maintain and develop its Reformed pastors training program. However, it was agreeable to Boer teaching at TCNN.

After considerable debate these reports were set aside and the Synod's own committee, set up after Synod had convened, presented its findings. In the end the Synod decided as follows:

1. The Christian Reformed Church *participate in TCNN only to the extent of loaning* Dr. H. Boer as teacher of Reformed Theology in the TCNN.

2. The Christian Reformed Church make funds available to pay the full cost of Dr. Boer's teaching for salary, housing, and traveling, according to the normal procedure of the Christian Reformed Board of Missions.

3. That Synod declare that a Missionary-Teacher loaned to teach at TCNN is not thereby violating his ordination vows.

> *Grounds:* a. The Christian Reformed Church does not assume responsibility for the teachings of others in such a school.
>
> b. The constitution of the TCNN guarantees the teacher freedom to present his doctrinal convictions and to refute all error.

4. In view of its decisions on the Theological College of Northern Nigeria Synod declares the following:

> In response to the invitation to be a member of the TCNN Synod expresses its appreciation, but regrets that in view of its total commitment to the Reformed faith it cannot see its way clear to be co-responsible for the college which may present many different doctrines. However, it would like to be helpful, especially because the Tiv and Benue churches are interested in the college.

It is glad to offer the services of a minister on its teaching staff and to support him and provide him with a home.

5. Synod instruct the Christian Reformed Board of Missions and the Nigerian General Conference to maintain and develop the Reformed Pastors' Training program in Nigeria with a view to hopefully establishing a Reformed Theological Seminary.[13]

Point number 5 above, especially the last line, which was an amendment introduced on the floor of Synod, created lengthy discussion and a sharp division of opinion, passing by the slimmest of margins. The decisions showed that Synod had taken a position contrary to that held by the Board of Missions and by the NGC, namely that the CRC should be part of the TCNN. In addition, Synod instructed Board and Mission to develop its work with a view to hopefully establishing a Reformed Theological Seminary.

The reaction of NGC to all of this is reflected in its statement to the Board. After assuring the Board that it was developing its leadership and pastors' training programs, Conference went on to say, "At the same time Conference reluctantly expresses disappointment at the action of Synod with respect to the extent of its participation in TCNN. We have from the beginning believed that in the Nigerian situation, the TCNN offered us the best opportunity to give leadership in theological education. We still believe so. We also believe that the encouragements we have repeatedly received from the Board and from previous Synods do not permit us to limit our participation to teaching only. We feel that until it becomes evident that the training received by prospective pastors proves to be inadequate, we are morally bound to support it also with the modest financial support that is asked of us."[14]

The following April NGC said to the Board that pastors' training in the vernacular, a Bible school, and a preseminary course "should in no way be construed as steps towards an eventual establishment of a separate seminary in competition with the TCNN." It then added "that it [NGC] takes note of the action of the Tiv Church Synod of April 1960 which, when confronted with a choice between the TCNN and a separate school, decided in the interests of her solidarity with her sister churches of the Tarayya, to continue her participation in the TCNN, and so has asked the CRC to pay her [viz. the CRC's] proportionate share of the financial support of the TCNN." NGC went on further to say, "We adhere to the position regarding the desirability of a united theological seminary which we have held from the beginning. In view of these considerations and considering that the Tiv and East Benue churches have consistently supported the TCNN and that strained relationships would be formed between our mission and these churches, and between these churches and their sister churches in the Tarayya; NGC cannot in good conscience support the founding of a separate seminary in competition with the TCNN and therefore requests counsel from the Home Board." [15] Thus, ten months after the Synod had made its decision, the missionaries on the field felt quite unable to turn away from TCNN and unable to implement the decision to work towards a Reformed Seminary. With reluctance NGC turned to the Board telling it of its dilemma and seeking its advice.

The matter was handled by the executive committee of the Board and it "decided to inform Synod of the concern of our missionaries as shown in this minute. We would impress on Synod that this is, in our opinion, a sincere and honest response of our missionaries arising from their convictions that they cannot comply with that decision of the Synod of 1959 as it pertains to the establishing of a separate seminary apart from and in competition with TCNN. The question now is what action the missionaries, feeling themselves unable to comply with the decision of 1959, should take. Our missionaries are burdened by the strained relation this decision will cause on the field and how it will impair the unity of the work." [16]

By this communication the Synod of 1960 was clearly aware of the impasse that had been reached between it and NGC and that the missionaries were not carrying out the mandate of 1959. It also knew that that mandate was contrary to the wishes of the Board of Missions. However, it did not see its way clear to offer immediate counsel but referred the matter to a full meeting of the Board "for consideration and action as soon as possible." That same Synod decided not to establish a special gift fund for TCNN, but it did agree to aid the Benue Church in meeting her share of the capital expenses of TCNN as had been promised by the Synod of 1958. It also agreed to give financial aid to Tiv and Benue students for their fees, "until a Reformed Theological Seminary has been established." Synod did this, it said, because "such support is given to the students personally and is not to be construed as implying our participation in the schools involved," and, secondly, "the TCNN is the only school at present where the native students on our Nigerian field can obtain higher theological education." [17] So, in addition to giving a teacher and supplying his home, the CRC was paying the Benue Church's share of the college's capital expenditure and was giving financial aid to students who studied there. However, this visible participation was not actual participation. The SUM (CRC) had become a member

254

body of the college and appointed a member to its board of governors and NGC did not revoke this after the meeting of the Synod of 1959. This membership was retained and the SUM (CRC) representative became the chairman of the board of governors at its inception and retained that position for many years.

An extraordinary meeting of the full Board of Foreign Missions was held in September 1960 and replied to NGC's request for counsel. It said to NGC, "The specific goal of Synod, that a Reformed seminary be established, shall be kept in view and held before the churches in Nigeria as the desired objective; but the autonomy.of the national churches shall be respectfully recognized in this matter. The TCNN shall be recognized by our Board and NGC as serving the best interests of the churches of Northern Nigeria, at the present time, for advanced theological training. We continue our participation in TCNN as defined by Synod, so long as the door remains open for Reformed teaching."[18]

At this point let us recall that the CRC had called Dr. Boer to go to Nigeria at the request of NGC and the branches of the SUM to propose means whereby the theological needs of all of Northern Nigeria might be met. After a careful survey and numerous consultations with all sorts of churches and missions he made his proposals. They centered on the Tekas Fellowship and the missions related thereto but also included the Tiv Church and the DRCM. The missions, of which SUM(CRC) was one, and the Fellowship heartily endorsed the idea. Because Boer was a CRC minister and because Smith, who had been Field Secretary of the branches of SUM in Nigeria was another, everyone in Nigeria assumed not only that the CRC was behind it but that it was an active proponent of the plan. This was emphasized when the mission and missionaries of NGC were so heartily in favor of it. The churches and missions concerned believed TCNN to be a means of cementing the fellowship which they enjoyed. These historical facts must be understood and considered by those who plead for a Reformed seminary in Nigeria.

The statement of the Board to NGC, which was the fruit of its special meeting convened in September 1960, received a very brief reply. NGC said, "NGC expresses thanks to the Home Board for its statement of confidence regarding our theological programs. We assure the Board that we shall continue our training along the lines stated in NGC 3304 and 3305, and in the response given in Board Minute 1057, with full respect for the autonomy of the local churches."[19] The Synod of June 1961 considered the Board's work of September 1960 and accepted it but made two changes. It said, "The TCNN shall be recognized by our Board and NGC as serving the

The Theological College of Northern Nigeria (TCNN) is owned by the Tekas Fellowship of Churches. Shown here is the chapel of the college.

NKST and EKAS Benue students of TCNN and their principal, Dr. H. R. Boer (right), meet with Rev. H. J. Evenhouse, Board Secretary, in 1962.

present interest of the churches of Northern Nigeria for advanced theological training *in the absence of a Reformed Theological Seminary.*"[20] The words in italics, so marked by the author, indicate the changes and the addition which Synod made. Synod also reiterated to the Board and NGC its decision of 1959 and reminded the missionaries of its concern with respect to the dangers of a union seminary. After a further period of eight months the Board conveyed these decisions to NGC.[21] NGC does not appear to have replied to this.

When the time came to finalize the constitution of the TCNN Dr. Boer requested the CRC Board to "take note of the constitution as revised, and express its satisfaction with it as the instrument under which he, as one of its missionaries, is called to work." In response the Board declared "that it is assured that Dr. Boer can work as an instructor in TCNN under this Constitution and in accord with the decision of Synod and the Board of Foreign Missions."[22]

Upon reflection we can see that NGC had explained clearly in 1960 that it could not implement the decisions of the Synod of 1959 where the promotion of a Reformed seminary was concerned. Counsel had been sought and the replies granted did not alter that situation at all. Through 1964 the position remained the same and was not altered later on.

Expansion at TCNN

By 1965 it became apparent that more buildings would be required at the TCNN in order to meet the need of enlarged student enrollments. Each of the churches served by the united seminary was asked to contribute $1680 per annum for three years. The Tiv and Benue churches in their need turned to NGC for help and it proposed to help them to the extent of 50 percent of the total amount. The following month, December 1965, a committee from the Board visited Nigeria and in its report it referred to this matter and concluded by saying:

> There are two reasons why we consider it right that this appeal be given favorable response:
> 1. The consideration that we have a separate and specifically Reformed seminary in Nigeria is not feasible. The will to retain the fellowship of churches on the part of two denominations comes to expression in the TCNN, and the establishment of a separate seminary would be a sword into the very heart of this cherished fellowship.

257

2. The proposal that we establish a seminary of our own would place us into the most difficult position of intertribal arbitration which could only result in establishing two seminaries, one in each of the respective church areas now being served by our mission. As it is there is with neither of the two church bodies any discussion of establishing an English language theological seminary, and anything less than that would be far below the needs of the modern situation; also, neither of the two churches want to consider a seminary training that would isolate them from neighboring Christians on lines established by foreign mission agencies. This they would consider foreign intrusion and an unworthy imposition. For us to press for a separate seminary would be to precipitate a tragic inter-church and tribal confusion.

It seems to us that we should recognize the TCNN as the school of TEKAS and be thankful to be able to have a significant opportunity for training leadership; and, that we should express willingness to help our Nigerian Church as to provide additional facilities as they have requested it.[23]

This report made by men who had been to the scene of action was not accepted by the Board which sent them and aid was not forthcoming to the Tiv and Benue churches for expansion at the TCNN. Instead it urged "our mission to develop the existing Reformed Pastors' Training Program." The effect of this advice on NGC was to make another full statement on theological training in the Nigerian field "in the interest of truth." It said:

Conference does not believe that the C.R.C. Mission should establish a seminary in Benue Province. We have said before and now reiterate that the seminary owned and operated by the eight Churches of the T.E.K.A.S. fellowship is in every way adequate to meet the needs of the Churches which we serve.

Specifically we adduce the following reasons for our position:

1. Both E.K.A.S. Benue and N.K.S.T. are joint owners of T.C.N.N. along with six other Churches. We do not feel that we have the right to ask them to relinquish this interest and ownership in the absence of any expressed desire on their part for a separate school.

2. The offer to establish a seminary in Benue Province while no conscious need of it exists among the Churches

and while they are co-owners of a seminary cannot but be viewed as a form of temptation to them to obtain still another institution.

3. The acceptance by them of such a seminary would threaten serious damage to the T.E.K.A.S. fellowship and it does not seem right to us to expose the T.E.K.A.S. to such damage.

4. The Christian Church and community in Northern Nigeria are keenly conscious of the need of a united front over against the overwhelming Muslim and pagan environment in the midst of which they live and witness.

5. The benefits derived from four years of fellowship at the College on the part of future leaders of the Church, existing as it does in a sectionally and tribally divided country, can hardly be overestimated.

6. The offer of a separate seminary which was not occasioned by an expressed desire on the part of the Churches, seems to us to constitute an infringement on their autonomy since they already are co-owners of a seminary.

7. The E.K.A.S. Benue and N.K.S.T. students at T.C.N.N. are given instruction in Reformed Doctrine and Church Polity while they are at the College.

8. We consider significant in the highest degree the fact that both those who are most identified with the work on the field and also the Home Board Committee which visited us in December, 1965, collectively feel that T.C.N.N. should continue to receive our wholehearted support.

It is for these reasons that we are compelled to say that we cannot in good conscience promote the establishment of a separate seminary in Benue Province. It is difficult for us to say this as we all have a sense of real loyalty to our home Church and dislike anything that affects the harmony of our relationship with her.

We, therefore, respectfully but urgently appeal to the Home Board to reconsider the request for financial aid made in behalf of the E.K.A.S. Benue and N.K.S.T. Churches. If it finds that it cannot do so, N.G.C. requests the Board to bring this minute to the attention of Synod at its meeting in June of this year.[24]

This is quoted in full in order to show that six years subsequent to the synodical decision of 1959, the SUM(CRC) mission conference continued to hold solidly to the conviction that the TCNN was the right way to go. The reasons were cogently and concisely stated and there could be no doubt in the mind of the CRC at home as to the position which the missionaries held. It was a conviction so deeply felt that NGC said, "It is difficult for us to say this as we all have a sense of real loyalty to our home Church and dislike anything that affects the harmony of our relationship with her." The Conference asked the Board if it found itself unable to grant the request for financial aid made by the two churches to bring the matter to the attention of Synod. For that reason the Synod of 1966 did consider it and instructed the Board to review the Church's policy regarding seminary training in Nigeria and to report to the Synod of 1967.

During the year 1966 one of the missionaries conducted an inquiry as to the future needs of ordained men in the NKST. The conclusion was that the Tiv Church would need an estimated seventy more pastors by 1973. Benue Church also said that it planned to expand. The TCNN was asked whether it was prepared to accept the large increase and was requested to "make plans for the expansion of its facilities so that additional qualified men from Ekas Benue and NKST areas can be admitted."[25] The following month, December 1966, NGC informed the Board of "the Tiv Church's request for a separate school."[26] The Conference gave no details but since the request introduced "a new dimension into the TCNN discussion" it asked the Board to allow time to consider this and to hear what reply TCNN would give concerning increased student intake. The Synod of 1967 as well as the Board was agreeable to this request and so the statement of policy on seminary training in Nigeria was delayed until 1968.

Although NGC had mentioned the Tiv Church's request for a separate seminary NKST had not approached NGC on this issue. It wrote directly to the CRC Board of Foreign Missions. The letter was held in abeyance pending a full meeting of the Board which took place in Feburary 1968. Although NGC did not know the contents of the NKST letter nevertheless it felt that it should again state its position. It recognized that the CRC had had reservations regarding full participation in TCNN for some years, yet it urged the Board and Synod to declare "their willingness to support the TCNN as our primary institution of theological instruction in Nigeria." It did this because TCNN was intertribal, and at a time when Nigeria was in the throes of civil war mainly caused by tribalism, it felt that this could "make a great contribution to brotherly love." A tribal institution would not do this. It was expected that the expansion of TCNN would provide "sufficient room for all qualified students from NKST" and it still felt that the Reformed emphasis was well safeguarded.[27] For twelve years and with repeated and considerable risk of being unpopular with the church at home the missionaries consistently held a position which they felt to be the only one which could bring glory to God.

The Board at its annual meeting in February 1968 considered the NGC material, the letter of the Tiv Church, and many other documents. After hearing and tabling a number of motions it decided to "inform NKST of our decision to ask the Synod of the CRC to approve the expansion of TCNN as a step in meeting the existing need for the training of pastors." It also asked "NKST to reconsider her request for a Reformed Seminary in the Benue in the light of the fact that we have not yet been informed of any consultation with other bodies who are affected by their request." The Board "further decided to request [the CRC] Synod to declare that we actively participate in TCNN and declare it worthy of our full support. . . ."[28] Thus yet again the Board gave its encouragement to the missionaries in Nigeria.

When the Synod considered the request of NKST that it have its own Reformed seminary it had before it two reports, seven overtures, two appeals, and a letter. The letter was from the NKST Synod addressed directly to the CRC Synod and not to, or through, the Board of Foreign Missions. This was correspondence from one sister church to another not feeling the need of an intermediary. It asked the CRC to give it the money with which to build a Reformed seminary. It referred to TCNN and said that it did not think the college could train all the Tiv students nor did it feel that it could give a positive Reformed training. However, it said, "Know this, we do not outright reject the TCNN. In fact, we will support it, but it is not adequate for our needs and desires for the Reformed faith. This does not mean we want to break our fellowship with the other churches in TEKAS. In fact, we know it will not, for each church is an independent body."[29]

The CRC Synod took sympathetic and careful notice of the NKST's request and charged the Board of Missions "to re-evaluate this request in the light of the conditions on the Nigerian field, the plan of reorganization of the missions, and the great need for pastors, and then to serve a future synod with advice."[30]

At the same time the CRC Synod also considered the request of the Board and NGC to help the TCNN. Synod decided to "accede to the request of the Board of Foreign Missions to participate in the TCNN according to the provisions of the TCNN constitution."[31] Six reasons were given and adopted for this decision. Briefly stated they were, 1) Boer's service to TCNN was seen to be in harmony with "cooperation membership" as described in the college's constitution.

2) The constitution protects the integrity of its constituent bodies, provides for mutual responsibility between them, and allows for orderly withdrawal upon notification. 3) The constitution allowed freedom to teach the Reformed faith without restriction. 4) "The present need for African pastors necessitates the commitment of our resources to enable the Board of Governors of the TCNN to plan for expansion and administration." 5) "The NKST and Ekas Benue churches hold 'permanent' membership in the TCNN and continue to look to the TCNN to supply pastors for their churches." 6) The urgent appeal of NGC "to promote the unity of the churches and of the nation through the TCNN should be heeded."[31] These reasons reveal a great deal but the decision itself was to aid TCNN in its seven-year building expansion program with a proportionate share of the expenses that would be involved.

The reader will have noted the changed attitude of the NKST shown at the end of 1966 when it wrote to the Board of Foreign Missions in America asking for a Reformed seminary. It was at this time that one or two missionaries, though very much in the minority, disagreed with the stand of NGC. Their attempts to change the mind of the Conference did not prevail and so they approached the NKST church. One of them, the Rev. C. Persenaire, explained this in an article in *The Banner*. Speaking of the estimated need of seventy new pastors by 1973 he said, "I then outlined a way whereby it could train enough pastors to meet the challenge of the future. I gave them a three-point plan: 1. They must begin a vernacular Tiv pastors class in February 1969; 2. Continue to send students to TCNN; 3. Prepare to open an English Seminary in the Benue for continuous theological education for its students in the future.

"The delegates listened and heartily endorsed the plan, and told the Executive Committee of the Synod to bring this plan into effect in the future. And so the request came from the Tiv church Executive Committee to the Foreign Mission Board." He added, "When the Board turned down the request, I advised the Executive Committee of Synod to communicate directly to the Synod of the CRC of 1968."[32] The author of the article was a member of NGC and, like every other missionary subject to it, but he was also a member of NKST and an officer of its Synod and executive committee. In this latter capacity he introduced to the Tiv Church the proposal for it to have an English language seminary in the Benue area and proposed to it that it communicate directly with the Foreign Mission Board, and later, the CRC Synod.

Charges Against TCNN

Some charges were brought against the teaching at TCNN by one of the SUM(CRC) missionaries, the Rev. T. Monsma. In 1969 the NGC executive committee took cognizance of these and set up a committee comprised of practically all of the theologically trained men on the CRC staff. The committee was told "to study, for the purpose of evaluation, the charges made by Rev. T. Monsma concerning the teachings of TCNN 'that higher critical theories regarding the authorship, inspiration, unity and reliability of Scripture are being taught.'"[33] This committee spent many hours and days and its individual members many more hours and days studying the teaching notes of TCNN. It is worthy of note that the college allowed them to have all these notes for such a critical evaluation. After seven months of work the committee of theologians sent its unanimous report to NGC and the Conference's executive committee said, "NGC notes that none of the charges brought by Rev. T. Monsma have been substantiated. Inasmuch as the charges brought by Rev. T. Monsma concerning non-evangelical teaching at TCNN have caused suspicion and embarrassment amongst the member bodies of TCNN, the NKST, EKAS Benue, the TCNN staff, and the CRC, we apologize. We are sorry for having caused unnecessary suspicion and heartache to those concerned. We have been strengthened in the conviction that God will continue to use TCNN to train pastors for His glory."[34] This needs no further comment.

In 1970 it was anticipated that the Benue and Tiv churches would have thirty suitable men ready to enter TCNN in 1971. However, it was felt that at that time the college would only be able to absorb twelve or fourteen of them. Therefore NGC proposed as an interim measure that one four-year course for the remaining students be set up in Benue Province. The CRC Synod agreed to this proposal and " . . . humbly request[ed] the NKST Synod to accept this decision as Synod's answer to their request for assistance to establish a Reformed Seminary." The request for assistance had been made in person by the President of NKST, the Rev. J. K. Manyam, who came to America from Nigeria to ask in person for £N25,000 ($70,000) as a gift to NKST so that it could build its own seminary.

This exhaustive rundown on the official actions related to theological training in the English language has been given because it has continually been a matter creating much comment throughout the years. The CRC missionaries, with very few exceptions, who actually live within the context of the Nigerian situation always have favored the TCNN. In general and with due caution the Board favored the stand taken by NGC. Within Synod and the CRC at large, opinions were divided and often came to emphatic expression.

In conclusion we have this statement made by the principal of the TCNN:

> The establishing of TCNN has had, I believe, a most beneficent effect on all the Churches that share in its life. It has given them a large and significant program to execute together. It is providing for them a constantly increasing segment in their ministry which has been trained together over a period of four years. Those students who are married bring their wives to the College with them to be trained and thus enriched for their own service and witness in their home communities.
>
> At TCNN, over the four year training period, tribe meets tribe and Church meets Church. There is exposure to the life and teaching of the Churches of the West through the missionary teachers. All this cannot fail to point to and hold as an ideal both the unity of the Church of Christ and her variety in liturgical, theological, tribal, and national background, within the framework of a common evangelical faith.
>
> In this experience both the Benue and the Tiv Churches have shared richly. Each has received into its ministry a number of TCNN graduates, most of them married, and all of them now serving their Church in various capacities. It has been particularly significant for them in view of their relative isolation in the southern part of the northern States. It is my belief that in the twelve years of TCNN's ministry patterns have been established which have had and will in the future have their effect on the development of the Churches we serve. Especially may it be expected that their membership in TEKAS will continue to take on added dimension because of the role which TCNN plays in the life of TEKAS.[35]

Notes

1. CRC Acts of Synod, p. 85 (especially D, 2, m.), June 1953.
2. Board minute 7636, 4, June 1954.
3. NGC minute 1287, November 1954.
4. Executive Committee of the Board minute 7887, November 1954.
5. Board minute 8049, February 1955.
6. NGC minute 1570, November 1955.
7. NGC minute 1723, April 1956.
8. NGC minute 1865, November 1956.
9. Board minute 9110 (1), February 1957.
10. NGC minutes 2200-2203, November 1957.
11. Board minutes 9637-9640, February 1958.

12. Acts of Synod, Article 113, C, June 1958.
13. Acts of Synod, Article 110 and 115, June 1959.
14. NGC minute 3035, November 1959.
15. NGC minute 3161, April 1960.
16. Executive Committee of the Board minute 984, June 1960.
17. Acts of Synod, Article 141, C, D, E, June 1960.
18. Board minute 1057, 3, 4, 5, September 1960.
19. NGC minute 3342, November 1960.
20. Acts of Synod, pp. 48 f. June 1961.
21. Board minute 2046, February 1962.
22. Board minute 2674, February 1963.
23. Report of February in Acts of Synod, p. 300, June 1966.
24. NGC minute 5521, April 1966.
25. NGC minute 5740, 6, November 1966.
26. NGC minute 5834, December 1966.
27. NGC minute 6089, November 1967.
28. Quotations from Board minute 7138, February 1968.
29. Reported in Acts of Synod, pp. 96 f. June 1968.
30. Acts of Synod p. 97, C, 2, June 1968.
31. Acts of Synod p. 98, 4, and a-f, June 1968.
32. *The Banner*, p. 10, March 1969.
33. NGC minute 6435, March 28, 1969.
34. NGC minute 6670, b, December 1969.
35. H. R. Boer, report to Smith, April 1971.

A healthy child—the coming of the gospel of Christ and its attendant ministries has brought a tremendous blessing to Nigeria's children.

20

Some Other Activities at Mkar

The Orphanage

Not infrequently Tiv mothers died at childbirth. When this happened the life of the newly born infant was in grave jeopardy. Modern means of saving such lives are not easily available in a Nigerian bush situation even today. The possibility of another nursing mother sharing her milk was very unlikely. Seeing so many infants die caused the DRCM to save a few of them by setting up a baby clinic at Sevav and bottle feeding the children. Eventually, in 1953, this led to the opening of an orphanage at Mkar. This was soon after the CRC had agreed to take over the work of the DRCM in Western Tiv. In 1958 the SUM(CRC) told the DRCM that it did not contemplate becoming involved in this institution, saying, "It is not a cold indifference to the serious plight of the babes but a feeling that it must give preference to such work as seems most profitable for the glory of God under its limited resources."[1]

Not long afterwards the DRCM built a better building to house the motherless babes on the higher slopes of Mkar beyond the teachers' college. However the SUM(CRC) felt that it must retain its position of nonparticipation and urged the Tiv Christians themselves to rise to this challenge. However, the South African Home Board regretted this and indicated, "It does not want an established work and department to vanish for it feels that in doing so it might create unpleasant opposition by the Tiv people."[1] But it was pointed out by SUM(CRC) "that right from the beginning of the proposed transfer

Children at the Mkar orphanage, relatives, and friends are shown here with Charles Jansen. Mr. Jansen is now field secretary of the SUM(CRC).

of Western Tiv it had clearly indicated its unwillingness to take the orphanage even when it was a very small institution. . . ."[1] However at the end of 1960 the SUM(CRC) agreed to take over the orphanage "while holding to the ideal that the Church assume responsibility in 1965."

In actual fact the transfer of the orphanage to the church took place in January 1969. The church was willing to do this and the mission promised to help NKST financially, cutting down the amount given each year. Mrs. Peter Bulthuis, who did so much to help at the orphanage, as did the Jansen family before her, tells us, "It is still an institution maintained for the purpose of helping those who have lost a mother in childbirth and are unable to raise the baby themselves. They ask for financial help from the family in the way of an initial fee. It is run completely by the Nigerians. Six months ago (i.e., June 1970) there was a staff of about ten people and there were approximately twelve children."[2]

At the present time the availability of powdered milk together with a more enlightened community may lessen the need for the orphanage in the future. In its place people can be taught to use sterile bottle-feeding methods at simple infant-feeding stations.

Benue Leprosy Settlement

The southern base of Mkar "mountain" is occupied by the mission station, the hospital and the primary school. The teachers' college and orphanage are situated towards the west of the station. In the 1930s leprosy was greatly feared and when the DRCM developed a treatment center for it they did so in a separate location east of the hospital. In the forties the government was pleased to grant a large tract of land extending outwards from the southern slopes of the mountain. Most of this was used as farmland by the patients but the corner nearest the road and the mission station was used for the homes and buildings of the treatment center. Today at the Benue Leprosy Settlement (BLS) in addition to three homes for senior staff members there is a four-ward, seventy-bed hospital, an operating theater, laboratory, a building for physiotherapy and one for occupational therapy, a shoe shop, laundry, and chapel. Further away there is a full primary school and a school for women. Beyond these again is a church which serves some seven hundred worshipers each Sunday. The church is a congregation of the NKST.

The early years of treating leprosy were hard and discouraging. The hydnocarpus oil treatment then used was by no means as successful as dapsone which was introduced later. The oil was messy and smelly and the deep punctures into the lesions sometimes led to tetanus and death. For several years, then, the work was difficult, but after World War II the DRCM builder, M. P. Loedolff, and his wife felt the call of God to devote their lives to this work. The testimony of all, especially those of the medical profession, was that he made a great success of it.

He quickly learned to diagnose the disease. He was an able administrator. (During the war he built a British air force base at Makurdi and demonstrated his ability to make more than a thousand men work at high speed for several weeks). This ability stood him in good stead and his strictness as a disciplinarian became well known and accepted by the people. Under him and with the advantage of knowing how to build well and cheaply the leprosy settlement evolved. At one point it cared for as many as fifteen hundred residents. He also developed the school, and later the church so as to meet the mental and spiritual needs of all who were interested. He saw to it that all lepers who were able worked their allotted farms and in addition produced food for those too maimed to be able to do so. His devout and motherly wife was well suited to her husband and was spiritual friend and counselor to hundreds of people.

During his leadership at BLS Mr. Loedolff developed segregation villages in the Benue Province and visited them regularly. These villages, a first step away from segregation in the settlement which was a long way from home for most of the residents, became more feasible once the oral treatment took the place of the injections of oil. Several other missions in the province—among them SUM(CRC) at Lupwe and Baissa locations—established segregation villages. Loedolff was appointed overseer of them all.

Subsequent to the establishment of local segregation villages, roadside treatment booths were set up and used once a week. Patients living near them would gather at a specified hour, mobile leprosy workers would meet them, examine them, tell them the gospel message and give them the medicine required for the next seven days. These roadside centers reduced the need both for the central settlement and the segregation villages. In other words the passage of time was demonstrating that leprosy is not the dreadful disease it has been made out to be. It is now known to be no more infectious than most other diseases with which we have contact every day. The patient may stay in the locality of his own home and carry on a normal and useful life. Today those who shrink back and think of leprosy as a loathsome disease only display their ignorance. Such an attitude is quite unjustified.

Mr. Loedolff was a ruler who found it easiest to keep everything pertaining to the settlement under his own control. But in 1962, after forty years of missionary service and after the DRCM had ceased to be a mission in Nigeria, he retired to South Africa, his wife having died some years earlier. Dr. Herman Gray and Dr. Susan Kok served patiently with Mr. Loedolff for many years. Dr. Kok, DRCM, continued as medical officer in charge under the SUM(CRC) until ill health forced her to retire in 1968. By that time she with the other doctors and nurses had developed fine physiotherapy and occupational therapy departments. Many successful operations were performed and with therapeutic aids the use of limbs, hands, fingers, etc. was restored. The cured people were no longer a drain on society; moreover, they were very thankful for the ability to take up a normal life. Another innovation was a shoeshop where simple sandals and corrective shoes for deformed feet were made. Because limbs affected by leprosy lose their sense of feeling, often the sufferer would injure himself unawares. With sandals or shoes these people could walk about more freely.

The apex figure of 1500 residents at the central settlement began to drop as local villages were opened, and did so much more when roadside treatment booths were set up. At the end of 1968 the number at BLS had dropped to 235. Many of these required operations or close supervision. For instance the hospital beds were used for 47 who needed help because of acute reactions to treatment, nearly 100 needed total rest for a time to help ulcers to heal, while 81 were surgical patients. At the end of that year 9 children who had stayed at Mkar for an average of five years were dismissed as cured. Thirteen adults also were discharged—they had stayed for an average of fifteen years each. An average stay in the hospital itself was twenty-four weeks.[3] Most leprosy patients are cheerful and grateful and cooperate well with the physical, farm, educational, and spiritual programs provided. The Christian teachers, evangelists, and Bible women had weeks and often years in which to labor with a resident of the settlement; as a consequence this ministry brought a large number of them to a firm and lasting faith in Christ. They were not only restored to their homes well and able to take an active part in the life of the community, but also as most valuable members of the church of Jesus Christ. The ministry is one of mercy and love, and God's Spirit arranges that it pays off large dividends to His glory.

In 1971 Emily Duyst completed eleven years of devoted service, nearly all of which had been contributed to the BLS. At that time the Rev. J. Kotze, formerly of the DRCM, was serving as administrator, ably assisted by his wife Lillian. There is no longer a separate doctor for the leprosy ministry on the Benue field; this work is now done by those working at the general hospitals. The Nigerian local authorities are more and more absorbing responsibility for this health problem. The Nigerian government and world leprosy organizations have borne almost 100 percent of the financial costs of such an operation as the Benue Leprosy Settlement. However, the CRC and DRCM paid all the salaries and expenses of the personnel they seconded to the work. This also is a part of the "Nigerian Harvest."

Notes

1. Collaboration committee minute 222, August 1958.
2. Correspondence, Mrs. Peter Bulthuis to Smith, January 1971.
3. Satistics from BLS Annual Report, 1968.

21

Nongo u Kristu hen Sudan ken Tiv

The DRCM Completes Its Nigerian Ministry

As a prelude to Nigerian national independence, which was due in 1960, there were indications by the government in 1958 that the issue of visas to foreigners would be under entirely new management. At the time missions were informed that there would be quotas and the quotas would be assessed according to the number of missionaries working in an accredited mission in 1958. For this reason the SUM(CRC) included thirty-six DRCM workers in its total number of missionaries for that year. This was to assure the CRC that it had official permission for enough personnel to maintain the Tiv work at the level which it had reached in 1958 should the South African workers leave the country.

The collaboration committee of the two missions had been working steadily on the plans for the final withdrawal of the DRCM. Each institution and segment of the work still in DRCM hands had its fixed date of transfer. The plans were that the printing press and bookshop were to change hands in 1961; the girls' school and primary schools in 1962, the leprosy work and orphanage in 1963 together with Mkar, Makurdi, and the remaining mission stations. New and vacated positions were to be staffed by the CRC, and financial responsibility at the rate of an additional 20 percent of the total each year was to be carried by it. All was to be completed by the end of 1963.[1] In retrospect the Lord's sovereign omniscience is seen in all of this.

All was well in hand and proceeding according to plan when there was political upheaval in the continent of Africa. One part of this occurred when the Republic of South Africa left the British Commonwealth of Nations in 1961. By this move her people in Nigeria became aliens instead of being favored British citizens. This situation was aggravated by the serious Sharpville affair in South Africa, which brought that country a great deal of adverse publicity and offended the other African nations.

In August of 1961 a high-level white Christian official of the Nigerian government realized the dangers in the situation and confidentially warned the field secretary of the SUM. He in turn advised the SUM(CRC) and DRCM. Private conversations took place between mission representatives and government servants which resulted in the DRCM decision to cease to exist in Nigeria forthwith. It held its final council at Mkar on September 2, 1961. Of this meeting the Rev. E. Casaleggio tells us that the chairman, the Rev. W. D. Gerryts, wrote to his General Mission Board saying, "This means that we have here no longer a Field Council, a Council Committee nor a Council Chairman. All responsibility has gone over into the hands of the SUM(CRC) into whose service our missionaries were taken. Temporarily we are now members of the SUM, we are represented in their council. . . ."[2]

In reality, however, this decision required the action of others also. The day before the DRCM Council met, NGC had decided to advance the date of transfer from December 31, 1963 to September 30, 1961. Even so the General Council in South Africa had to act and it made the date of transfer November 1, 1961. This choice was agreeable to the two missions in Nigeria and they sent out a notice to all concerned telling of the " . . . completion of transfer of Dutch Reformed Church Mission to Sudan United Mission (Christian Reformed Church Branch)" and saying, " . . . the transfer has been completed effective the 1st of November, 1961. The Dutch Reformed Church Mission has now ceased to be an official, incorporated mission body in Nigeria." The transfer included all properties, schools, and leprosy facilities. All bank credits were transferred to the SUM(CRC). More significant and praiseworthy than everything else was the transfer of all DRC missionary personnel in Nigeria to the CRC. The NGC and the DRCM were agreeable to this and it was more remarkable still that the Nigerian government transferred en bloc and in record time all of these workers of South African origin to the employment of the CRC.

When sudden and unexpected political action endangered the gospel ministry among the Tiv, God had arranged and found His children ready to effect a complete change of ownership so that it barely ruffled the surface of the ongoing life of the Tiv Church and Christian people. Let it be clearly understood that the Tiv leaders were very unhappy officially to lose the ministry of a band of men and women who under the banner of the DRCM had so faithfully served God and them for fifty years. Unofficially some thirty-six workers were still retained who would only slowly fade out of the picture through the years that followed.

When the Nigerian senate debated South Africa's withdrawal from the British Commonwealth on November 26, 1961, the Minister of Internal Affairs spoke about the DRCM and in concluding his remarks said, " . . . I thought I should allow them to be in Nigeria up to April 1962. . . ."[3] He was referring to a conversation with mission representatives but the date of the conversation is not known. Since the DRCM had ceased to exist in Nigeria on November 1, 1961, and all of her missionaries were now employees of a North American mission—the SUM(CRC)—there was no further talk of them leaving in April 1962. The whole incident of the transfer of the DRCM to the SUM(CRC) is worthy of praise to God.

Prelude to Organization of NKST

We will now review the development and legal establishment of the Nongo u Kristu hen Sudan ken Tiv (NKST) Church. The title in English is "The Church of Christ in the Sudan among the Tiv." This church was the outcome of the ministry of the DRCM and up until 1961 was very largely influenced by it. Earlier we have referred to the distinctive influence of South African Dutch culture where black Africans are concerned. This was reflected in the relationship between the DRCM and the Tiv Christians. It was a paternal and authoritative relationship, a relationship which did not appear to be resented by the Tiv Christians.

In the closing years of its ministry the DRCM saw the formal establishment of the Tiv Church and celebrated the jubilee of the arrival of the first missionaries at Sai. A few months later came the final transfer to the CRC and then in 1964, the dedication of the complete Tiv Bible, the Mission's farewell gift to the Tiv people.

It takes many years to formally establish a Christian church. Twenty years after starting their work at Sai the DRCM settled at Mkar. It was another twenty-four years before a splendid church building was dedicated at Mkar. This itself took many years of thought and preparation. The Rev. A. J. Brink was the mainstay of this practical project. Eight years before the building was opened he had purchased the roofing materials because they were available at the time at bargain prices. At the dedication it was reported that the building had cost nearly $5,000 of which the Tiv people had given one-third, the missionaries (not the mission) a third, and interested friends the remainder. In 1947 the service of consecration was held with 2,000 people present and, of these, 240 partook of the Lord's Supper. The building centralized the entire Tiv Church and here the annual synods and important meetings of the church were and still are held. It is situated at the verge of the Mkar mission station within a stone's throw of the late Mr. Brink's home.

By 1950, when the CRC was taking its first step into partnership with the DRCM and Tiv ministry, there was a general church council and NGC decided, "The present unity of the Tiv Church situated on both sides of the Katsina Ala River is recognized and it is agreed that this unity be maintained. . . ."[4] At that time CRC ministers in charge of Tiv districts were members of the NKST's General Church Council. Of these one or another has served on the church's executive committee throughout the years.

The ordained missionaries of the DRCM and the SUM(CRC) met in July 1954 to discuss the rules and regulations of the church. They, although there were no Tiv present as there were no ordained Tiv pastors or elders at the time, recommended that a document of rules and regulations become a guide for the conduct of Tiv Christian affairs. They suggested that Tiv leaders in the church now become elders and that some of them together with missionary ministers plan for the ordination of Tiv men into the ministry and also set up a tentative constitution for the Tiv Church. At the time there were nine organized Tiv congregations.[5]

Formal Organization of NKST

January 9, 1957, is described by the Rev. H. J. Evenhouse as "a day of precious remembrance in the work of missions in the Sudan. . . . a day of rejoicing for the 2,000 members of the newly organized group . . . no less a day of great rejoicing and thanksgiving for the missionaries present." This referred to the formal organization of the Church of Christ in the Sudan among the Tiv (NKST) and every January 9 that church celebrates its inauguration. The Church is autonomous, self-sustaining, self-governing, and self-propagating. Its acceptance of its constitution enabled it to immediately institute proceedings for its recognition by the Nigerian government as a legal entity and it became an incorporated body in the country. The name of the church comes very near to marking it as a church of only one tribe and the use of the Tiv language tends to make it that. However, the word *among* (*keñ*) was placed in the title to seek to leave a way whereby others could be included in it.

The creed of NKST is worded, "The Church accepts the Word of God as it is written in the Old and New Testaments as the supreme rule of faith and life of a Christian. It also accepts the confession of faith as expressed in the Apostles' Creed and as explained in the Heidelberg Catechism and shall in due time exercise its right to frame its own Confession of Faith in agreement with the Word of God, and the fundamental doctrines of the Christian faith as set forth in these standards."[6]

The collaboration committee noted in 1956, "the mission should not have a place in the body of the constitution inasmuch as it is a temporary organization having no legal position in the Tiv Church." The committee also said, "It was felt that from now on in an increasing measure the ordained missionaries will be simply counsellors of the Tiv Church."[7] Article XI of the NKST Constitution allows ordained missionaries to serve the church and its councils "for such time as the Church may find it necessary."

As one index of church growth we note the figures for communicant church members. Speaking at the time of the DRCM Jubilee, the Rev. W. D. Gerryts reported that "after twenty-five years [of gospel witnessing] there was the meagre harvest of not more than twenty-five baptized Christians." This was an average of one for each year of mission service. When the church building was dedicated at Mkar in 1947 there were 240 who partook of the Lord's Supper, or ten times as many as there were in 1936. In 1957 when the NKST was organized mention is made of more than 2,000 communicant members, again almost ten times as many as in 1947. Five years later the Tiv church reported to TEKAS that there were 4,000 and, again, five years later (1967), the number was given as almost 12,000 or six times as many as there were ten years before. In 1970 the number had risen to 15,974. The harvest that is being gathered steadily increases.

The following statistics are gleaned from the figures submitted by the NKST to the Tekas Fellowship. There is no record available to the author before 1962.

NKST Church	1962	1970	Percent of increase
Places of worship	979	1,407	43
Attendance, Sunday worship	78,140	134,052	72
Organized congregations	16	43	169
Ordained pastors	16	43	169
Other workers	20	160	700
Communicant members	3,933	15,974	308
Confessions of faith	921	2,113	130
Children baptized	474	1,478	227
Offerings	$19,768	$94,920	380

Mission Headquarters Transferred to Mkar

With the formal organization of the Tiv Church the SUM(CRC) had to make adjustments also. In increasing numbers CRC missionaries were being involved in the Tiv work as over against that of the Benue Church. The unexpectedly quick transfer of the Mkar Hospital to the CRC was too sudden for the peace of mind of the Tiv Church. It was felt that the NGC secretary should be closer to Mkar where both the NKST and the DRCM had their centers. He was transferred from Lupwe and the headquarters of the mission went with him. This move made no particular impression upon the Tiv Christians as they had been used to Mkar being the center of mission activity for a long time. But it made a considerable impression upon the Benue Church which had also been mission headquarters for a long time for now these were taken away. It felt that the SUM(CRC) was deserting it in favor of a newcomer, the NKST.

The transfer of SUM(CRC) headquarters from Lupwe to Mkar brought the leaders of the mission into much closer contact with the Tiv Church. At the time the DRCM was still the mission in charge and for a while the transfer did not bring NKST and SUM(CRC) into open confrontation. But the sudden transfer of the total DRCM to the SUM(CRC) in 1961, which was forced by Nigerian political considerations over which neither mission had any control, placed SUM(CRC) in the saddle of authority. This was something the NKST had to realize even though there were many DRCM missionaries still working near at hand. The dispute over the location of nurses' training and agitation for the SUM(CRC) to become two missions immediately arose.

As an autonomous church the NKST felt it had the right to determine which CRC missionaries should return to work in Tivland after a period of furlough in North America. It did not see the need for discussion about this with the missionaries concerned, nor with the mission, and did not give the reasons for its action.[9] NGC said, "We are grieved as a mission that several of our staff have been dealt with so summarily and, as we feel, in an un-Biblical manner." It asked the church to assume a responsible attitude in the work of Christ's church. There was no fruitful communication between the two bodies for six months and at the end of that time NGC told NKST it believed "any prolonging of the discussion will serve no useful purpose, and now wishes to commit the matter into the hands of our Lord."[10] Such happenings as these made it clear to the SUM(CRC) that the Tiv Church was in a fraternal and not a filial relationship with her. However, curtly to dismiss missionaries with-

These officers and trustees of the Tekas Fellowship of Churches in 1967 represent five hundred thousand regular churchgoers. The Tiv and Benue trustees are standing fourth and fifth from the left. Rev. Ed Smith was then the secretary.

Rev. J. Orffer, Sr. working on the translation of the Old Testament into the Tiv language.

out reason was hard for the mission and more especially for the aggrieved missionaries to take. It was a humbling process similar in effect to that of the NKST corresponding directly with the CRC Board and Synod without informing the NGC that such steps were taken. The mission is striving with no little difficulty to adjust to these changes recognizing that other cultures have other ways of doing things.

The Tiv Bible

The Tiv Church was a very happy church when it received the complete Bible in its own mother tongue. It was a labor of love, the love and devotion of many South African missionaries spread over fifty years. First of all the language had to be reduced to writing and the first book in it was published by A. S. Judd just three years after the mission began its work. Two years later the first Gospel in Tiv was published and twenty years after that, in 1936, the New Testament was finished. This first appeared as a single book in 1942. Of the Old Testament we are told, "the Rev. J. E. Orffer, the translator, began translating Genesis in December 1938 and in 1951 he wrote the last verses in Malachi . . . 1600 handwritten pages." For the revision Mr. Orffer was joined by the Rev. W. M. Scott and two Tiv assistants, Mr. Shawon and Mr. Buter.

The revision of the Old Testament took several years and while it was being done it was seen that the New Testament needed revision also. This was given to the DRCM workers but continuity was in part ensured by the use of the two assistants mentioned above. We are told "the translation and the revision were done entirely with the help of the Tiv Christians. No part was considered to be concluded unless it satisfied them as far as language was concerned."[11] On January 23, 1961, fifty years after the work began, a special prayer service was held and then "the complete manuscript was carefully sealed, registered and flown to England to be printed by the British and Foreign Bible Society."

The first shipments of the printed Tiv Bible reached Nigeria in the autumn of 1964. The entire Tiv Church was invited to meet at Mkar to celebrate this most auspicious occasion in the history of the Tiv people. On November 4, 1964, thousands of Christians crowded inside and outside of the large Mkar Church to dedicate to God His precious Word in the Tiv language. The Chairman of the former DRCM, Rev. W. D. Gerryts, assisted by the Home Representative of the CRC, Mr. A. Huibregtse, and the Field Representative of the United Bible Societies, Dr. W. Reyburn gave the Bible to the Chairman of NKST, Rev. J. E. I. Sai, and two of his fellow ministers. The whole congregation joined audibly in the dedication, offering prayer after each of six portions of Scripture were read by the minister in charge. It was a memorable day and set the fast pace for the sale of the new Bible, thousands of which were sold in the first few weeks. Tiv is the seventh Nigerian language in which the whole Bible has been printed. The church celebrates on November 4 each year in commemoration of the event.

The Ordained Ministry

Very soon after the establishment of the Tiv Church, and really a concomitant of it, four of its members were ordained into the ministry. About two years later three others were added. By 1970 the total number of Tiv ministers was forty-three, some being graduates of the TCNN and others having had their training in the Tiv vernacular. That year another big class began its training in the vernacular and there were also many more studying at the TCNN. The Rev. A. Nevkar was the first chairman of the Synod, an active office which continued throughout the twelve months of the year. Mr. Nevkar was succeeded by the Rev. J. E. I. Sai, who served for a long time. While doing so he visited the United States and South Africa on church business. He was a son of Mr. Sai who founded the village of that name where the mission began its work. The present chairman is the Rev. J. K. Manyam, a graduate of TCNN, who has visited the Netherlands and America. Some of these overseas visits were related to the Reformed Ecumenical Synod of which both the Tiv and Benue churches are members.

The CRC method of calling and ordaining men into the ministry was adopted by both churches in Nigeria. A man had to receive and accept a call from a local congregation to serve it or to serve in some position approved by the NKST Synod. When a new Tiv minister took up work in a locality cared for by a missionary within a few months the missionary was given a new assignment most often requiring that he be transferred to a new location. In time it meant that most of the ordained missionaries served as teachers in training Christian leaders and pastors. One or two became writers or developed the sale of Christian literature. By 1970 it was clear that teaching positions also would be taken over by qualified Nigerians.

Work Among Women and Youth

Ordained missionaries were not set aside for work among the women

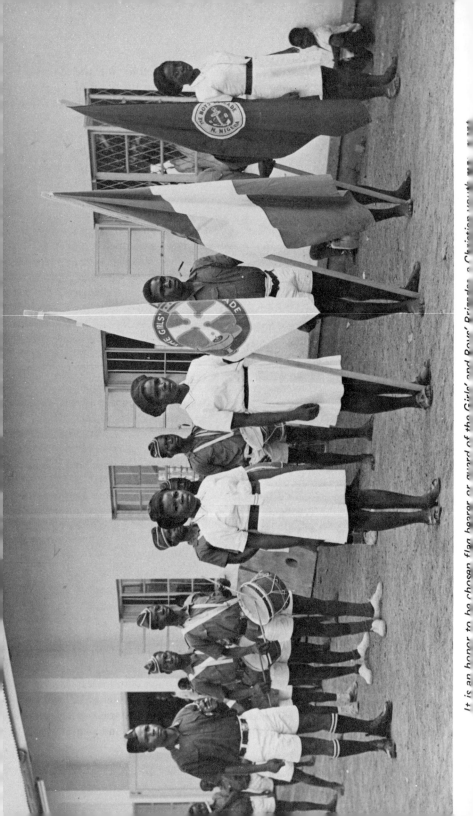

It is an honor to be chosen flag bearer or guard of the Girls' and Boys' Brigades, a Christian youth activity.

or youth of the two churches. A great deal was done for the Christian women by CRC women, some of whom were the wives of missionaries. Moreover, whenever men were being trained for church work, their wives, if they were married, were given training to the measure of their ability. In both Tiv and Benue churches the fellowships of Christian women are an important and powerful force to be taken into consideration. Study materials for the weekly gatherings were produced by women missionaries. The study books produced by Mrs. Nelle Smith enjoyed a wide circulation in many other churches also.

By and large it seems as if Sunday school work, while carried on everywhere, has not received any prime emphasis by mission or church. Sunday school materials have been consistently supplied but the records of this aspect of the work are not very vocal. Christian Brigade work for the young people, known by the CRC as Calvinist Cadets and Calvinettes, has been carried on and in these last few years concentrated efforts have been put into village youth work by Rachie Moolman of South Africa and Evelyn Vredevoogd. This is proving to be valuable and is adopted by the younger leaders of the church, promising well for the future.

In these latter years there has been a heavy drift of the young people away from their farms and villages and away from the control of parents to the so-called freedom of urban and city life. Among the Tiv the cities of Makurdi and Gboko are proving to be very attractive. Under the mission and in close cooperation with the church, Mr. and Mrs. W. Lemcke have set up a youth center with a fine building in the heart of Gboko town. It is proving to be popular, but it is too early yet to assess its value. Undoubtedly something has to be done in all the cities to effectively reach for Christ this youthful and better-educated element of society.

Civil Strife among the Tiv

For the Tiv people the transition of Nigeria from British supremacy to national independence in 1960 was marred by internal strife. The new authority throughout the Northern Region was largely in the hands of Muslims. Some of the Tiv leaders, though not Muslims, were favorable toward the new regime and profited by it. Of the rest of the people a large majority were not favorable to Muslims; strife within the tribe began in 1960 as a result. It continued with increasing bitterness for the next five years. Pillage and destruction with some murder threw a pall of fear and despair over the whole tribe.

Historically in pre-British times the Tiv were a fiercely independent and conservative race, but after the riots at Abinsi in 1906, there was a long period of peaceful colonial penetration. This was disturbed in 1939 by the temporary rise of the Inyambuan cult which caused rioting throughout the tribe and in 1947 by a serious uprising in Makurdi. Then came the prolonged happenings of 1960 to 1965 which toward the end spilled over to affect neighboring tribes, bringing reprisals from them.

In the sixties the Tiv Church was a real force for good. Even though the troubles covered every part of Tivland, very few Christians were directly involved. The statistician can note that it was in this decade that there was a sharp rise in attendance at church services on a Sunday and hundreds of new places of worship were opened. It is reasonable to suppose that the strife drove many people to seek the comfort of gatherings of people which met for peaceful purposes and did not promote political opinions. On August 23, 1964, the chairman of NKST wrote, " . . . peace has not yet come to Tivland. In the center and the east and south things are a little easier. But to the west and north around Makurdi there is no let-up and people are being driven from their homes and are killing each other. Now the work of the church is much more difficult and meetings are difficult as it is dangerous to travel the roads." In response to this letter the mission found a way whereby the chairman, his wife, and one or two others were able to visit every part of the church to comfort the believers.

It was toward the end of that year that other tribes became involved. This was especially so in the region of Takum. For a few days things were black indeed. Kuteb and Jukun people, not Christians, became involved. Intertribal relationships reached a very low point and the aftermath even affected the fellowship between the NKST and Benue churches. But it was a victory of the Lord's grace that soon afterward the two groups were able to meet with the rest of the Tekas Fellowship at Lupwe for its annual meeting in January 1965.

It was at this meeting of the Fellowship that Tiv singers sang some of their special hymns to the delight of all the delegates. This is the other thing which contributed very much to the increased church attendance among the Tiv in the 1960s—the use in moderation and under the supervision of Tiv Church elders of Tiv musical instruments playing Tiv tribal tunes at meetings of worship. Accompanying this music were new songs quite unrelated to foreign hymnology. In 1971 a revised book of some four hundred Tiv hymns was published. Many of the earlier edition of 150 hymns were produced by a blind Christian who, with the aid of his sister, toured the churches and introduced these hymns to the people who memorized them. In many Tiv churches the instruments were used and the songs sung as a prelude to the worship service and also at the time of the offering. Psalms and hymns written by missionaries are still used during part of the service. All Tiv people love their own music and sing their own songs without tiring. It is certain that the new singing attracted many outsiders to the services.

The last population census taken in Nigeria was unsatisfactory and has not been freely published. Therefore it is uncertain how many Tiv people there were then, but it is possible that there are today one and a quarter million. The figures given by the church for those attending Sunday morning worship services are also erratic. In 1968 NKST gave the total as 262,138, but in 1969 the church reported 148,169, and in 1970 134,052. The 1970 number indicates that approximately one Tiv person out of eight goes to an NKST church and calls himself a Christian. But of the churchgoers, less than 16,000 were on the communicant roll; or one person in eight going to church regularly had publicly confessed his faith. Of the remainder a portion would be children and another portion would be attending one level or another in preconfession classes. It takes two or more years of study before a person is accepted into the full membership of the church. It is not improbable that of those attending church in 1970 perhaps nine out of each twelve people have yet to show some greater sign of faith than that of entering the church doors. This sets both a formidable but also a challenging task to the confessing membership to lead the others to true faith in the Lord.

It is a great harvest! One hundred and thirty four thousand in church hear the Word of God every week. Sixteen thousand communicant members have publicly declared their faith and intention to follow the Lord Jesus. These members belong to a branch of the church militant and have promised their allegiance to it. Thinking on this we cry, "This is the Lord's doings and it is marvellous in our eyes."

Notes

1. Collaboration committee minute 247, March 1959.
2. E. Casaleggio, *The Land Shall Yield Its Fruit*, p. 115.
3. Lagos Hansard record p. 842, November 25, 1961.
4. NGC minute 434, August 1950.
5. Collaboration committee minute 41, July 1954.
6. NKST constitution Article III.
7. Collaboration committee minute 140.
8. Collaboration committee minute 144 (appended letter), August 1957.
9. NGC minute 4519, May 1963.
10. NGC minute 4610, b, November 1963.
11. *The Coming of the Gospel into Tivland*, pp. 24-28.

22

Other Ministries and Supporting Services

Mass Evangelism

Speaking of the diverse services of the department of evangelism in 1962, the NGC notes, "One medium which has recently been put into practice is a sight-sound truck with an electric generator, projector, speakers, and recorder. Although this project is a rather new venture, as far as we are able to judge it is a very effective way of reaching the masses."[1]

This ministry has continued up to the present time. In these later years Le Roy Baas has been in charge, ably assisted by Nigerians. In the dry season of 1967 Mr. Baas was spending two weeks out of every three "on the road" and the other at home. This was quite a concession for Mrs. Baas to make as very often when her husband was absent she had no missionary colleague nearer than thirty miles away. Mr. Baas reports that people came from every direction to attend the two-night programs in their area. "Perhaps it is a market place, maybe it is a church center, or a school compound, and then it might be a small village, wherever we are the Lord has showered blessings. I know, numbers don't mean a lot; yet they are very encouraging. In the past months of the dry season we have been averaging 2,000 people every night. Think of that! Some nights it is close to 3,000 and then other nights about 1,500 but that is the lowest it has been. All of these people listening to the Gospel of Salvation through Jesus Christ in their language. Each night's program consists of a Biblical film strip, a prevention of disease picture of some type, and some pertinent evangelistic message built around a slide or film strip presentation."[2] This mobile ministry reaching many places and many people who otherwise would not be touched, is being used extensively throughout the Tiv area of our work.

Agricultural Outreach Program

From the early days of its occupation of Nigeria some fifty years ago, the British government set up agricultural centers in each province to teach the people improved farming techniques. The usefulness of these is not discussed here except to say that the one near to Mkar supplied the mission with hundreds of citrus and other tropical fruit trees which were a great blessing to the missionaries. Even villages far distant from the mission stations were benefited for the missionary trekkers planted trees which are still yielding fruit today.

With an eye to improving nutritional standards and helping economic progress of an essentially rural people the NGC proposed in 1964 to "initiate two programs of agricultural outreach: one to be in direct conjunction with the Benue Bible School in the NKST area, the second, to be at a Bible School in the EKAS area."[3] In February 1966, after lengthy consideration by a subcommittee, the Mission Board concurred "in the proposal of NGC that an Agricultural Outreach Program be furthered to assist the members of the churches in Nigeria in the development of agriculture." It felt that "this assistance is considered necessary in order that the indigenous principle of self-propagation and self-support be advanced with maximum involvement of the Christian nationals and the Christian church communities." At the same time it said quite plainly, and in doing so repeated the advice sent from the field, " . . . it is not envisioned that agricultural outreach of the mission take on the form of establishing any type of new and separate agricultural institutions, either practical or theoretical in nature."[4]

The Christian Reformed World Relief Committee was already established, so the Mission Board referred the whole proposal to it for possible implementation. Just over a year later the NGC wished to begin this agricultural extension work and that it be supervised by the evangelism department. It asked the Board to send a missionary with a Bachelor of Science degree in agriculture and extra training in extension work. It also wished to employ a trained Nigerian assistant. To start, NGC estimated it would need $10,000 exclusive of the missionary's salary and other expenses. He and his Nigerian colleague were to travel extensively, giving advice, selling supplies, and holding short courses in improved farming methods in church communities.

Eventually the CRWRC through the Board sent Lou Haveman to do this work.

At an earlier date the Benue Bible Institute students had profited much from the zealous and "green-thumbed" ability of the Rev. R. Baker. BBI has a well-developed program for its students and many of them return to their communities as both farmer-evangelists and religious class leaders.

Mr. Havemen settled at the Benue Baissa Bible School and carried out his work from that center. For a time the Ekas Benue Church was not amenable to the idea and as early as March 1968 said, "The Regional Church Council does not wish the agricultural project to be related to a Bible school. The Council wishes [the mission] to build a big institute exclusively for agriculture." In November of that same year it said, "RCC wishes the missionary to establish a school for agriculture where our children will be taught." But it added, "He shall also visit the villages to teach them how to farm and to bring them the Gospel."[5] The SUM(CRC) and its board had been so clear in stating their intention "not to establish any type of new and separate agricultural institutions" that it is difficult to see how this arose. By the close of 1970 the problem was resolved and Mr. Haveman was due to resume his work at Baissa in 1971.

"Islam in Africa Project" and the Mission

The SUM(CRC) has not restricted herself to her own corner of Nigeria. When there was need and it was able, workers have been loaned to other missions and spheres. Many CRC ministers served the Tekas churches at TCNN. Teachers have helped at other colleges and nurses and doctors have given months and sometimes years to other hospitals. Smith was allowed to serve the Tekas Fellowship for many years. In 1960 that Fellowship accepted the offer of the services of Dr. Willem A. Bijlefeld to instruct the churches of Tekas how to minister to Muslims. This led to the involvement of CRC's Rev. Peter Ipema in Christian-Islamic work.

It is possible that there are twenty-five million Muslims in Nigeria. The majority of these live in the far northern provinces of the country. For sixty years the British government restrained missionaries of Christ from penetrating into these areas except for the establishment of a few leprosaria and a Christian bookshop or two. With the coming of national independence in 1960 the new government, which in the north was largely in the hands of Muslims, did not turn against Christian missions. Religious freedom had been clearly written into the new constitution and it was soon made plain that the new authorities meant to respect this freedom. After six years Smith's report to the CRC Board said, "To the praise of God one thing is abundantly clear . . . there is far more liberty to proclaim the gospel everywhere. This includes the Muslim States and there have been many instances of us being allowed to proceed freely where before this was not the case. Let me hasten to add that compared with many places in the world there has always been great freedom in Nigeria. . . . We hear from several places of the conversion of Muslims to the Christian faith."[6]

In 1965 the premier of the Northern Region of Nigeria was Alhaji Sir Ahmadu Bello. He was also vice-president of the World Islamic League. Although he was the premier yet he instituted no legislation to restrict Christian missions. To the contrary he took the positive attitude of propagating his own faith and set up "a Torch of Islam Fund for the education of Muslims and the spread of Islam in hearts that have not yet received its light."[7] In June, seven months before his untimely death, "he announced the conversion of 189,216 people into the religion [of Islam] within the past eighteen months."[8] This total resulted from mass conversions of a thousand or two at a time. An Islamic conversion is not similar to a Christian conversion. This spurt of Islamic missionary endeavor by the head of the Region ended when he was killed in January 1966.

The fact that the door to Islam opened wider in 1960 instead of being closed, showed how timely was God's provision in setting up the Islam in Africa Project in 1959. Its aim is "to keep before the churches of Africa (south of the Sahara) their responsibility for understanding Islam and the Muslims of their religion, in view of the Church's task of interpreting faithfully in the Muslim world, the Gospel of Jesus Christ; and to effect the research and education necessary for this."[9] The project is not related to any ecumenical or other movement and is open to the participation of any church which considers its task to be that of interpreting faithfully in the Muslim world, the gospel of Jesus Christ. Dr. Bijlefeld described its prime emphasis when he said, "Our starting point of all our planning should be that the Islam-apostolate in each area is a matter for the indigenous Christians."[10] The whole purpose of the IAP movement, which is now active in several countries in sub-Saharan Africa, is to enlighten and encourage African Christians to witness the gospel to Muslims and to help them replace the fear and dislike which they inherited from their pagan forefathers with a positive and sympathetic attitude toward the many millions who are their Muslim neighbors.

In May and June 1963 the NGC and the IAP made a mutual

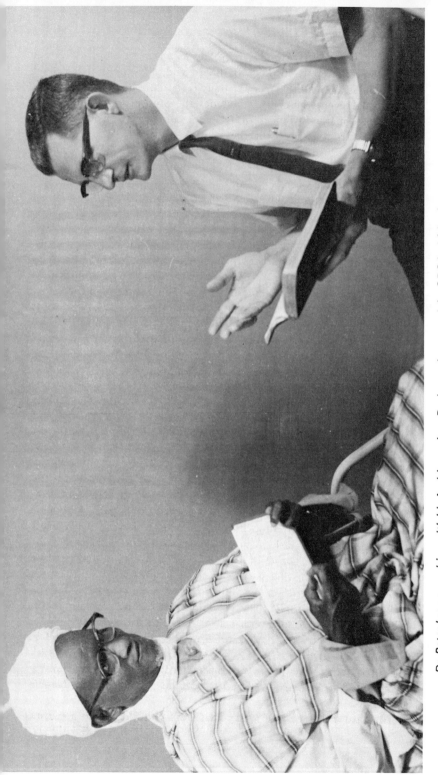

Dr. Peter Ipema working with his Arabic teacher. Dr. Ipema has served the CRC in Africa for over twenty years.

agreement whereby Mr. Ipema was set aside to serve the churches throughout Northern Nigeria by giving them short courses on the Christian's approach to Islam. He joined Dr. Bijlefeld and others in this ministry. After some very full years of service Mr. Ipema was encouraged by the Mission Board to take further studies in Islamics and Arabic. He obtained his doctor's degree from the Hartford Seminary Foundation early in 1971 and was appointed the principal of the IAP Study Center in Ibadan, Nigeria. This center serves African students and missionaries from many parts of the continent. These students become teachers in the areas from which they come. The CRC, through Dr. Ipema and others, is making a significant contribution to the glory of God in the conversion of Muslims throughout Africa.

Supporting Services—Building and Maintenance

In pre-European days architecture in the Benue Province was very simple. A half a dozen round rooms, each separated from the others, were clustered together in patterns differing with each tribe. These would form a home. For greater protection or privacy some would link these together with connecting walls of rocks or fences of woven grass. Material for the walls and floor would be dug from the ground nearby, which, when dampened, formed a malleable clay that was easily shaped into walls that soon dried hard in the sun. Poles and grass gathered from the forest and bushland served as a covering for the home, and a hole in the wall sufficed for light and ventilation as well as an entrance.

Missionaries and others introduced sun-dried bricks, rectangular buildings, hinged doors, and window shutters. They discovered that the male fan palm tree split into scantlings of twenty feet in length made very strong roofs. They also used granite or laterite rock to form a tough foundation which resisted the torrents of rain which fell for six months of each year. These simple and available improvements were soon adopted by the local people.

When missionaries and money were scarce it was necessary for the available men to turn their hand to every practical task waiting to be done. But as the number of our missionary personnel increased it became obvious that full-time help was needed for the erection of homes and other facilities. In 1952 Ray Grissen was our first full-time building overseer. In 1955 Ray Browneye took over where Grissen left off. Browneye headed this very practical aspect of the work for several years and, with J. T. Yusufu as his right-hand man, was responsible for building Takum Christian Hospital. Eventually

Browneye was transferred to the field of flying. Gordon Vander Bie carried the construction load for a long time with Benue Bible Institute and the Mkar Hospital as memorials to his meticulous care. Harvey Poel is remembered for his work at the Gboko Secondary School and in Jos. Don Branderhorst was an able coworker with Vander Bie at Mkar Hospital in which venture George Schutt also lent a hand. This was in the late sixties and the changed times and better health conditions are illustrated for us when we know that Schutt, although he was a retired business man and a grandfather, went to Nigeria to care for the many engines and generators which were in use throughout the mission. To build and keep in good repair so many buildings and to keep contented so many families with only makeshift supplies is no mean task. The builders and mechanics with their African assistants deserve our hearty thanks. They set others free to perform their primary tasks of bringing the evangel and health and education to the people.

Transport, Planes, and Radio

Transport is a necessary aspect of life anywhere. Without delays at transfer points it used to take six weeks of travel from North America to Takum. After twenty-six days on ocean steamers there would be two weeks in a flat-bottomed barge or a dug-out canoe rowed or poled against the current of the Benue River. Nights would be spent beneath the stars on a sand bank at the river's edge with one eye half open towards the east to see whether a storm was brewing. This exceedingly slow journey would end at Ibi and be followed by a day in the sun riding the hot roads on a motorcycle to Takum. If it was very wet weather the canoe would be abandoned for a paddle-wheeled steamer and then only four days would be spent on the river instead of fourteen. But if there were no motorcycle then the use of a bicycle became necessary and the journey took two or three days instead of one. Nowadays, granted good transfer timing, it is possible to leave America one day and be in Takum the next.

When the main connection between two towns is only a foot track and the way is intersected with many streams, then walking or, with some difficulty, cycling are the only ways to go. Bridge the streams and a light weight motorcycle might be used. But slowly throughout the years roads for cars and trucks have been built, some of them by missionaries. An abundant supply of nodules of red laterite make an excellent and colorful road but in very wet weather any such road is a tiresome problem for the traveler. In 1970 there were only seventy miles of tarred surface roads in the Benue Province. Bridges improved, and apart from those on a few bush roads, all of them are of reinforced concrete. The three great rivers, Benue, Donga and Taraba, have been bridged but the Katsina Ala must be crossed by ferry boat.

The fleet of cars and motorcycles now in use in the SUM(CRC) is a very large one, so the mission has a workshop and gasoline supply center at Mkar. To help keep these in some sort of repair the mission supplies missionary mechanics and Nigerian assistants and apprentices. Because of rugged roads and the fact that some drivers have not yet adjusted to the Nigerian conditions, cars and trucks take a terrible beating. All journeys by road are very hazardous and there have been many accidents but we are thankful to our heavenly Father that throughout the years no one has been killed. Travel on dirt roads in Nigeria is a heavy strain for drivers and passengers and excessive heat with dust or mud and bumpy conditions leaves even the most sturdy person weary, dehydrated, and nervous after a long journey.

It was in 1953, when a case of serious illness required speedy action, that a report was made to the CRC Board urging it to consider placing an air strip at Takum. The following March the Board approved "the construction of an airstrip at Lupwe and to accept the offer of a construction firm working in the Lupwe area to survey a site and level out an area half a mile long by 300 feet wide."[11] Although for a time no progress was made, by April 1956 NGC was able to report that the government had granted use of a strip of land near to the town of Takum and the Sudan Interior Mission was willing to make available the services of their aviation department. It was a year later that NGC decided "to proceed with the preparation of this strip on the understanding that the local community be requested to actively help the Mission in making it." The chief of Takum was so pleased at the possibility of an airplane being able to land at his own town, that he had no difficulty in getting the people to voluntarily clear the land of its trees and roots. This made a good contribution to the success of the project.

During the Second World War planes began to land at Makurdi and by 1958 the SIM air arm was graciously helping our missionaries by bringing them to Takum or taking them to Jos and Kano. The value of such air service when set against rough road transportation is incalculable. The fair-minded critic has only to travel Nigeria's roads for a few days in March or September and then make the same journeys by plane to know that the pilot and plane are God's gift to enable the missionary to make much better use of his time and strength. To drive 340 miles by road from Takum to Jos is a hard day's work whereas by plane the journey is 195 miles and it takes an hour and a half, without dust or heat. The passengers are fresh and can tackle a day's work upon arrival and the pilot can add three or more hours of flying, which he often does. The provision of the plane is good stewardship on the part of the Mission Board.

At the annual Board meeting of 1959, "It was decided to provide air service for our Sudan field." The four reasons given were "a. This will save the time and physical strength of our missionaries; b. This will be a great help in transporting children and those going to and from the field; c. This will serve to reduce the wear and tear of the cars used on the field; d. This will be welcome in case of medical emergencies."[12] In the first instance friends of the mission in Iowa supplied the means to buy a Cessna 170 aircraft from the air arm of the SIM and to erect a small hangar at the Takum airstrip. In 1962 a new single engine Piper 250 Comanche was purchased and the Cessna was sold to another mission. By 1966 air travel in the mission field in Nigeria had become sufficiently heavy that the Board authorized the purchase of a twin-engine Aztec with weather avoidance radar and other special equipment. This was made possible by friends in Michigan. The Comanche was not sold and both planes are now serving the mission.

The Nigerian government put in airfields at Wukari and Gboko, road makers put one in at Beli, and the mission with the help of local communities put in strips at Baissa, Bete, Jibu, and Serti. The Jibu and Bete strips were made to help the doctors superintend rural health clinics at these places and Baissa and Serti have been used extensively for sending medical emergencies to our hospitals. On one occasion the Serti strip was very useful to the former premier of the North and he ordered it to be made into an ample airfield suitable for larger craft. Our planes also serve other missions, landing at their fields. Some of these are in foreign territories surrounding Nigeria.

It would be difficult to overestimate the value of bush medical air service as a demonstration of Christian sympathy. Consider, for instance, a swift air journey instead of a jarring ride in a truck for a woman long in labor, or the speedy delivery to the hospital of someone seriously hurt in an accident. Such service has saved lives and has earned the lifelong gratitude of many besides the ones directly involved. Obtaining such aid is made possible by radio contact.

Radio contact between mission stations began concurrently with the interest in planes. It was April 1956 when the first radio transmitter was proposed for the CRC.[13] In time transmitters were set up at Lupwe, Mkar, Kunav, Baissa, Serti, and Jos. The law did not permit these to be used for broadcasting to the general public. They could be used for sending messages between the places mentioned and, for a long time, between the airplane and those stations. Before 7:00 A.M. the Sudanum[14] transmitters are on the air and anyone with an ordinary receiving set can tune in and listen. Flight schedules and important but not confidential information can be sent and acknowledged. The messages are to some extent a daily bulletin of mission news. This was a boost to lonely missionaries on stations where there were no transmitters. There are two other regular standby times during the day with someone listening at each transmitter to catch urgent messages which cannot wait until the following morning. This convenience makes up somewhat for the lack of telegraph or long distance telephone.

One illustration of the value of quick radio transmission and the emergency use of the planes is representative of many others. When Brian Scholten was very ill in Jos a radio call was put out for his father, Herman, to come to him immediately. The pilot of one of the planes was airborne. He picked up this message, turned the plane in its tracks, and half an hour later had picked up Mr. Scholten. Within two hours he was with his son in Jos. Brian died that day. That evening the radio carried the sad news to the CRC stations and three carloads of missionaries made an all-night journey to attend the funeral held the following morning. With some difficulty Ray Browneye was contacted four hundred miles away late that evening. The following morning he brought several more missionaries to join the family in their bereavement. The CRC missionaries in Nigeria are one family and what affects one affects all. It was due to radio, planes, and automobiles that they were able to express their loving concern to the family in their loss.

There are hazards in the air as there are on the ground but CRC planes have had only three accidents and no one has been hurt. The planes are kept in tiptop condition with all air worthiness rules being observed and every part of the planes and engines being regularly examined. Ray Browneye was appointed as the first pilot in 1959 and has continued in that position up to the present. He has flown in every kind of tropical weather—which says a great deal in a very few words. There are frequent and vicious storms with some line squalls extending for more than two hundred miles. Then there are days with cloudless skies and not a bit of turbulence—but insidiously the Sahara dust closes in and visibility is cut to a few hundred feet, and a return to base is made necessary. Mr. Browneye flew the twin-engine Aztec to Nigeria from America alone and without incident except for a nerve straining cutout of the engines while switching from the normal gas tanks to reserve tanks carried in the cab. As one of many

Ray Browneye, pilot, prepares to take a sick lad to hospital by plane.

hundreds of people I have flown with him for tens of thousands of miles and have had no qualms at all.

For a time the SIM air arm helped out during Browneye's absences in America. Then CRC's Gordon Kooistra piloted the plane at furlough time and finished his term as airplane mechanic. Later Gordon Buys switched from teaching and became pilot with Browneye. From available figures one gleans that over a period of six years our planes have flown nearly one million air miles and have carried fourteen thousand people. Seen on a graph this would show a steady rise, beginning with less than a thousand persons a year and ending with almost four thousand. Every takeoff is preceded by audible prayer in which the journey, the craft and pilot, and the purpose of the flight are entrusted to God. The missionaries cannot adequately express their gratitude to God for His goodness in providing planes and radio and willing pilots to help them in their needs.

Mission Finance

Another supporting ministry of the mission is the care of finances. Even though the institutions have their own business administrators for the internal workings of schools or hospitals, yet all are related to a central office. The first full-time worker for the business office was Evelyn Vredevoogd. W. J. Lemcke took over from her and served as business manager for many years, first at Lupwe and later on at Mkar. More recently Harry Meyer has borne this responsibility, being assisted for one term of service by John Zuidema. This department also employs several Nigerians, some of whom have become very able assistants. In the year 1969 the CRC paid out $1,484,622 for the mission in Nigeria and probably an added $140,000 for services rendered for Africa by the Board's office in Grand Rapids. This is a large sum of money and considerably more than the $4,667 spent in 1940, the first year of operation. All accounts in Nigeria are audited annually by a professional firm. If the Nigerian government feels it is necessary the accounts have to be made available for its scrutiny also.

The missionaries are adequately paid for their services, and their family needs, medical services, pensions, and travel are all cared for by the Board. Nigerians who serve in the business office are able to compare their own wage scales with those of the missionaries, and in their estimation the missionaries are highly paid. They cannot see that the missionary workers are making financial sacrifices for there is no doubt that many of them with their specialized training could command far higher salaries at home.

In the thirty years from 1940 to 1969 the CRC spent a total of $10,667,643 for its Nigerian field, an average of $355,000 per year.

In 1945 it passed $10,000, in 1954 it passed $100,000, by 1961 it was well over half a million dollars, and by 1967 it reached one million. In 1970 it reached almost $1,500,000. To run a mission demands funds and also those who are skilled in keeping the accounts in order. The CRC members in North America who give their quota and some far above their quota may rest assured that their gifts are carefully and faithfully used in God's work in Africa.

In the "good old days" of the 1940s the missionary on furlough was instructed, when he was sent out to speak to the churches, not to appeal for money since this was well taken care of by the quota paid by each congregation. As late as 1949 Dr. J. C. De Korne told the Synod, "It would not be necessary for the missionaries to seek special gifts from the audiences which they addressed but they may if the project is approved by the Board and Synod." However, early in the next decade special gifts for above-quota items became a necessary and important part of the mission budget. It was a great help when congregations decided to be responsible, above their mission quota obligation, to pay the whole or part of one or more missionaries' salaries. In 1970 for Nigeria alone, no less than 131 CRC congregations were financially involved in the payment of missionary salaries. A blessing resulting from this involvement was that the supporting congregations came into close contact with its missionaries and the countries which they served. On the other hand the missionary had congregations where he or she felt particularly at home.

Special projects are dependent on above-quota gifts. There are, for example, medical wards, schoolrooms, vehicles, planes, and all sorts of things on the mission field which have been given by individuals, societies, Sunday schools, and others. In 1970 the amount of money collected by quotas from the churches was only about 45 percent of the total given and as much as 55 percent was given as special gifts. This trend is expected to continue and is a long way from the ideas held so firmly twenty-five years ago. God runs His work so well. He gives faith to board members, home office staff, and missionaries so that His people loyally support the work which He has told the CRC to do, not only in Nigeria but in North America and around the world. All praise and glory be to Him!

The General Secretary and Conference

The most demanding and important job on the mission field is that of being general secretary to the SUM(CRC). He must coordinate all the work of the mission and keep the Home Board and every missionary informed as to what is taking place. This position has been held by Rev. E. H. Smith (1940-1954), Rev. R. R. Recker (1954-1957), Rev. P. Ipema (1957-1963), Mr. P. Bulthuis twice (1963-1964 and 1969-1970), Mr. W. Bierma (1964), Rev. H. Vander Aa (1964-1969) and Mr. C. Jansen (1970-   ). The Secretary attends nearly all departmental meetings and committees—and these are legion. He arranges for and attends the monthly meeting of NGC and then carries out its wishes. He is available to every missionary, sharing their joys and sorrows, guiding them, and sometimes rebuking them in the most tactful way that he knows. He is the bridge to the Board at home and to the Benue and Tiv churches on the field. He is the official spokesman to the government and serves as liaison with the other missions and churches. His is the key position in the mission in Nigeria. Because of his heavy responsibilities he, like his counterpart at home, the Rev. H. J. Evenhouse, needs the frequent and earnest prayers of the church.

The executive authority on the field is in the hands of the Nigeria General Conference (NGC). For about fourteen years every worker on the field had a say at NGC. In 1954 this was changed and a conference of nine people was elected; at its second meeting only five were present. But a few months later the number of official delegates rose to fifteen. This number continued to increase. In 1960 Nigerians were included for the first time. At the last meeting of this type, which was held in April 1967, the total number of delegates could have been thirty-six but three of the eight Nigerians were absent. Of those present twenty-eight were missionaries. For some time during Nigeria's civil war the five-man executive committee of NGC carried on, and in April 1968 it added to its number three others to help it conduct the work of the mission. Under the Board's guidance this eventually became a nine-man committee when it also became the new type of NGC. There are no Nigerians on this Conference. It meets once a month instead of twice yearly and so does not need an interim subcommittee. All the missionaries and high officials of the two churches receive copies of the NGC minutes. Missionaries also receive departmental minutes and so, apart from confidential matters, they keep fully informed of all that is happening.

Some Notes on Mission Personnel

Reference has been made to the millions of dollars spent by the CRC for Christ in Nigeria. This is an indication of a much greater gift made by some members of the church when they become missionaries. Men and women have felt the call of God to this work and have given years of service to God and His church. Including the few who went to Nigeria prior to 1940 no less than 156 workers from the CRC have served in Africa. On an average they each contributed just under nine years of missionary service. Owing to poor health a few were unable to complete one year on the field and for the same reason a few were only able to give a term of two and a half years of service. At the other extreme 5 workers gave over twenty years and 3 of these are still going strong. The author and his wife were there for nearly forty years, thirty of these with the CRC.

One hundred and four of the missionaries were married. Many of the wives contributed to the missionary cause in various ways. During their service in Nigeria these couples were the happy parents of no less than 277 children. The other fifty-two workers were unmarried and nearly all of them were women. Twenty-four of the single workers served for an average of almost sixteen years each. The mission owes a great deal to its single workers, and their service takes on a deeper meaning when we recall that they do not have the comfort of a partner and children to fall back on in times of stress which can be many in a foreign land.

Some workers served in more than one capacity while in Nigeria but in the following categories they have been included under that heading to which they gave the greater portion of their time. Of the 156 workers mentioned 58 served in education, 48 in the medical field, 34 in evangelism and religious teaching and 16 in other services. There were 16 doctors and 16 ordained ministers. Ten additional doctors gave most useful service for a few months each. From Calvin Seminary 6 men served a year of internship teaching religious knowledge in the schools.

The list published by the Board in September 1970 shows that there were 94 workers for Nigeria in its employ at that time. Eighteen of these were in North America or studying elsewhere. From the beginning of 1969 there has been difficulty in obtaining visas for new workers from the United States. Some acceptable applicants have been unable to go to Nigeria for this reason. Discussions arising over this make one thing plain, namely that the Nigerian government is determined to have Nigerians who it thinks are capable do the work which is at present being done by missionaries. Almost without exception missionaries coming home for a period of rest are able to return to Nigeria if they do so before twelve months have elapsed. In 1970 the president of our Mission Board was asked by the Nigerian ambassador in Washington to arrange that each missionary train a Nigerian to take his or her place.

Matters which are confidential to the Board are not known to the author. Nevertheless I firmly believe that to a very large measure the behavior of missionaries towards each other, to the Nigerian Christians and churches, and to the government has been exemplary. Generally there has been a tone of well-being and harmony in the mission and on the mission stations. The mission workers make up a family with each member being closely knit to the others. This has been manifest in those annual gatherings in America and Nigeria where workers, past as well as present, have come together to fellowship in the Lord. In Nigeria this usually takes place in August and lasts for four days. The study of God's Word and prayer predominates. The climax is a celebration of the Lord's Supper, which includes Nigerians and is a precious blessing that carries over into the following year.

Naturally there have been problems with individuals and within the mission community, but these do not alter the general quality of Christian comradeship and love which has prevailed. Because the mission is a family it did not make a success of the CRC tradition of home visitation once a year. The missionaries are so close to one another that a visit to a family or a single worker causes difficulties. Sometimes the Mission Board overcomes this by asking its delegates to Nigeria to carry out this function.

With very few exceptions the missionaries are confessing members of congregations in Canada or the United States. It is reckoned that responsibility for their spiritual life rests with the consistory where they have their membership. The ordained men are responsible to the congregation which calls them and installs them for service in Nigeria. It is true that each one tells the Mission Board that God has directed him or her to go to Nigeria. The Board also obtains medical and psychiatric advice on all the adults who go abroad. But the Board does not require that a prospective worker have general missionary training for the foreign field. Some laymen have had such training, and ministers have attended a theological seminary. But apart from a brief course in the Grand Rapids office, training in principles and practices of missions and orientation to a foreign situation is not required. In this the CRC differs from other Christian missions.

Contact with Other Missions

Contact between the CRC missionaries and those of other denominations was inevitable and desirable. The CRC field of labor is remote from the large cities of the land, but business, health, or vacation needs sent the missionaries to one or other of them. The swimming

Ninety members of the SUM(CRC), their children, and some of their Nigerian colleagues meet at the annual conference in 1965.

pools at Harga or Makurdi bring a day's relief from the heat from time to time; January fishing or a stay at Obadu ranch can be a highlight in the year. Jos, presently the capital of Benue-Plateau State and situated four thousand feet above sea level, is a fine place for a vacation. Its climate is pleasant and there the parents can be near their children at Hillcrest School. In Jos there are stores to be visited and there seriously ill missionaries and expectant mothers find help at the SIM hospital. The kindness of doctors and nurses and the efficiency of their care bringing new health to most is a heartwarming memory for dozens of families.

In Jos there are many churches where the CRC missionaries worship and enjoy the preaching of the Word even though it does not always fit the Reformed pattern. In Jos also there are facilities of other missions for entertaining guests and these have been used by CRC families thousands of times. Hospitals, transport, churches, and vacation accommodations all kindly supplied by strange missions and missionaries inevitably brings an appreciative response from those who use them. To many it is a happy discovery that there is a host of very fine Christians who do not belong to CRC circles. These contacts have a broadening effect so that most CRC missionaries and those of other missions show a much greater appreciation of and display a less parochial attitude towards people of other denominations after a few years. These contacts have been reciprocal and benefits have been bestowed by the CRC missionaries as liberally as they have been received from others. For missionaries in other lands this is a special blessing which seems to elude those at home.

Contact with the Government

The SUM(CRC) has maintained good relationships with the British and Nigerian governments. As early as 1944 Dr. De Korne quoted the governor of Nigeria who had written to the British Colonial Office saying, "The Lupwe station is an undoubted power for good within its sphere of influence. Not only is the medical and educational work of value but the mission, in the evangelical field, adopts the wise policy of concentrating on older men and women rather than on youths; from the Mission's point of view this is desirable, and from an administrative point of view it is eminently so, as the sanctions of tribal life continue to evert side by side with progressive ideas. All the activities of this Mission are marked by a sober spirit of patient endeavour which in some other cases is badly wanting."[15]

It has been mentioned that throughout the rule of Britain in Nigeria, Christian missions had not been free to operate in the northern emirates. In 1949 the Richard's Constitution was being discussed and the formation of a federal government for Nigeria was expected. At that time the head of the SUM, the Rev. G. Muir, wrote, " . . . the North will be governed by a body almost entirely Moslem and I fear that missionary work by non-natives will be further restricted. The next ten years may possibly be the *zenith period* of Missions in N.P. before the country follows the pattern of Egypt, Persia, and Pakistan."[16] This latter prediction has not proved to be true but throughout the closing decade of British rule in Nigeria the fears entertained by missions were kept very much alive. To combat these fears, leaders of missions took all steps possible in consultation with the churches to keep a way open for the Christian faith.

In 1954 the entire Nigerian SUM was very upset when two of her missionaries were forced to leave their stations and large numbers of Christians were imprisoned. The charges were based on fiction and an attempt seemed to be in the making for a general opposition to Christian missions. The trouble was not in the CRC field but further to the east. The following year the government took another position and introduced a certificate of permission for missionaries to operate. It contained five points restricting the missionary in his activities; the missionary was required to sign this certificate showing his agreement therewith. The SUM(CRC) joined with the others in seeking modifications of these restrictions. The efforts were successful and the certificate was changed. It was then worded to refer to all religious beliefs, specifically Muslim as well as Christian, and not to Christians alone. It was reduced to two points and the head of the mission was required to sign instead of each individual missionary.[17]

It was in February 1956 that Her Majesty, Queen Elizabeth of England, addressed the government of the Northern Region and said, "The people of the Northern Region vary in character, in background and in religion. Whatever the differences in religious beliefs, I would ask you to remember that those beliefs form the background of national standards of integrity and morality. I am sure that the Government of the Northern Region will always allow men freedom to worship God in the way that the conscience of each dictates. Tolerance is necessary not only in religious matters but also towards those whose views and traditions differ. It is by this spirit of understanding that the people of varied races and tribes will be brought together."[18] This was a high level encouragement to Christian missions and helped them to press on with the request for a religious freedom clause to be incorporated into the new constitution then being considered.

At the same time J. T. Yusufu and I. Usuman were elected to office—the former as a member of the Northern House of Representatives and the latter as a member of the federal government. Both were members of Ekas Benue Church. Other Christians also were elected to office. By February 1958 it was possible for the African Protestant Christians of the North to approach an official commission set up "to study the position of minorities in the colony of Nigeria." This was an all-Nigerian delegation and worked out its stand with the aid of African lawyers. Its ten-point program was very far reaching; among other matters it asked for freedom of religion to speak, print literature, preach, and listen to preaching anywhere in public. It asked that freedom be granted to any individual to change his religion and not to lose his inheritance if he did so. It desired "the right of citizenship for all natives" and "the right for anyone to travel and to reside wherever he sees fit."[19] These references are sufficient to indicate that the earlier anxieties and activities of the missions had now become the concern of Nigerian Christians and that they with their representatives in office were able to handle their own affairs.

The human rights clause with its section on freedom of religion is now firmly entrenched in the constitution of the Republic of Nigeria and is respected by the authorities. When, in 1964, there were some indications that it might be ignored the Christians of every section of the community banded together and formed a Northern Christian Association. It was an association of individuals and not of churches or Christian councils, and foreigners were not included. J. T. Yusufu was very active in its formation and made use of its influence to reopen churches which had been closed by one government official or another.

Apart from the churches, missions continued to have their own problems. In 1958 the numbers of allowable missionaries for each mission were restricted by the Nigerian government. The SUM(CRC) was allowed forty-one which was the current number of missionaries on its active list. However, our membership as part of the SUM now was helpful in this matter as it was soon stated by the government to the entire mission, "that [the SUM] will not be under a quota for missionaries because of its reputation."[20] It will be remembered that in 1961 the government allowed the inclusion of over thirty South Africans into the SUM(CRC) list without any question or hesitation. It was only in 1969 that some classifications of missionaries belonging to the United States were not allowed visas.

When war broke out within Nigeria in 1967 it was the American government that advised its citizens living south of the River Benue and west of the Katsina Ala River to move elsewhere if their presence was not vital to the mission's ministry. The fighting was not far from that area at the time and in order to lessen congestion should a sudden exodus of missionaries become necessary it was suggested that wives and children should move. This was done and some went to the Takum area, others to Jos. It was an inconvenience, but it was for the well-being of all concerned. The separations lasted for only a few months; after that it was possible for families to be together again.

It was in 1966 that many Nigerians, some of them living at Gboko, Makurdi, and Jos, lost their lives in the violence related to the civil war. The foreigners, some of them missionaries, did everything they could to return the people whose lives were being threatened to their tribal homelands. Mercy was also displayed by many Nigerians, in some cases to a far greater extent than by the foreigners. Although these efforts were made by individuals, both black and white, sometimes the missions were blamed for interfering. The violence came so suddenly that there was not time to deliberate; each person reacted individually—some felt they must help, others felt they should not. The conscience of each must answer to his God.

The circumstances were of a most unusual nature and Nigerians hope they will never recur. The policy of the SUM(CRC) is clearly one of noninterference in the national affairs of the countries in which it is a guest. In the Missionary Manual of 1961 the general secretary says about political involvement:

> We are usually respected guests, and our opinions are often favourably considered by many people because we are often in positions of leadership. There is one thing we are asked to be very careful about in this connection. Nigeria is a self-determining nation. This responsible privilege is a prized possession of Nigerians. It is the privilege and the duty of the people of Nigeria carefully to consider the alternatives offered them and to choose wisely those who will govern them. Any attempt on the part of any one of us missionaries to influence any Nigerian to choose or reject a certain candidate for public office, or a political party will be regarded as an infringement of the rights of Nigerian self-determination.
>
> This mission does not favor or sponsor, or advise adherence to, any Nigerian political party. Members of many diverse political parties are equally respected employees of the Mission. No man may be discriminated against because of his party affiliations. We should never seek to favor one party against another by any of our words or actions. This

307

is a very important matter, and even the slightest violation of this non-political rule of the Mission (cf. Rules and Regulations, Article XIII, February 1951) may damage the good name and relationship of the Mission with the peoples and Government of Nigeria. . . . We are being most carefully observed on this score. . . .[21]

This strong reminder was especially necessary in 1961 when high political feelings were causing much distress among the people on the Nigerian field. The Mission has always held this position and, although not 100 percent successful, the Secretary has usually succeeded in seeing that it was carried out.

The Children of Missionaries

The biggest problem for any missionary couple serving in a foreign country is that of the well-being of their children. More married foreign missionaries find it necessary to return to their homelands because of their children's needs than for any other reason. In each case it is strictly a parental matter and each couple with their children in consultation with the Lord has to decide from time to time whether to continue in the work or to go home. In 1950 there were a few preschool children in the CRC mission. That year the NGC asked the Mission Board what part it "will play in the education of the children of Sudan missionaries. Several children in a few years will reach school age. Parents express themselves as desiring to have their children on the field with them. We have neither lodging nor school accommodations and staff. Hillcrest School . . . offers an excellent opening to us."[22]

Fifteen months later the Board agreed to give Hillcrest School $280 each year. At the end of 1953 the NGC again spoke of Hillcrest School as being the best opportunity which Nigeria had to offer and asked permission to carry on conversations with the Church of the Brethren Mission (CBM) which owned and operated the school. The Board agreed but also said, " . . . if they [NGC] desire to go the way of having our own covenantal school, the Executive Committee of the Board would support such action."[23] When the full Board met three months later it said, "The Board favors the establishment of our own covenantal-type school and would request General Conference advice."[24] The Board reiterated this feeling in 1959 but, on the other hand, NGC continued to recommend "that the only practical course to follow for the education of missionary children is to cooperate fully in the Hillcrest School project."[25]

The school to which reference is made is located on the high plateau, on the crest of a hill near the southern limits of Jos township. It was started in July 1942 by the Church of the Brethren Mission and had at that time a teacher and twelve pupils, only two of the children being of the CBM. Four years later its pupils represented no less than nine nations including Syrian, Turkish, Danish, Scotch, American, English, and Canadian. A headline in the *Nigerian Daily Times* said, "No Color Bar in Brethren Mission School."

As early as 1947 two of the students connected with the school were doing high school work in connection with an American college. This continued and their numbers increased. By 1960 there were 25 high school students at Hillcrest sending their work to America. In 1963 this correspondence work ceased and the next year there were 59 enrolled at Hillcrest High School. By 1968 this number had risen to 121 with the total enrollment for the twelve grades at 400.

Each year missionaries' children, such as those of the CRC, lived on the Hillcrest campus during the two eighteen-week periods of school. In 1964 a change was made for High School students when they moved to hostels off the campus. Soon there were seven hostels run by different missions. CRC's "Mountain View" located about half a mile from the school is one of these. In 1967 the outside hostels cared for a total of 139 students and there were 137 younger children living at the school itself. There were also 92 day students living in their homes or with friends in the town. At the time there was an expatriate staff of 46, of which 19 were full-time teachers.

The CBM sought the cooperation of other missions in the Hillcrest venture. In November 1955 the first meeting of the Board of Governors was held; one of the member bodies present was the SUM (CRC). The school's purpose was "to provide in a private Christian Day and Boarding School, suitable education facilities for children of the missionaries of the cooperating missions, and other children for whom accommodations may be available. . . ." Each cooperating mission or branch of a mission was a member body and had a seat at the Board of Governors. Since the CBM was the originating mission, for many years it had three members on the Board and had the privilege of nominating the principal. All cooperating missions had the responsibility of subscribing to the frequent capital expansion which became necessary. School and, where necessary, boarding fees are required of all students. More was required of an associate but noncooperating member mission and even more of parents whose child belonged to neither group.

Another requirement for membership was to supply a member or members of the staff according to the ratio of the number of a particular mission's children to the total number attending the school. In 1970 the SUM(CRC) had three full-time teachers and one part-time, a single woman serving part-time in a children's hostel, a married couple doing the same work full-time, and a married couple in charge of catering and cooking and helping in the administration. Off campus there was a married couple in charge of the Mountain View Hostel. If the CRC mission supplied no workers at all for this important ministry then it is certain it would have no missionaries with school-age children serving in the Benue and Tiv fields. The intermingling of CRC workers with those of some ten other missions and of their children with the CRC children is an exercise in tolerance; one result is in a wealth of love and understanding. Fears which were entertained by some for such a fellowship have proved to be groundless and the meeting of Hillcrest alumni every third year in North America, including members from other lands, is a testimony to the depth of Christian love which exists between those who attended the school as children and workers.

It is a severe trial when parents leave their six-year-olds at the school for the first time. For a few weeks the little ones feel it keenly but after a time this is overcome so that when they are on vacation the children look forward to the day when they may return to school again. For the parents the ache continues. It is a cross they bear, but they do so with considerable peace because they know the satisfactory situation to which they have committed their children at Hillcrest School. Outside of the classroom all the missionaries become "uncles" and "aunts" to the children. This lessens the coldness of formality and retains the dignity of a family relationship.

Elsie Vander Brug (now Mrs. Peter Dekker) served as the first CRC teacher at Hillcrest and the Henry Driesengas were the first houseparents for the children. Gertrude Van Haitsma, formerly of the CRC mission in New Mexico, has served the school for eleven years as a teacher. In all some twenty-six workers of the CRC have served for greater or lesser periods in the school and hostels; this is about 20 percent of the whole staff. The education absorbed by the normal student is excellent and it proves very adequate when he or she has to merge into an American or Canadian situation. The outside sports and cultural activities leave nothing to be desired. The spiritual needs are well cared for day by day and Sunday by Sunday. In recent years it has given cause for much joy that many CRC young people have publicly declared their faith in Jesus Christ.

The organization of Hillcrest School to serve the children of missionaries and others was born of a vision given to Dr. H. Stover Kulp. He promoted it; and Mary Dadisman, Lucile and "Uncle"

Heckman, and later the Weavers, Wilma Schrag, and Martha Underwood were prominent in making it into the fine institution which it is today.

Notes

1. NGC minute 4212, November 1962.
2. Le Roy Baas, report, February 1967.
3. Appendix to NGC minutes (G, 1, 5, B,) April 1964.
4. Board minute 5307, A. 3. B. 2, February 1966.
5. Ekas Benue RCC minutes 84 and 1532, 1968 (translated).
6. E. H. Smith, report to Board, May 1966.
7. Nigerian "Morning Post," p. 12, April 20, 1965.
8. "Nigerian Citizen," p. 1, June 1965.
9. Islam in Africa Project constitution, 1970.
10. W. A. Bijlefeld correspondence, January 1960.
11. Board minute 7488, March 1954.
12. Board minute 229, February 1959.
13. NGC minute 1760, April 1956.
14. "Sudanum" is the radio call sign for the Sudan United Mission.
15. De Korne to Smith correspondence September 26, 1944.
16. Gordon Muir to Board correspondence, October 1, 1949.
17. Appendices to NGC minutes March 1955 and April 1956.
18. *Nigerian Citizen,* February 4, 1956.
19. Appendix to NGC minutes April 1958.
20. NGC minute 2340, April 1958.
21. CRC "Missionary Manual," pp. 5 f., February 1961.
22. Conference minute 491, December 1950.
23. Board minute 7848, November 1954.
24. Board minute 8046, February 1955.
25. NGC minute 2849, April 1959.

The Wukari church building was erected in 1966 on the site of the original missionary's home which was built in 1905.

23

To God Be the Glory

In Conclusion

Let me draw to a close this history of the first thirty years of the Christian Reformed Church in Nigeria. In 1970 the large majority of the missionaries were serving in institutions. These included two hospitals, a teachers' college, two secondary schools (one of which belonged to the Benue Church), a Bible institute, some Bible schools, a pastors' training school and a preseminary school. It also had workers at a theological college, a school for missionaries' children, and another hospital. Other workers were engaged in practical services by which the whole mission was kept moving. There were also others working as linguists, some in literature production and distribution, some among the youth, and others as district church missionaries.

The SUM(CRC) is closely involved with two Nigerian churches. The Ekas Benue Church is an autonomous Reformed body which the CRC was directly responsible for bringing into being. It serves eight or ten tribes of Nigerian people. Then there is the NKST Church of the Tiv tribe, an autonomous Reformed church brought into being by the DRCM. Both churches are member bodies of the Reformed Ecumenical Synod and the Benue Church is in official fraternal relations with the CRC. Unofficially the NKST is in a similar relationship. Both of these churches are members of the Tekas Fellowship and are copartners with the other churches in the Theological College of Northern Nigeria.

After sixty-six years of an ever increasing volume of gospel witnessing which included thirty years of CRC influence there is cause for much praise to God. Our heavenly Father established the ministry in the north of Nigeria and Jesus Christ was pleased by the Holy Spirit and through the witness of His children to redeem Nigerian lives. By 1970 in the Benue Province of the Benue-Plateau State two churches had been organized with a total of 24,000 communicant members and about 153,000 attending church every Sunday. Worship services were being conducted in sixteen hundred places and there were 63 ordained men and 267 evangelists serving them. It was a goal of the SUM to establish an African union church. The Tekas Fellowship of Churches is the nearest it has come to reaching this goal.

The two churches of Benue and Tiv are realities. They are Nigerian, and do not depend upon the CRC or other foreign sources for the day-by-day running of their ecclesiastical life. However, the services which the CRC is now rendering are most valuable for the physical, mental, and spiritual life of the Christians, churches, and community. The wish is often expressed by the people and their leaders that missionaries will continue to help them. A survey made in 1970 by the various mission departments indicate the expectation that there will be but little diminishing of their numbers in the next five years.

The devotion of the present missionaries and their predecessors together with abundant giving by CRC laymen at home has made all of this possible. Nor does one forget the dedicated services of the workers in the office of the Foreign Mission Board in Grand Rapids. There were the long pioneer years of Dr. Henry Beets, and then those of Dr. J. C. De Korne, Reta De Boer (now Mrs. W. Hendriksen), and Mr. Harry Boersma working over the store on Eastern Avenue. Then we move on to 2850 Kalamazoo Avenue with the Rev. H. J. Evenhouse. He made his first foot-slogging through the African bush when he was President of the Mission Board. Since the torch of foreign missions was passed on to him from Dr. De Korne his visits to Nigeria have been many. He has carried the light of truth nobly and well for over twenty years, and in that time has seen the globe circled with a CRC testimony to Christ in a dozen different lands. He and his assistant, A. Huibregtse, have faithfully served the CRC, its Mission Board, the missions, and their missionaries, and have earned the gratitude of all. Space will not permit the mention of many who, like Henry Denkema and Henry Hekman in the years of long ago, gave of their time, talent, and wisdom to the progress of the gospel by serving in a thousand meetings of committees or boards. Currently twenty such men serve every month and with them another twenty for four days every year to keep the Nigerian and all the other foreign missions functioning. The missionaries and the church at home are thankful to them.

It is to the praise of Almighty God—Father, Son, and Holy Spirit—that scores of thousands of men and women, boys and girls of Nigeria have become the children of God through faith in Jesus Christ and that a dozen "tribes and tongues" who hitherto were not His people have now become the people of God.

"To God be the glory,
Great things He hath done."

A list of Christian Reformed Church members who served the mission of that Church in Nigeria for more than twelve months (to December 1970). (There were also a great many missionaries from South Africa and some from North America and Europe who served Christ in the Tiv and Benue mission fields.)

Baas, Mr. Le Roy W., Youth Work, 1965—

Baker, Rev. Ralph, 1953—

Beelen, Miss Laura, Teacher, 1957—

Bergsma, Mr. Harold, Teacher, 1955-1967

Bergsma, Mr. Stuart Kenneth, Teacher, 1954-1960

Bierenga, Mr. John, 1927-1929

Bierling, Mr. Albert, Teacher, 1962—

Bierma, Mr. William, Teacher, 1959-1965

Boer, Miss Ella, Nurse, 1959-1965

Boer, Rev. Dr. Harry R., 1947-1950; 1955—

Boer, Rev. John, 1965—

Bouma, Mr. Reanard, Teacher, 1964—

Branderhorst, Mr. Donald, Builder, 1967-1969

Branderhorst, Dr. Joyce, 1953-1956

Brandsen, Mr. and Mrs. Preston, Houseparents, 1961-1964

Bremer, Mr. Donald, Builder, 1970—

Brouwer, Mr. Norman, Teacher, 1961—

Browneye, Mr. Raymond, Pilot, 1955—

Bulthuis, Mr. Peter, Teacher, 1955-1964; 1968-1970

Buys, Mr. Gordon, Teacher and Pilot, 1963—

Chapel, Miss Nancy, Teacher, 1959—

Cok, Mr. Ralph, Teacher, 1959—

Danford, Miss Cloe Ann, Nurse, 1964-1968

De Boer, Dr. Arthur, 1961-1964

De Groot, Rev. Harold, 1955-1970

De Jong, Mr. Fred, Treasurer, 1970—

De Jong, Mr. Harold, Teacher, 1968-1971, (ordained) 1971—

De Jong, Miss Jessie, Nurse, 1958-1970

De Jong, Mr. William, Teacher, 1969—

Dekker, Rev. Peter, 1947-1961

Den Besten, Dr. Lawrence, 1957-1960; 1965-1966

Deters, Mr. Ellis, Teacher, 1964-1967

De Vries, Miss Neva, Nurse, 1954

De Vries, Mr. and Mrs. Richard, Houseparents, 1965–

Dik, Mr. Ralph, Teacher, 1956-1965

Driesenga, Mr. and Mrs. Henry, Houseparents, 1957-1962

Duyst, Miss Emily, Nurse, 1960–

Dykgraaf, Mr. David, Teacher, 1968–

Dykstra, Miss Margaret, Linguist, 1946–

Evenhouse, Mr. Aldrich, Teacher, 1967–

Evenhouse, Mr. William, Linguist, 1965–

Faber, Mr. Harry, Mechanic, 1970–

Feikema, Mr. Fred, Builder, 1968–

Franz, Miss Marjorie Ann, Hospital Office, 1961–

Friend, Miss Nancy, Nurse, 1963–

Gabrielse, Mr. Leonard, Medical Technician, 1968–

Geleynse, Miss Geraldine, Nurse, 1958–

Gray, Dr. Herman, 1953–

Grissen, Mr. Raymond, Builder, 1952-1954

Groen, Dr. G. Paul, 1964–

Haarsma, Miss Ruth, Nurse, 1967-1970

Haveman, Mr. Louis, Agriculturalist, 1969–

Hoekstra, Mr. Robert, Teacher, 1968-1969

Holkeboer, Mr. Gilbert, Teacher, 1949-1955. (ordained) 1958-1967

Holwerda, Dr. Harry, 1968–

Hoolsema, Miss Angie, Nurse, 1959–

Huizenga, Miss Tena, Nurse, 1937-1954

Ipema, Rev. Dr. Peter, 1948–

Jansen, Mr. Charles, Administrator, 1961–

Kass, Mr. Frank, Teacher, 1968–

Kaldeway, Miss Mary, Nurse, 1968–

Karnemaat, Miss Frances, Teacher, 1966–

Keegstra, Miss Jennie, Teacher, 1963-1966

Kiekover, Rev. Harvey, 1965–

Kingma, Dr. Stuart J., 1961–

Kok, Miss Bena, Nurse, 1952–

Kooiman, Miss Margaret, Nurse, 1957–

Kooistra, Mr. Gordon, Pilot-Mechanic, 1966-1969

Koops, Mr. Robert, Linguist, 1965–

Korhorn, Mr. Cornelius, Teacher, 1962–

Kortenhoven, Mr. Paul, Teacher, 1965-1968

Koster, Miss Janice Mae, Teacher, 1968–

Kredit, Miss Carolyn, Teacher, 1965-1968

Kuik, Mr. Gordon, Evangelist, 1961-1967

Kuiper, Mr. James, Teacher, 1968–

Kuipers, Mr. Gordon, Teacher, 1962-1968

Lambers, Mr. Stephen L., Teacher, 1955-1964

Lemcke, Mr. William, Youth Work, 1955–

Lodewyk, Mr. Bauke, Literature Work, 1966–

Lootsma, Miss Anna, Teacher, 1963-1966

Mast, Miss Mae Jerene, Nurse, 1954–

Meyer, Mr. Harry, Business Manager, 1967–

Monsma, Rev. Timothy, 1962—
Niemeyer, Mr. Elzo, Builder,
1960-1966
Nobel, Miss Faith, Teacher,
1969—
Ohlmann, Miss Maxine, Nurse,
1961-1965
Oosterhouse, Mr. Kenneth D.,
Teacher, 1968—
Ottens, Dr. Henry, (Short-term
1967); 1969—
Padding, Mr. Harold, Medical
Technician, 1957—
Persenaire, Rev. Cornelius, 1956-
1962; 1965—
Plate, Dr. Keith, 1966—
Poel, Mr. Harvey, Builder, 1958-
1966
Posthumus, Mr. Thomas, Teacher,
1968—
Pothoven, Miss Lois, Nurse,
1967—
Prins, Dr. Ray, Dentist, 1968—
Reberg, Mr. Alan, Hospital Administrator, 1967—
Recker, Rev. Robert, 1949-1965
Reedyk, Dr. Martinus, 1970—
Roos, Miss Christine, Nurse,
1967—
Rubingh, Rev. Eugene, 1957-1967
Salomons, Miss Ruth, Hospital
Office, 1966—
Scholten, Mr. Herman, Builder,
1964-1970
Schutt, Mr. George, Mechanic,
1967—
Sikkema, Dr. Donald, 1961-1963
Smit, Dr. Henry, 1960-1967
Smith, Rev. and Mrs. Edgar H.,
1930—
Spee, Rev. George, 1956—
Stehouwer, Dr. Edward, 1958-
1968
Sterken, Mr. Jacob, Hospital
Administrator, 1968-1970

Stielstra, Miss Jennie, Teacher,
1932-1956
Swartz, Mr. and Mrs. Marvin,
Houseparents, 1959-1961
Sytsma, Miss Dorothy, Teacher,
1954—
Tadema, Rev. Rits, 1955-1958
Terpstra, Rev. Gerard, 1952-1961,
(medical leave, 1961-1964),
1964—
Ubels, Mr. and Mrs. Engbert,
Houseparents, 1970—
Van Beek, Miss Jean, Nurse,
1959—
Vander Berg, Miss Geraldine,
Teacher, 1953—
Vandenberge, Miss Elizabeth,
Nurse, 1945-1960
Vanderaa, Rev. Harry, 1960-1969
Vander Bie, Mr. Gordon, Builder,
1961-1969
Vander Brug, Miss Elsie, Teacher,
1956-1965
Vander Meulen, Miss Ruth, Nurse,
1955—
Vander Steen, Mr. Dick, Teacher,
1965—
Vander Vaart, Miss Aleda, Nurse,
1952-1954
Vander Zwaag, Miss Frances,
Nurse, 1957—
Van Essen, Rev. Lester, 1961—
Van Haitsma, Miss Gertrude,
Teacher, 1959—
Van Heukelum, Miss Margaret,
Bible Woman, 1960-1966
Van Korlaar, Miss Lois, Teacher,
1962-1963
Vannette, Mr. Avert, Teacher,
1961—
Van Reken, Mr. Donald, Teacher,
1949-1958
Van Staalduinen, Miss Martina,
Teacher, 1961—
Van Tol, Rev. William, (Seminary
Intern 1965-1966); 1967—

Van Tongeren, Mr. Warren, Teacher, 1960-1966
Van Vugt, Mr. and Mrs. Gerrit, Houseparents, 1963-1970
Veenstra, Miss Johanna,1919-1933
Veenstra, Rev. Rolf L., 1957-1964
Veltkamp, Miss Ruth, Teacher, 1968—
Vermeer, Mr. Stanley, Teacher, (Short-term 1964-1965); 1969—
Visser, Mr. and Mrs. Henry, Houseparents, 1961-1969
Visser, Mr. Thomas, Teacher, 1964—
Vissia, Miss Anita, Nurse, 1941—

Volkema, Mr. Fred, Teacher, 1952-1955
Vredevoogd, Miss Evelyn, Youth Work, 1950—
Vreeke, Mr. Abe, Teacher, 1968—
Vroon, Dr. John, 1958-1961; 1964-1965
Winkle, Mr. Peter D., Teacher, 1964-1969
Wybenga, Miss Anna, Nurse, 1967-1969
Zagers, Miss Bertha, Nurse, 1932-1936
Zuidema, Mr. John, Treasurer, 1968-1970

A list of Christian Reformed Church members who served from three to twelve months in Nigeria.

Aukeman, Mr. Owen, Builder
Bratt, Dr. Harvey
Broersma, Mr. Thomas, Teacher
Davis, Dr. Roy A.
De Vries, Mr. Stanley, Seminary Intern
Dolislager, Dr. Donna
Geelhoed, Dr. Glenn W.
Hammink, Mr. Terry, Teacher
Hekstra, Mr. Fred, Builder
Heyboer, Mr. Marvin, Seminary Intern
Homan, Dr. Henry L., Dentist
Hoogewind, Mr. Allen Jay, Seminary Intern
Hutt, Mr. John, Seminary Intern

Lensink, Miss Sharon, Teacher
Mulder, Dr. Arthur G.
Mulder, Mr. Dennis, Seminary Intern
Oom, Dr. Robert, Dentist
Oosterhuis, Mr. Thomas, Seminary Intern
Paauwe, Dr. Donald
Plekker, Dr. Robert, Dentist
Postma, Dr. Edward Y.
Renzema, Dr. Robert, Dentist
Rottschafer, Dr. Owen
Salomons, Miss Joanne, Teacher
Van Dellen, Dr. Jerrian
Van Dyken, Dr. Charles, Dentist
Van Solkema, Dr. Andrew